Shades of White

Pamela Perry

Shades of White

White Kids and Racial Identities in High School

Duke University Press   Durham & London   2002

To my parents,

Marshall and Louise Perry

Contents

Acknowledgments

When I first entered graduate school, a rather shy woman of low confidence in her intellect, I was horrified by the common practice of submitting one's written work to scrutiny by professionals and other graduate students. What could be more humiliating! I quickly learned, however, that one of the most rewarding aspects of academic life is the relationships and communities it generates for intellectual dialogue and support. From the beginning, when the idea for this project was conceived over dinner with my good friend john powell, to the point when my tireless research assistant, James Todd, and I were pulling our hair out to get the manuscript to press by the deadline, the help of colleagues, friends, family, students, and institutions is what has made this book possible.

Troy Duster's encouragement fueled the research phase of this project, and his vision and insight guided the analysis of my field materials. I couldn't be more grateful for his wise mentorship, generous attention, and kind support throughout the whole course of this project. Barrie Thorne enlivened and emboldened me with her enthusiasm for my work and provided invaluable, in-depth comments on both early and later draft chapters of this book. Many thanks, Barrie. Michael Omi helped keep my head above water in the early phases of analysis and writing with his friendly encouragement and acute grasp of racial politics. Others who read and commented on all or parts of this book, and whose keen judgment and insights significantly shaped it include Kamau Birago, Bob Blauner, Robert Bulman, Teresa Gowan, Becky Chiyoko King, John Hartigan Jr., Nancy Palmer Jones, john powell, Jiannbin "J" Shiao, and David Wellman. My sincerest thanks to you all.

At the University of California, Berkeley, I was supported for two consecutive years by the Dean's Dissertation Fellowship, and a third by the Doreen B. Townsend Fellowship in the Humanities. In addition to financial support, the Townsend Fellowship provided the opportunity to share my work with the other Fellows, who were from various disciplines and helped strengthen the interdisciplinary approach of this research.

At Harvard University, as a Post-Doctoral Fellow in Evaluating Programs for Children, this work was supported by a grant from the Spencer Foundation. I am grateful to the post-doctoral Fellows there (another interdisciplinary group), namely, Kathy Boudett, Eliot Levine, Ana Yolanda Ramos-Zayas, Sean Reardon, Ana Cristina de Souza, and Stuart Yeh, for their feedback on presentations of this material. I also extend my deepest thanks and appreciation to Carol Weiss, Kay Merseth, and Mary Askew for their tremendous support and for giving me the time to finish this manuscript. Gary Orfield also gave much-needed and highly appreciated encouragement.

A project like this one requires detail work that would be crazy-making without the help of others. Marsha Grant transcribed interviews, Karen Feinberg provided writing and editorial counsel, and Zoe Sodja did proofreading/editing. James Todd carried out the tedious and often frustrating jobs of composing the endnote citations and bibliography, and formatting the final draft. He also ran frequent trips to the library and did last-minute research.

Many friends, family, and colleagues offered helpful feedback on ideas or drafts, and/or provided emotional-spiritual support. They include Fay and Herbert Aptheker, Michael Bittle, Aimee Chitayat, Marjorie Cusick, Maria Grahn-Farley, Anthony Farley, Jim Graydon, Tony Jefferson, Moira Killoran, Sally McKee, Bob McMichael, my sisters Cindy Perry Patterson and Marika Perry, Penny Stinson, Nancy Stoller, Michael Wilson, and my dear friend and love, Jeff Weintraub, who was taken by leukemia a month before this book went to press. I also want to acknowledge the support of my brother, Marshall Perry Jr. Although he passed away suddenly just as my research was getting underway, his lifelong, unswerving faith in me frequently nurtured the courage I needed to go on when self-denial threatened my resolve. And not enough can be said to express my gratitude sufficiently to my mother and father, Louise and Marshall Perry, for their generous, loving support and enthusiasm throughout this project.

Finally, this study would not have been possible without the kindness of all its participants. I deeply thank the administrators and teachers of the two high schools for making my time in the field easy, industrious, and pleasurable. Many went out of their way to help me out, and I am eternally grateful to them for that. And I give my most heartfelt and emphatic thanks to the youth in this study. No words can do justice to the scope of my appreciation for their openness, perspectives, and insights, and for how they influenced me. I would come home from a day in the field or an interview completely charged with their energy, creativity, sensitivity, and hunger for discovery. I started listening to music again, playing the piano after a ten-year hiatus, laughing louder, longer, and more often, and seeing common things with renewed attention and appreciation. What a gift you all gave me! Thank you so very much.

Introduction

The bell rings and students burst through classroom doors as if they just met depressurized space. Once-empty corridors are now swift rivers of bodies— bodies that are tall, short, wide, thin, brown, olive, pink, gray, chocolate, high-yellow, beige, bald, spiked, conked, limp, blue, wrapped, nappy, gangly, stocky, pierced, fierce, laughing. This heterogeneous mass flows out of the halls and into the open areas of the campus where the physics of "race" take over and fragment students into murky currents of "black," "white," "Asian," and "Latino." Black youth pool up in central spaces, whites and Asians in distinct off-center locales, Latinos and newly arrived immigrant groups in niches along the margins. Some youth grab french fries, corn dogs, and packaged snacks from cafeteria vendors, others take the time to greet friends. Before long, it is time to begin the slow trip, against the tide, to class.

This is Clavey High, a large, urban public school in a metropolitan area on the Pacific Coast of California.

Valley Groves is a large, suburban public school located not twenty miles from Clavey. At 10:30 A.M. "brunch," the savory smell of freshly baked cinnamon rolls beckons students into the Quad, a large patio area in the middle of campus. Students fly into the Quad like so many downy seeds of a cottonwood tree on a breezy day. They glide, dive, swoop, and twirl, hover in suspension momentarily, then resume gliding, diving, swooping, twirling. Everywhere, rosy-cheeked girls with hair that banners out into silky golden flags greet broadly grinning boys with sun-burned noses. Youth who look otherwise are not here, are elsewhere, beyond purview. The class bell rings and within moments the Quad is barren and quiet. All that remains are the last lingering smells from the kitchen.

A normal day at school.

From the winter of 1994 through spring 1996, I spent most weekdays at either Clavey or Valley Groves high school talking with students and participating in their daily activities. I was interested in what being "white" meant to European American students in those schools and curious to see if the racial consciousness and identities of white students in a multiracial school, like Clavey, differed from those of white students in a predominantly white school, like Valley Groves. I went into the schools equipped with some working assumptions, mainly that all identities spring from social relations and that one needs to confront a "racial other" for there to be a "racial self." Given this, I expected the white youth at Clavey to have reflected on their whiteness more than whites at Valley Groves. I also had a methodology—participant observation[1] and in-depth interviews that ideally would help me examine not only what students said about their identities, but what they meant by what they said, and what they could not say but only perform in daily, unexamined practice.

What I was not prepared for was the extent to which white youth's identities would differ and vary between whites in the same schools and even within individuals' minds. This was particularly true in the multiracial school, where some youth stumbled when trying to answer "What does it mean to be white?" and some spoke eloquently. Some could discuss white identity only as something with social-political meaning and not cultural meaning, others could do both. Most believed that to be white meant that you had no culture, all the while marking "white" boundaries in personal interests, clothing styles, musical tastes, and other cultural forms. Some felt victimized as whites, some felt privileged, many felt both. Some felt "racist," some felt nonracist, many felt both.

In this book, I present students' narratives and my observations and interpretations of the everyday, lived processes of white identity formation at Valley Groves and Clavey high schools. I argue that white students' identities, like all racial identities, were fickle, multiple, and often contradictory. They were so because, in order to make sense of race and one's own racial identity and social location, students looked to large- and small-scale local (in this case, school) social-political structures and their personal experiences of interracial relations. When their associations with racialized groups were impersonal and distant, as at Valley Groves, whites fashioned identities of a kind very different from those of whites at Clavey, who had personal and up-close relations with students of color. Moreover, in both cases, but at

Clavey especially, white students' experiences of racial-ethnic[2] difference was complicated by such things as the ways gender, class, age-group, and other identities influenced the experience of race in a given moment; the degree of diversity whites saw among people of color; and the different sentiments and meanings attached to different racialized relations, such as white-Asian or white-black relations.

Overall, this work supports contemporary theories of race and ethnicity that argue that race, culture, and identity are not static, immutable *things*; they are social *processes* that are created and recreated by people in their daily lives and social interactions.[3] Considerable research has illuminated the ways historical, political, and/or economic processes constitute and alter the meanings and ideologies of race and white domination,[4] but much less has been done with respect to the more intimate, everyday processes that link the self to the racial order.[5] Whereas the former tends to see change over long periods of time, the latter observes the daily shifts and turns identities can take as individuals negotiate their social landscapes.

My emphasis on the mutability and multiplicity of white identities has particular relevance for contemporary scholarship on "whiteness" and white racism, which have tended to represent white identities and attitudes as fixed and stable. Whiteness scholars have taken on the important task of revealing the invisibly pernicious ways that white cultural and political domination permeates people's lives, from interpersonal relationships, to classrooms, the law, the color of "flesh"-tone make-up, and commonsense notions of good and bad, right and wrong, the beautiful and the damned.[6] In the process of illuminating whiteness, however, scholars have tended to reify it into a monolithic "fact" that affects more or less all whites certainly and consistently.[7] Sociologists of "modern" or "new" racism similarly assign coherency and fixity to white racial consciousness. By their account, inconsistencies and contradictions in white people's attitudes, behaviors, and self-perceptions are nothing more than a contemporary form of anti-black sentiment that, because blatant racism is no longer socially accepted, hides behind egalitarian beliefs and good intentions.[8] This book seeks to challenge whiteness and "new racism" theories by vividly illuminating the ambivalences and contradictions in white identity and showing how they are products of the socially constructed nature of race. Furthermore, I assert that contradictions need not be seen as nefarious, but as potential inlets for nurturing antiracism.

To argue that race and white identities are more multiple, fickle, and complex than what is suggested in studies of whiteness and white racism is not to say that they are mere illusions of which we need only rid our consciousness. In the United States and many places around the globe, racial ascription holds very real consequences for people's well-being and life chances. This is evident in "racial profiling," the practice of singling out people of color[9] as criminally suspect for no other reason than their skin color, and riveting differences between whites and "nonwhites" in infant mortality, the number of children in poverty, unemployment, median income, and net worth.[10] Moreover, racial identities and the solidarities that come with them matter greatly as spiritual and political resources for surviving and confronting those inequalities. And finally, white privilege—advantages white-looking people accrue because of gross morphology alone—and white cultural-political domination are also very real, pervasive, and constant. This is particularly true when and where white culture and interests masquerade as the norms and standards by which others are judged.

However, without underestimating the deep roots that race and racial identities have anchored down over several centuries of white racial domination or the widespread pernicious effects of "whiteness," I suggest that if we are to form effective alliances for social change and advance out of the racial polarizations and inequalities we are now embedded in, we must more firmly embrace the notion that "race" and racial categories, including white identities, are unstable, mutable, and variable by context. They are shaped, on the one hand, by the distinct social, geographical, political, and historical matrix of a given context and, on the other, by the contingencies of daily life and one's relationships to racialized others.

As a device for imagining and understanding the everyday relational processes of racial identity formation, I have found the metaphor of a river useful. Rivers are basically composed of water, rocks, and a stream bed. Where the stream bed is relatively flat, the river's waters will move slowly and imperceptibly, and the river surface will appear still and coherent. But once the bed drops or turns or narrows, microcurrents begin to interact with each other and move in contrary directions to others, churning the water at the surface. Add to these dynamics rocks of different shapes and sizes. These, too, set microcurrents in motions that influence the surface of the water.

Racial identities, like the surface of a river, can hold relatively constant at one moment and change the next, even turn chaotic, depending on the wider social-political context in which individuals are embedded and the nature of their interpersonal relationships. For a while scholars of color have argued the need to move away from the idea that race is predicated on biological or other essential differences between people. They urge greater understanding of the socially and culturally constructed nature of race and the heterogeneity of people that are corralled behind putatively homogeneous categories.[11] Such a perspective not only challenges stereotypes, on which many forms of discrimination and exclusion are based, but also opens doors toward linking people along lines of identification other than "race." The same perspective applied to white people can, I believe, reveal the weak links and fissures in the reproduction of whiteness in daily life, begin eroding hard-and-fast white-other dualisms,[12] and open up necessary coalitions for fostering transformative change in race relations.

Identity and Whiteness:
Personal, Historical, and Political Obsessions

I chose to focus this work on identities and not attitudes, the more common subject of research on white racism, for a list of reasons ranging from the personal to the politically theoretical. Before elaborating on that, let me explain what I mean by *identity*, specifically *racial* or *white identity*. By my definition, racial identity is a self-concept that is defined by racial ascription. Hence, "white identity" is a self-concept defined by the racial ascription "white." The degree of investment in the ascription/identity runs along a continuum of personal significance, from the self-concept shaped by little more than an awareness that one carries a racial ascription to full internalization and passionate identification with it.[13] In this book, I explore both ends of this continuum with white youth. For analytical purposes, I call identities at the "awareness" end "social," because they seem to respond purely to how one is socially *identified* within a system of categorical locations and distribution of resources,[14] and identities at the opposite end "cultural," because they tend to engage some level of *identification* with the peoples, practices, and/or histories of the "racial" group.

I became interested in identities while a graduate student in anthropology at the University of Texas, Austin, where my master's research explored the "ethnic" and other collective identities of a small group of Garifuna (also known as Black Caribs) on the Atlantic Coast of Nicaragua. I was interested in the ways identities were mobilized among the Garifuna to bring them into a war with the Sandinistas against their Miskitu and Creole neighbors.[15] So much reading, thinking, and writing about the construction of ethnic identities, the ways identities serve as a lens for making sense of the world and mobilizing action, led me to question my own identity as a white person. Looking into myself, I could not find a racial-ethnic identity; there was no "there" there. I would think about the answers my parents gave me as a child when I asked about our European heritage. I couldn't keep the list of ancestral nations in my head so asked several times, and every time the list would change, making it all the more difficult to remember. It always included England and Ireland, in varying proportions, and at one point I determined that if my mother was a quarter Irish and my father too, I must be *half* Irish. So when I was fifteen I decided to start being and doing Irish. I told people I was Irish, took up Irish step dancing, and began tagging along with a few Irish street bands that played at annual theme fairs around San Francisco. But when my dancing fancies shifted toward ballet and modern dance, my Irishness returned to the amorphous blur of racial-ethnic identity from which it came.

Now in graduate school and curious as hell about why the question "What is my racial-ethnic identity?" consistently drew up a cavernous void in my mind, I started asking other adult whites what they thought about it, and they, too, said they felt like they had no identity as a white person. Only the "ethnic" groups did. An answer began to take shape for me when I began reading Michel Foucault and other critical theorists concerned with the ways the "norm" in societies is constructed. Within this paradigm, white people, by virtue of being members of the dominant group in this society, construct identities defined as "normal" and that set the standard by which racial-ethnic "others" are measured and marked.[16] To be defined as "normal" means to not be defined at all, to just "be." This understanding of my own racelessness, however, made me complicit, despite my intentions, in the social reproduction of white racial dominance. I had to learn for myself how I got that way. That was the first catalyst for this research. Indeed, this study was as much a personal inquiry as it was an academic one. Valley Groves was located just over the hill from the suburban high school I attended in my youth.

The Historical

The second and definitive catalyst for this research came when two reports appeared simultaneously on the front page of my local newspaper. One announced that the Census Bureau had predicted that by the year 2050, "whites" will decline from over 75 percent of the national population to close to 50 percent or less. The other report told about a "European American" club that had opened in a southern California high school. According to the report, a group of white youth in the school felt that they, like the students of color in the school, needed a forum in which to discuss economic and academic issues of concern to them as a racial-ethnic group. An underlying belief of the students was that we now lived in a world that was culturally pluralist and in which whites needed to assume their place at the multicultural table. These two articles fascinated me and I wondered if they were related, given that the youth in southern California were already living in the diverse world the census predicted for the next century. Would increasing contact with racial-ethnic difference challenge whites to depart from the "norm" and consciously construct white identities? If so, what shape might those identities take and with what implications for race relations? These were the questions that gave rise to my research methods and focus in the field.

The "European American Club" and my own personal engagement with white as an undefined and illusive identity are both historically constituted. Since the Civil Rights movement of the 1960s, *identity* has arguably been one of the most salient buzz words pertaining to personal and cultural politics. Black mobilizations in the sixties reframed the issues of race and racial injustice to no longer be "black problems" but *white* problems. And African Americans, in claiming and redefining the term *black* as a social identity of pride, gave new meaning to the concept of race by shifting it from a stigmatized category comprised of the putatively culturally inferior and powerless, to a category that marks one of a number of relative cultural *identities*. Emblazoned in my mind are sharp images from that era that, I believe, attest to its impact on white racial consciousness: an anonymous white woman in her thirties, her face twisted in anger, her right arm pitching a rock at a busload of black children; a white policeman repeatedly striking a defenseless black protester with a night stick; a Black Panther in a beret with his fist raised, shouting "Black power!"; a poster of a young black woman in profile, her hair meticulously combed into a six-inch afro and a large hoop earring dangling from her ear—the caption reads "Black is beautiful."

Moreover, the sixties engendered a new model of political mobilization that we now recognize as "identity politics," where *identity* has come to be a key term by which issues of "culture" and difference are discussed and battles for political representation and power waged.[17] Identity politics has drawn other racial-ethnic minorities, as well as women, gays and lesbians, the disabled, and other historically marginalized groups into the political arena, focusing yet more attention on the "white" (middle-class, male, able-bodied, heterosexual) *norm,* the standard by which the margins have been defined.

Finally, the 1965 Immigration Act, which opened U.S. borders to unprecedented numbers of people from Asia, Latin America, and the Caribbean, was the beginning of the demographic shifts we are experiencing today and projecting into the future. Through the course of this immigration, multiculturalism, which envisions a culturally diverse America, has replaced the old "melting pot" model of assimilation. Through this process, the values of cultural retention and cultural identities have been so celebrated as to make them seem like given facts and necessities for everyone, including white people.

Only a few sociologists and anthropologists have stopped to question and empirically analyze the impact of these processes on white racial consciousness and identities. Those who have done so have mostly focused on white racial attitudes, prejudices, and racism in the post–civil rights era,[18] but not identities, which involves a more holistic view of white racial consciousness. Others have been more or less concerned with the "crisis in identity"[19] among whites, how whites are dealing with the fear of losing racial dominance.[20] Only recently have scholars begun to examine white identities not from the perspective of how whites are *reacting* to new racial politics and practices but rather the perspective of how those things are themselves *reconstituting* white identities.[21] This book seeks to contribute to this latter concern with a comparative focus on the processes of white identity formation among white youth in high schools.

The Political

Finally, identities make interesting and important analytical subjects because they serve as guides for action and interpretive frameworks with which individuals make sense of the world and their social relations. Analyzing racial identities, white identities in particular, is an effort to develop a well-rounded and complex understanding of race and the reproduction of racial inequalities in daily life. Attitudes and prejudices are not sufficient to account for the political behaviors of whites because attitudes and prejudices are themselves the results of identity-making processes, processes of formulating a positive image of the self and the collectivities with which the individual identifies;[22] of defining and regulating the boundaries between "me" and "you," "us" and "them"; and claiming a position from which to speak politically.[23] Revealing those processes can tell us much about how attitudes, prejudice, race categories, and inequalities are reproduced and, hence, where the weak links might lie in their reproduction.

Moreover, identities are not only constructed through intra- and intergroup sameness and difference, but also with respect to wider processes of social reproduction. In this respect, identities are engaged in relations of power and the focus on identities brings this dimension into the analysis as well. Individuals in U.S. society have their place—such as gender, racial, and class locations. Knitting individuals to their social location requires a process whereby, on the one hand, social-discursive processes exert pressure on individuals to take up certain subject positions and, on the other, the individual responds by more or less internalizing a social location into a definition of the self.[24] Stuart Hall defines *identity* as the "suture" that links the societal call with the individual "self."[25]

These understandings of the social construction of identity, then, place identities squarely at the site in which individuals are most engaged in interactive relations with others *and* the social-discursive structures that seek to summon all into their social locations, in this case, their racial locations. Often, when scholars of race speak of the relationship between the "social" and the "self," they fail to recognize the role played by interracial interaction in conditioning and mediating the relationship between the individual and wider social structures.

Identity and High School

I decided to conduct this research in high schools for two main reasons. First, teenagers attend high schools. Contrary to common stereotypes, teens are bold and resourceful human beings with keen insights into society that are too often dismissed. Moreover, adolescence is an excellent age for observing and analyzing identity formation. It is the time when youth must face the fact of impending adult status and embody the rules, values, and roles the society calls them to fulfill.[26] That embodiment translates, in part, into the quest for personal and collective identities outside of the family. What's more, identity making is not only central to youth, but is also very public, performative, and, often, spectacular. Indeed, the very category *teenager* defines a consumer category to which specific commodities, styles, types of music, and leisure activities are marketed for the sake of circumscribing (and in many respects, constituting) "youth" and the subcategories of identities youth explore.[27]

Second, no other public institution is as critical for the development of the identities youth will carry into their adulthood as schools. A large corps of research in primary and secondary education shows that schools are primary sites for the construction and reproduction of race, class, and gender norms, social identities and inequalities. The bulk of that research theorizes, in a nutshell, that the types of values, assumptions, language skills, behaviors, and/or parental involvement that are encouraged and rewarded in schools are culturally biased toward a white, European American, middle-class, patriarchal culture.[28] Such biases can disadvantage students who are not white, middle class, or male in a number of ways, from devaluing their work and demoting them,[29] to instilling expectations of what is possible to obtain academically,[30] to engendering resistance to school practices that result in students opting out of acceptable performance in school.[31] A slightly different genre of research examines the ways teacher and societal expectations become self-fulfilling prophesies for negatively stereotyped students.[32] And yet another line of argument exposes the ways school norms and expectations become played out and reinforced by students themselves in their daily peer interactions and practices.[33] Related to this is a view that schools do more than merely standardize and enforce dominant norms and expectations; they embed youth in a matrix of social and institutional relationships that provide the symbolic material with which youth fashion social and collective identities.[34]

I carried these theories in mind while conducting this fieldwork. While each came to bear upon my analysis of the ways schools influenced the construction of "white" identities among European American students at Valley Groves and Clavey, my focus landed most squarely on the ways youth negotiated racial meanings and identities among themselves, calling upon institutional structures and practices to guide their way.

The Schools

Valley Groves

To get to Valley Groves High, one has to drive several miles through a meticulously planned commercial and residential suburb, over a low range of hills carpeted in amber, ash, and green, and down again into a populated valley surrounded on three sides by rolling terrain. Years ago, this valley was the home of Chupcan Indian tribes who shared the land with elk, antelope, and grizzly bears. In the early 1800s, Spanish *rancheros* staked a claim on the land and founded early Valley Groves, which served as an agricultural support community for the wider area. By the 1950s, Valley Groves was a firmly established working-class bedroom community for workers in outlying lime and coal mines, oil refineries, and shipping industries. Shortly thereafter, modern-day Valley Groves sprang up, becoming a large commuter community with its own light industry, retail, and business economy.[35] Residents of Valley Groves today work largely in service and manufacturing industries and enjoy a lifestyle suburban in character, but where horse farms are not far away and wild pigs occasionally roam down from the hills to check out the metropolitan night life. In 1990 the median household income of the city's 111,400 residents was $41,675.[36]

Adjacent to Valley Groves, and within the catchment area for Valley Groves High School, is the quaint city of Rancho Nuevo, with a population of about 10,000. Although Rancho Nuevo predated Valley Groves as a coal-mining town and stagecoach stop, it had all but disappeared by the time the latter was officially incorporated in the early 1900s. With no major high-ways leading directly to it and no other towns contiguous except Valley Groves on its northwest end, Rancho Nuevo has an expansive, small-town, rural flavor to it. While Valley Groves was burgeoning into a densely popu-lated commuter community, Rancho Nuevo remained a quiet, pastoral area with orchards, cattle, and dairy farms. In the late 1980s, however, that began to change as developers sought to capitalize on the natural beauty and seclusion of the town by attracting moneyed professionals and managers seeking a controlled community without an iron gate. Although there are still downtown saddlery shops and large ranches and horse stables at the base of the southeastern hills of Rancho Nuevo, today nearly half of the working population is in executive, managerial, or professional jobs. According to the census, the median household income of Rancho Nuevo residents in 1990 was nearly $70,000. In 1999, estimated median household income was $100,000.

Valley Groves High School is located in southeastern Valley Groves, near Rancho Nuevo. It is surrounded by modest but nice single-family homes with either crisply manicured lawns or easy-maintenance rock gardens dressing up the front yards. Streets and sidewalks are clean, and parking ample. The air smells alternately earthy, fragrant, and homespun. The school opened in 1959 as the first of a major expansion in public school facilities in response to the post–World War II population boom. It triangulated with two other high schools in the area to cover the expanding community more effectively. Since then, four other public high schools and two private schools have come to serve the city population.

The students of Valley Groves High School are drawn from Rancho Nuevo and adjacent working- and middle-class neighborhoods of Valley Groves, bringing considerable economic diversity to the school. According to some lore I picked up from a grounds supervisor on my last visit to Val-ley Groves in 1999, in the early 1980s the high school comprised largely working- and middle-class students and was dominated by a large group of cowboys from Rancho Nuevo. The cowboys, in ten-gallon hats and tooled-leather boots, would spend lunch and break hours in the center of the school Quad, chewing and spitting tobacco and making Valley Groves "real colorful," in the supervisor's words. As the class and economic character of Valley Groves and, especially, Rancho Nuevo changed, more youth from professional, middle- to upper-middle-class families began attending the high school. The cowboys slowly diminished while moving their territory farther and farther out to the margins of the campus. At the time I did my research, 1994–1996, there was a group of about ten cowboys and girls who regularly hung out on the backs of Chevy and Dodge pickup trucks in the student parking lot. By 1999 they were all gone. While the cowboys were moving out, the center of the Quad became, and remains, territorialized by athletes, cheerleaders, student council members, and other more mainstream youth.

While I was at Valley Groves High, it was composed of students from a broad range of the middle class, along with some working-class and upper-class students. The school curriculum reflected (and possibly played a role in constructing) this diversity, offering something for everybody—from advanced placement college preparatory classes, accounting and other business courses, to "industrial technology," which included a professional autobody shop course, wood and metal craft, and radio broadcasting.

Like so many other suburban communities across the nation, Valley Groves and Rancho Nuevo became the cities they are today as a result of economic and residential shifts in the post–World War II period. Nascent deindustrialization, the rapid influx of African Americans seeking work and housing in already overcrowded cities, discriminatory local and federal housing loans, and healthy savings accounts resulted in "white flight" to the suburbs.[37] Between 1950 and 1970, the population of Valley Groves grew twelvefold, from 6,953 to 85,164 people, and remained around 99 percent white through that transition. In the same period, the population of the neighboring industrial city of Clavey decreased only slightly, from 384,575 to 361,651 (a 6 percent decrease), but changed demographically from 85.5 to 59.1 percent native and foreign-born white.[38] Since the '70s, more non-white minorities have been moving to the suburbs, but suburban communities remain predominantly white.

The city of Valley Groves in 1990 was 83 percent white; in 2000 it was 71 percent white.[39] This mirrored a decrease in the white population nationwide, but whites in Valley Groves remained a hearty majority. In 1990 Rancho Nuevo was 93 percent white.[40] In the years I was doing my research, Valley Groves High, with 1,600 students, was the "whitest" public school of its size in the region. Non-Hispanic white youth made up 83 percent of the school population, followed by Hispanics (7 percent), Asians (5 percent), Filipinos (2 percent), and African Americans (2 percent). The teachers, administrators, campus supervisors, service and other staff were also overwhelmingly white.

Clavey High

While Valley Groves was slowly transitioning from a *ranchero* to an agricultural economy in the mid-to-late 1800s, Clavey was quickly growing from a bayside settlement canopied with ancient oak trees into a bustling city. First the gold rush then the transcontinental railroad brought in large waves of immigrants from diverse ethnic, racial, and geographical backgrounds. By the turn of the century, Clavey had a thriving industrial economy based on manufacturing, lumber, coastal trade, and processing agricultural goods from places in the rural outskirts like Valley Groves. African Americans, who today form the largest racial-ethnic group in Clavey, began populating the city at this time. They came in as Pullman porters and hotel workers and lived in the western part of the city along with largely foreign-born Irish, Portuguese, Italian, and eastern European laborers. The majority of the population of Clavey was northern Europeans who dominated small business and skilled crafts, railroad, and building trades.[41]

World War II dramatically changed the demographics of Clavey. The demand for labor in shipbuilding and other war industries resulted in a 30 percent increase in the population of the city, including greater numbers of women and people of color. The African American population, already the largest nonwhite group, tripled, reaching 12.4 percent of the population by 1950. In the following decade, "white flight" to the suburbs reduced the total white population of Clavey by one-fifth.

The movement toward greater racial-ethnic diversity took another leap forward after the passing of the 1965 Immigration Act, which brought into Clavey unprecedented numbers of people from Asian, Caribbean, and Latin American countries. Today Clavey is one of the topmost diverse cities in the nation. In 2000, 24 percent of Clavey's 399,484 residents were non-Hispanic white, 36 percent were black, 22 percent were Latino (of any race), 15 percent were Asian, 17 percent were "some other race," 5 percent were two or more races, 1 percent was Native American, and 1 percent was Pacific Islander.

At the time of my research, Clavey's workforce was fairly evenly distributed across the range of occupations, from white-collar executives to blue-collar manual laborers, with a little over half of the workforce concentrated in the clerical, service, and manufacturing industries. This meant a wide range in economic diversity. Median family income in 1989 was $27,095, but the average was $37,100, reflecting the fact that over 16 percent of Clavey families lived in poverty (thus driving the median down) while a smaller percentage enjoyed very high incomes (pulling the average up). In 1989 Clavey had the second largest African American middle class in the nation.[42]

Unlike many cities of its kind in the United States, Clavey citizens enjoy a significant degree of racial and ethnic social integration in its neighborhoods, work spaces, and leisure activities. However, de facto segregation is also prevalent, most vividly by geographical location within the city. The "flats," the neighborhoods closest to the bay shores and old shipbuilding yards, are populated mostly by poor African Americans. As you move toward the "lower hills," integrated spaces pop up that mix working- and middle-class whites, African Americans, Asians, and Latinos. As you move higher up the hills, income levels rise and skin colors whiten, until you get to the top, where mostly white and wealthy people live.

This racial geography was no accident. In the early 1900s a massive earthquake leveled a nearby city, causing many of that city's elite to seek homes in Clavey, particularly in the hills area because of its woodsy terrain and splendid views. New properties and homes began to spring up that were specifically targeted to the white upper class and zoned to keep nonwhites out, particularly those of African or Asian descent. In recent years African American, Latino, and Asian American professionals have moved into the hills, shifting the character of the area toward greater racial-ethnic diversity. However, whites still predominate, making up about 67 percent of the hills population in 1990, compared to only 28 percent of the city at large. More than half of all hills residents work in executive, managerial, and professional occupations.[43]

Clavey High School sits perched, fortresslike, atop a ridge in one of Clavey's "hills" neighborhoods. From the school cafeteria on the east end of the campus, students enjoy a bucolic view of a forested regional park with undulating terrain that appears untouched by humankind. From the football field on the west end of campus is a spectacular panoramic view of the city and the Pacific waters that mark its western boundary.

The school went under construction in 1957 with great fanfare and a promise of being "second to none."[44] Four years and $5 million later, Clavey High School opened, relieving the pressure from overcrowding in three other high schools down in the flats. Not unexpectedly, the transfer of youth left the previous schools with virtually no white students and Clavey High predominantly white. This was anticipated and strongly protested by the NAACP and other civil rights groups because from the onset the boundaries for Clavey High's catchment area were drawn around the ridge line of the hills, surrounding the predominantly white neighborhoods of the city. Proponents of the boundaries touted the virtues of the "neighborhood school" while opponents claimed that the city was building a "private prep school supported by public funds."[45] The debate over the boundaries went on for several years, and in May 1964 the school board agreed to allow restricted out-of-district enrollment into Clavey High from the city's fifteen junior high schools. That change, they estimated, would make the incoming tenth grade class about 8 percent black. This did not assuage the opponents, who continued to press for shifting the boundaries in a way that would send some of the hills' white youth back into the predominantly black schools in the lower hills and flats. Parental opposition to such a change eventually made the issue moot, but not before the school board decided to allow unlimited open enrollment into Clavey High from the city's predominantly black junior high schools.

Over the last ten to twenty years, between the above measures, the creation of a citywide open enrollment program, the establishment of two magnet academies[46] at Clavey High, the arrival of more families of color into Clavey's catchment area, and the departure of many white youth to private schools, the racial-ethnic demographics of Clavey High School have shifted to make it the most racially and socioeconomically diverse high school in the city. At the time I did my research, the majority of students were African American, but they made up just over half of the school population (54 percent). They were followed in numbers by Asians (23 percent), whites (12 percent), "Hispanics" (8 percent), Filipinos (2 percent), Pacific Islanders (1 percent), and Native Americans (1 percent). The individuals within these broadly defined categories differed in national origin and/or ethnicity. So, for example, among "Asians" were Chinese, Vietnamese, Koreans, and Hmong; among "Hispanics" were Chicanos, immigrant Mexicans, Cubans, Salvadoreans, and other Central Americans. At any given moment during lunch break one could tour the campus and hear Standard English, Black English ("Ebonics"), Eritrean, Cantonese, Mandarin, Korean, Spanish, Spanglish, Tagalog, Samoan, Russian, and Vietnamese, among others. According to school records, 14 percent of Clavey youth were classed Limited English Proficiency (LEP).

The racial composition of the administrative and teaching staff, while not perfectly representative of the school population, was nonetheless quite diverse. The principal of the school was a white male, but the other top administrators, two assistant principals and the dean, were African American. Of all the administrators and their staff, 50 percent were African American, 25 percent were Asian, and 25 percent were white. Clavey teachers were 53 percent white, 30 percent African American, 8 percent Asian, 3 percent Pacific Islander, and 6 percent Hispanic.

Clavey students were about as socioeconomically diverse as they were racially and ethnically diverse. The district's open enrollment policies drew students to Clavey from the wealthy hills and the poverty-stricken "flats." Moreover, one of Clavey's magnet academies, Performing Arts, appealed to youth from both economically advantaged and disadvantaged backgrounds. The other, Future Teachers, attracted a lot of working- and middle-class African American students. However, the income gap between the wealthiest and poorest students at Clavey was not as wide as it could be because the wealthiest students in the area tended to go to private school and, for whatever reasons, a lot of the poorest youth did not apply. This is reflected in the fact that Clavey rated above the district norm in the California Learning Assessment socioeconomic index for high school sophomores and had the lowest AFDC and free or reduced lunch statistics in the city: 5 percent and 14 percent respectively. The next-lowest AFDC and lunch statistics in Clavey city were 29 percent and 39 percent, respectively. A counselor at Clavey High told me that there were as many wealthy white students at Clavey as wealthy black students and Clavey's attendance zone gave it a substantial, multiracial, middle-class student body.

Why Valley Groves and Clavey?

Making the choice to focus on Valley Groves and Clavey as the sites on which to conduct my research was not difficult. Significant for me was, first, the fact that white students at Valley Groves were a racial majority in the school *and* the wider community, and at Clavey white students were a minority in both of those places. Since my main interest was the role of interracial association in the ways white youth made sense of race and their identities as whites, it was important that the demographics of the schools and their communities be fairly consistent. Of course, there were some kids at Valley Groves who lived in neighborhoods that had people of color in them, and students at Clavey who lived in predominantly white neighborhoods. However, with perhaps one exception, white students I spoke to at Valley Groves and Clavey said that they experienced themselves as the racial majority and minority, respectively, in their school and city.

Second, the socioeconomic composition of students at Valley Groves and Clavey was a relatively close match, especially given that suburban schools tend to have a lot of middle- and upper-middle-class students, and urban schools tend to have more working-class and poor students.[47] Both schools had a range of working- to upper-class students, with middle-class students firmly at the core. This allowed me to spend a lot of time with and interview middle- and working-class white students at both schools in order to gauge the influence of class background on the ways youth experienced and defined their racial experiences and identities. Moreover, I was especially interested in the ways white identity was constructed as the norm among middle-class whites in particular. Therefore, I was pleased that the majority of white students at Clavey were from middle-class homes. This allowed me to focus on middle-class whites in the two schools.

Finally, after I had a chance to spend time observing school life in Valley Groves and Clavey and compare those schools to other possibilities, my gut feeling told me that Valley Groves and Clavey were the best choices for doing research with far-reaching implications. Valley Groves struck me as a school like so many other American suburban schools: predominantly white, fairly sheltered, a conventional curricula, all-around no frills. It seemed to me that the racial and other social dynamics of the school might be familiar to just about anyone who had attended a suburban high school. Clavey High, on the other hand, with its racially diverse but significantly middle-class student body struck me as a place where I might witness dynamics more indicative of the direction many suburban schools may be heading in the near future. Since completing the research, I have discovered, through feedback from students and recent studies with findings similar to mine, that my hunches were good ones.[48]

Reading This Book

Although the main objective of this book is to make a theoretical argument about the processes of white identity formation and to suggest new strategies for addressing the reproduction of racial inequalities in schooling, I have sought to make the book appealing and accessible to readers who may only be interested in gaining insights into how white youth in different school contexts think about race and their whiteness. For that reason, in each chapter I have placed the ethnographic and interview material in the foreground and confined my theoretical framings and analysis to, respectively, the introductions to each part of the book and discussions at the end of each chapter.

The book is divided into three parts. Part one consists of ethnographic analyses of school life at Valley Groves and Clavey high schools. I examine the ways students broadly categorized themselves in the school and the extent to which racial differences played a part in those categorizations. Theoretically, the two chapters in this section introduce the roles of interracial association and school norms in helping white students define race and their identities as whites. Here and throughout the book I emphasize the utility of thinking in terms of "*proximities*" of interracial association rather than interracial association alone,[49] because modern media technologies allow the most segregated and isolated of whites to experience constructions of racial-ethnic difference on television, in the press, or at the movies. I argue in this book that significant distinctions in racial identities obtain between those whites who experience daily, direct, and up-close association with people of color and those whose experience of people of color is indirect and distant. However, it is not interaction with racialized difference alone that constructs identities, but that in concert with how semiarbitrary differences are social-politically marked and defined. That is where school norms, practices, and expectation come in: they provide the symbolic materials that students draw on to make sense of their experience and define themselves.

Chapter 1 focuses on Valley Groves. I argue that students there had little to no direct association with students of color and that school practices, expectations, and cultural assumptions were drawn from the dominant, European American suburban culture. This meant that (white)[50] students experienced themselves as "normal" and viewed race as an insignificant social and political category. Chapter 2 focuses on Clavey High. White students there had face-to-face association with a variety of racially and ethnically charged identities, and racialized school practices, like tracking, reinforced the significance of race as a social category. I argue that, therefore, "race" was the primary principle by which all youth at Clavey, including whites, categorized themselves and who was who at school.

Part two, "Culture and Identity," explores the ways white youth reflected on and defined white identity as something with which they personally identified and/or that brought them some meaningful sense of membership in a community. In these chapters, while continuing to emphasize the roles of school structures and interracial association, I introduce two everyday processes by which white youth defined their racial identities. The first regards the ways students define their relationship to racial-ethnic others, what I call the "us-them" relationship. For example, in chapter 3, I examine what white students at Valley Groves and Clavey explicitly said about white identity as a cultural identity. When I asked white students at Valley Groves to describe white culture, most of them drew a blank. They understood "white" to mean that you were, simply, the majority and had no cultural ties. "Minorities," on the other hand, did have culture; it was their apparent culture-fulness that put the culture-lessness of whites in relief. In contrast, white students at Clavey had multiple ways to define the cultural meanings of white identity. Their conception of whiteness shifted from being an empty cultural category, to "white" meaning that you had certain European American cultural traits, to its meaning that you lived in the present and eschewed the relevance of the past. These different meanings of white cultural identity tended to correspond with sentiments or experiences associated with particular racial-ethnic, "us-them" relationships. This was because, I propose, at Clavey High white students did not merge all students of color into a single category, but differentiated students by distinct racial and ethnic groups. Each intergroup relationship, like white/Asian or white/black, invoked different feelings about white identity.

Chapter 4 looks at the meanings youth gave to their clothing styles, tastes in music, and leisure activities and examines the extent to which racial meanings were embedded in those practices. The focus on youth cultures nicely illuminates the dialogical processes of identity formation that fall between the self and other, or "us" and "them,"[51] and the different meanings cultural forms take when that dialogue is face-to-face or distant and impersonal. For example, I argue that at Valley Groves white students could wear hip-hop clothing and listen to rap music without sanctions from white, black, or other students of color. They associated those cultural forms with being "tough" or "cool" and not "black" per se. Those were meanings they acquired through mass media representations of blackness. At Clavey, on the contrary, cultural forms from hip hop to rock were charged with racial-ethnic meanings and marked racial-ethnic identity boundaries. Crossing those boundaries in clothing or music consumption could be strictly sanctioned by both inside and outside group members. At Clavey, then, most whites consumed hip hop selectively and usually only when they wished to signify African American identity or group identification.

In chapter 4 I also introduce a second relational process that youth cultures give crystalline light to: the relationship between the self and the "other" within. As James Baldwin once wrote, "each of us, helplessly and forever, contains the other—male in female, female in male, white in black and black in white."[52] I refer to this as the "multiracial self" and in the discussion section elaborate on this concept in light of material presented earlier in the chapter.

If you have not found white youth's racial consciousness and identities multiple, ambiguous, and contradictory after reading parts one and two, you will after reading part three. The two chapters in this section address white identity according to how youth experience the social implications of being a white person within a social-political, white-dominant racial hierarchy.[53] The material in these chapters continues to address the roles of social-institutional structures, proximities of association with racialized groups, us-them constructs, and the multiracial self in shaping and complicating racial identity formation while spotlighting yet more processes. Chapter 5 examines the responses both Valley Groves and Clavey High students had to the Million Man March on Washington, which took place on 16 October 1995. Chapter 6 focuses on what youth had to say about the social and political implications of being white. In both chapters, I show marked differences between white students at Valley Groves and Clavey. Up to this point I mostly illuminate the ways wider institutional and political structures shape the meanings youth gave to their racial interactions; these chapters illustrate how communities—composed in the Valley Groves case of white people and in the Clavey case of racially diverse people—shaped the ways people interpret and make sense of racialized events, politics, and discourses. For instance, Valley Groves students tended not to be able to relate to or understand the purposes of the Million Man March nor support it. Whites at Clavey, on the other hand, had a lot of information about the March and tended to support it. These differences, I argue, had to do with the different types of knowledge and experiences youth acquired through their differently composed communities. However, different interpretations of the March, of whiteness, and other political matters ensued not only between Valley Groves and Clavey students but, at Clavey especially, between white boys and girls as well. Gender, like class and other social locations in which individuals stand, will influence the experience of community and the social implications of being white.

In the conclusion, I pull together the different pieces of my theoretical argument—proximities of interracial association, social-structural influence, us-them constructs, intersecting identities, and the multiracial self—and tie up any loose ends. Again, readers who are not interested in theory might want to skip over this section and go to the next, where I discuss some of the practical implications of this book, particularly with respect to schooling and antiracist organizing. I argue that the comparisons between Valley Groves, a predominantly white school, and Clavey, a multiracial school, speak strongly on behalf of reversing the current trend toward re-segregated schools and revitalizing efforts to integrate and reform our public schools.

part one

School Life and Social Meanings

Chapters 1 and 2 of this section set the ethnographic contexts of Valley Groves and Clavey High, the respective institutional, social, and cultural practices at the schools that helped constitute in-common discourses and understandings of race and whiteness. A focal point of each chapter is the common or normative culture of each of the schools and the extent to which that culture was derived from, reflected, or constituted white European American culture. By "white European American culture," I refer to three features of American culture, broadly. First, although the dominant culture in the United States is syncretic, that is, composed of the different cultures of the peoples that populate the United States, several of its core characteristics are of European origin. These include the values and practices derived from the European Enlightenment, Anglican Protestantism, and Western colonialism, namely individualism, personal responsibility, a strong work ethic, deferred gratification, self-effacement, mind over body, self-control, and the mastery of nature.[1] Other "carry-overs" from Europe include some of the material cultures of the Western, Eastern, and Southern Europeans who immigrated to the United States from the seventeenth to the twentieth centuries. Examples include types of food, like hamburgers, hot dogs, spaghetti, and cupcakes, and social activities, like line dancing, ceremonial parades, and state and county fairs.

A second feature of white culture is the dispositions, world views, and identities whites, especially those in predominantly white communities, tend to share by virtue of being numerically and politically dominant. Currently, examples of that include a race-neutral or "color blind" world view and a sense of oneself as "normal." Finally, I include in a definition of white European American culture particular cultural products or activities that are enjoyed principally by whites and have identity-defining or constitutive force. Examples are country music, modern (post-sixties) rock and roll, certain slang terms or ways of talking, and outdoor activities like backpacking. In what follows, I argue that to varying degrees these three features of white European American culture constituted a way of life at Valley Groves that was unmarked, undefined, and taken for granted. At Clavey, however, where African American and other students of color claimed cultural space, white culture and identity were marked and not entirely taken for granted nor undefined.

A second focus of these chapters is students' peer groups and the meanings youth ascribed to peer group or clique membership. Several ethnographic studies have observed the ways that peer group structures in schools resonate with wider social structures defined hierarchically by race, gender, and class[2] and form interpretive communities by which youth make sense of those structures.[3] Penny Eckert articulates this well:

> The culture of the peer group takes over where the individual student-school dynamics leave off. The variety of means by which classroom methods teach children their . . . place in the world are gradually incorporated into interactions among the children themselves. This occurs both through adaptive strategies within homogeneous groups and in the dynamics between groups. As childhood groups emerge into the politicized atmosphere of the secondary school, they take on differential roles in a highly structured peer society.[4]

In these chapters I analyze the meanings youth gave to peer group membership and the influence of interracial association on those meanings. In later chapters I examine how peer group structures, in turn, informed how white youth made sense of race and their identities as whites.

1. Valley Groves

"Normal. I'd say I'm just . . . normal."

PP: *How would you describe your group of friends?*

Billy: *Normal. We don't smoke or drink or anything and [we] wear clothes we would call normal.*

PP: *And what is that?*

Billy: *Not oversized, baggy clothes like the skaters wear, or, obviously, we don't wear cowboy hats or boots.*

Valley Groves High School sits on the floor of a verdant and woodsy valley, embraced on three sides by softly undulating hills. Inside the school boundaries the protected and nurturing feeling of the outer terrain is replicated in the campus layout: clean, wide, and expansive; game fields stretching out of sight; wide open vistas of the pastoral valley walls. When I first walked around the campus, I marveled at what felt like a tribute to youth in the extraordinary resources devoted to their play and to the development of their physical and intellectual competencies.

Also contributing to the nurturing air of the school were the attitudes and self-presentations of the school authorities. The campus supervisors were not the burly, tough-looking male figures I had come to expect of security. They were all white, middle-aged, and graying women who roamed the grounds with walkie-talkies, guarding the borders from outside intruders, keeping the smokers on their toes, and rallying students on to class. While not particularly popular among all the youth, they were seen in more of a parental than a policing role. The oldest of the supervisors was affectionately called "grandma."

The principal, a white male, was friendly and personable with a competence for and informality about his work that made him seem more like a hip uncle than an authoritarian, fatherly figure. At lunch he walked around and chatted with students, calling them by their first names. When he and I spoke, I sensed a genuine love for youth and a desire to provide them with the safest and best possible experience at his school. The other administrators—two vice-principals, the dean, and counselors—matched the principal's avuncular demeanor and feelings about the students. They told me that Valley Groves students were "great kids," and it seemed to me that they treated the students with the kind of respect that "greatness" deserves.

School Geography: Center White

At 10:30 A.M., when the bell for a fifteen-minute "brunch" rang, the campus came alive as students filed out of the classrooms to meet up with friends in the outside spaces of the campus. The bulk of the school's population, it seemed, amassed in the Quad—a deep and wide paved patio area in the center of campus—and its immediate periphery, where snacks and drinks were sold. Every day, mouth-watering smells from the cafeteria ovens summoned students to little pastry stands in the center of the Quad where staff sold fresh cinnamon rolls and cheese buns. On special occasions, students put up a cappuccino stand or sold other warm beverages that also went over well with the youth. Too quickly, it seemed, the break would end, but students always headed off to class with little apparent complaint.

Two hours later was lunch. The school provided a daily special lunch menu that featured such things as meatloaf and potatoes, fried chicken, hamburgers, tacos, or spaghetti. At outdoor stands, students could also buy french fries, nachos, or slices of pizza. Frequently, however, a student club sold food as a fundraiser. On those days, homemade types of foods appeared, including baked goods like cupcakes, Rice Crispy bars, fruit pies, and fudge, and other sweets like candied apples and caramel corn. At "Oktoberfest" early in the school year, school clubs sold foods to raise funds for their respective activities. An Asian students' club sold chicken teriyaki and Thai iced tea. A Mexican American club, MESCLA, sold tacos and Pepsi. The Earth Club sold chicken noodle soup. Conflict Management sold clam chowder.

Lunch break offered time for students to find their friends and disperse to their favorite niche on campus. Most students settled into the Quad and its immediate vicinities. As young people bounded onto the patio, they tossed their backpacks and book bags on the ground and freely danced around, laughing and joking with friends, or else sat quietly and conversed. Under the "juniors' tree" in the south-central part of the Quad, the cheerleaders would talk louder than necessary, giggle, scream, and then flash their eyes to make sure such-and-such a boy was watching. The boys would either stand tall in controlled, cool composure (aware of the girls' gazes) or directly engage girls in their flirtatious play. The seniors claimed the space under a large oak tree that overhung a patch of grass and some benches. Boys and girls generally stood or sat there with relative physical restraint and stately demeanors. Elsewhere around the Quad, students of all grade levels huddled together with friends, munching food and catching up with one another.

The students in the centermost part of the Quad were overwhelmingly, if not exclusively, white, and dressed in styles like those sold at the Gap, a popular store among white youth that features styles with basic, gendered distinctions in colors and cuts that are conservative, no frills, conformist.[1] Most boys in the Quad wore loose-fit (but not oversized), faded blue jeans or sweat pants with either button-up flannel or polo shirts, or clean, un-tucked t-shirts sporting the names of rock groups or commodities manufac-turers. These were accessorized with a pair of white athletic shoes. Girls exhibited more variety in styles. The most casual wear was a sweat outfit or slim to loose-fit, faded blue jeans or cut-offs with a cotton blouse tucked in. Sun dresses or mini-skirts with a high cropped blouse were common for a more dressy look. Valley Groves girls also tended to wear their hair very long, no bangs, and always clean and shimmering—suitable for a Vidal Sassoon commercial. This look was so prevalent that, during P.E., as girls ran laps around the football field, their combined manes seemed to knit into one, fifty-yard patchwork banner of shiny golden and brown hair.

Elsewhere on campus, other groups of kids, who in one way or another looked much different from the youth in the Quad, claimed their own spaces. To the east of campus, out in the parking lot, a group of white girls and boys in cowboy hats and tight denim jeans cinched up with large brass buckles gathered around Dodge and Chevy pickup trucks that blared coun-try music. To the north, between the two outermost classroom halls, the "E" and "D" halls, was frequently a group of kids who, as I approached, might yell "Narc!," snuff out cigarettes, and eyeball me suspiciously as I passed (*narc* is slang for narcotics officer, of course, but in this context it was the name youth gave to the campus security and anyone suspected of being security). And in a protected corner of the Quad, a group of predominantly white boys wearing oversized, torn, and dirty pants would practice various tricks on broad, battered skateboards.

Inside the cafeteria, to the south of the Quad, was where I would find most of the students of color. A group of five or six African American males typically sat on the indoor stage at its east end. The rows of tables on that same side of the hall were, one by one, semihomogeneously taken over by Filipino, Asian, Latino, and African American youth who huddled together to consume their midday sustenance. I say "semihomogeneously" only because commonly, within every group in the cafeteria, there would be at least one (usually only one) white youth, usually a white male.

Popular, Smokers, Hicks, Homies, and the Normal

Over time, I came to know more about the different students who hung out in the Quad, the parking lot, between the E and D halls, and in the cafeteria. By and large, the students in the Quad were the popular and "normal" kids. The normal kids tended to conform to a youthful rendition of the adult mainstream. They were middle-class, though not exclusively, listened primarily to "classic" and/or alternative rock and, according to Billy, whom I quoted at the beginning of this chapter, wore "normal" or conventional clothing. They were the silent majority that drew no particular attention to itself. When I first started my research and told administrators that I would be examining school cultures and racial identities, they immediately assumed I would be most interested in the "minority" groups who hung out in the cafeteria or the "hicks" in the parking lot. It seemed that, to them, the vast number of students who daily inhabited the Quad were without culture and race, and would thus be uninteresting to me.

The popular kids were a special designation among the normal kids. They were the supernormal: the best athletes with the best looks and physiques for boys, and the best personalities and looks for girls. Alternative names for them were "jocks," "preppies," and, for popular girls, "muffies." Apart from their popularity, the popular students were barely distinguishable in dress and musical tastes from the other "normal" students. Mormon and other religious kids were also among the normal and popular, but tended to stick together apart from the others. Overall, the normal and popular students were "good kids," for whom an important image was that they did not smoke, drink, or engage in other illicit activities. If they did do drugs, they did so surreptitiously. Laurie, a self-proclaimed popular girl, told me, "A lot of [popular] people smoke and drink and do drugs but just don't want it known. There are those that always do that [i.e., the smokers] and those that do it for fun and don't want you to know."[2]

The students who did engage in some kind of illicit, taboo, or unconventional activities looked markedly different from the normal and popular kids. They were the "hicks," "skaters," "punks," "hippies," "druggies," and "homies." Hicks dressed as if they had stepped off the set of an Old West movie. Boys and girls alike wore full-brimmed cowboy hats, pearl-buttoned shirts or blouses, leather belts with large metal buckles, butt-tight blue jeans, and pointy, tooled-leather boots. Some were "authentic" to the extent that their families lived on ranches and owned livestock, and they liked to ride horses and participate in rodeo competitions. Other hicks, according to a girl who identified herself as authentic, just "like[d] to dress Western." All had a reputation at Valley Groves for being "racist." I was told by nonhicks that hicks liked to brandish Confederate flags and had been responsible in the past for interracial fights on campus.

Skaters, who were all male at Valley Groves, always carried well-abused skateboards and took every opportunity to try a certain trick, even if—or in some cases, *especially* if—there was a prohibition against them doing so. They were marked by torn and ragged, superlarge, sagging-crotch trousers, and a thick layer of grime over all their clothes.

Punks, hippies, and druggies each had very distinctive styles and behaviors as well. Punks tended to be marked by spiked hair, studded clothing and accessories, and their love for punk rock music. By my count there was only one hardcore punk of this kind at Valley Groves; the rest were more typical of "glamor" punks, those who turn the edgy, rebellious styles of punk into hip fashion statements. At Valley Groves, these punks listened to some punk rock but mostly to underground alternative music, which is more melodic and pop-sounding than hardcore punk, which tends to overlay a raw, angry tone on a lightning-fast beat. They dyed their hair blue, purple, and other unusual colors and wore clean "retro" clothing, clothes that appeared like they were bought off the rack at a thrift store but actually went for top dollar at stores like Urban Outfitters. Hippies liked to smoke pot, listen to groups like the Grateful Dead, and wear colorful, frequently tie-dyed clothes. And the druggies were by and large the kids I ran into between the E and D halls. They were marked by conspicuous consumption of drugs—cigarettes, pot, or heavier stuff. Many spoke as though swimming through a dense haze, their eyes glazed and lips curled in a quizzical smile. Punks, hippies, and druggies were all mixed-gender groups.

And finally, the homies. They were externally defined by an affinity for rap music and wearing oversized, sagging pants (clean, not dirty), and poker faces. Many, but not all, were students of color, and although race-ethnic difference figured in homies being distinctly set apart from the other counterculture students, it was not the explicit reason, as I will discuss shortly. Homies carried the mantle of being the school's problem children, the students who were disruptive in class, prone to fights, and either involved in gang activity or at risk of being so.

Although each group on campus formed part of a diverse mosaic and had unique, identifying characteristics, a norm-other logic was the overarching principle by which students organized and made sense of their social world. The "normal" and popular students were, basically, those in compliance with school and adult mainstream expectations, and the "other" kids posed some contradiction to that. This type of norm-other dichotomy has been widely observed by other school ethnographers as a widespread and persistent culture in American schools.[3] To the extent that schools function to socialize youth into being productive and reproductive members of the adult mainstream, youth will situate themselves and others within a paradigm of who accommodates to school expectations and who does not.

The norm-other organizing principle was apparent in various ways in students' discourse. It shows itself in the words of Billy that open this chapter. Billy said that he was "normal" and wore "normal" clothes, which he defined in opposition to the types of clothes skaters and hicks wore. Laurie mentioned that although popular kids drank and did drugs, they wouldn't want anyone to know, presumably because that was the behavioral signature of druggies and other "others." A popular boy named Howie told me that the white kids he knew who were skaters or homies were the kids that nobody liked. He said, "People would look at them like nerds, that type of thing, and then they end up being skaters because they don't really care what or how they are." Finally, popular and normal students also tended to group druggies, skaters, hippies, and punks into one category, "smokers/ skaters," which, as I read it, cast a "deviant" ascription on those groups as a whole.

The students in the "other" side of the dichotomy also played up the differences between "rebel" and "mainstream" students. In my conversation with Carli, a self-identified hippie, she told me,

> "There's lots of appearance-loving people that dress really nice, care about what they wear, you know, go in the bathroom that's packed with girls fixing themselves; and guys are always making fun of each other when they do something wrong or stupid. . . . Then there's the rebels, who just sit around and complain all day [laughs.] And, you know, smoke pot at the tennis courts or whatever . . . I'd call them rebels 'cause they know that the system sucks, or they believe that the system sucks and they talk about it."

Later in our conversation, Carli and I were talking about skaters and their unkempt style. She said, "A skater's not a skater if he's not dirty, 'cause then he's pretty. . . ." I interpreted her to mean that if skaters were pretty, they would be buying into normative, mainstream behaviors and expectations.

This norm-other organizing principle was, in practice, race neutral and neutralizing. When I asked white students about cliques at Valley Groves, they tended not to mention the small groups of Filipino, Asian, Latino, and African American youth who routinely ate their lunch and socialized in the cafeteria. Those youth were rarely acknowledged because "race" was not the dominant form of social organization. During our interview, Maria, a middle-class senior of mixed Mexican American and German American descent, told me that the "first cut of students starts with who is popular" and who fits in the other cliques on campus. Secondarily, if at all, youth made racial distinctions between groups. Moreover, beyond the fact that "mainstream" may be arguably defined as culturally "white," the norm-other dichotomy was not a code for a "white-other" racial distinction. Cliques within the range of "normal" kids and those in the range of "other" were all predominantly white, with the exception of the homies. But even they were not entirely racially homogeneous nor particularly racially marked. African American, Filipino, and/or Latino youth were in every school category, such as in groups of popular kids, hicks, and skaters. Admittance into a group was not based on race but on conformity to the styles, values, and demeanors of the other members. Inside and outside members of these cliques looked at each other and saw internal sameness, not difference. If and when they acknowledged racial differences, students emphasized the race-neutralizing effects of the activities and interests shared by the group. For example, when I was talking to a skater one day, he proudly described skaters as "multi-cultural." He pointed out that among their crowd were an African American and an Asian American. Then he added, "But that doesn't make any difference. We all love to skate together, hang out together. . . ."

Similarly, when I would probe white students about the small, "ethnic" cliques, students would usually point out that they were not racially exclusive, suggesting that something other than race or ethnicity held them together. As Billy said, when I asked him if ethnic or racial groups on campus had their own cliques, "Hmmm. Yeah, some. They hang out [together], but then there's always another person of another race hanging out with them. I would say it's pretty much integrated. I know there's some African American kids that hang out, but they'll hang out with some white kids. It's pretty much integrated, I think."

During a group interview with ten African American youth at Valley Groves, we talked about cliques and friendship groups and what kind of kids the students in the group hung out with. All five of the girls said that their friends were either white or racially diverse, and the five boys said their friends were all black. They explained this gender divide as a result of black males being more subjected to racism by white males on campus. However, Ron, one of the boys, added, "One of the guys that hangs out with us is white. He's not a racist and we've known each other since seventh grade." He further commented that he had no problem with whites who were cool and not racist. I felt that by saying these things Ron was wanting to make sure that I understood that his group of friends was not exclusive in terms of *race* but in terms of ra*cists*.

To those outside Ron's clique, his was a group of homies. I confess that when I first heard about homies, I assumed that the term was a code for "blacks" or, at least, "minorities," but I came to believe that this was not exactly the case. Valley Groves youth, whether they were white, black, Latino, or Asian American, were tagged "homie" for their style and were not referred to as "white" homies or "Latino" homies as would occur if the term implicitly meant "black" (as the way "slave" implies *black* slave, making it difficult to speak of a white "slave" without specifying "white"). A kind of racelessness surrounded the homie term, as it did other social categories at Valley Groves.

To say that racial distinctions were not primarily at play in the social organization of Valley Groves, however, does not mean that the construction and reproduction of racial—and class[4]—meanings were not in process. Indeed they were, if surreptitiously or indirectly. They "spoke through"[5] and helped define social distinctions on campus. Characteristics that classified homies—criminal behavior, disidentification with school, nonstandard ways of talking and dressing—spoke "nonwhite" (even though homies were not all nonwhite) and "working-class" (even though they were not all working-class). Similarly, classifying hicks as "racist" invoked derogatory stereotypes of working-class whites (even though many hicks were not working-class). Oppositional identities need not be explicitly defined as "nonwhite" or "working-class" to be, simply, an "other" for constructing the untainted, normal self—in this case the middle-class, white self. My point is that, at Valley Groves, the logic of race-neutrality obscured the ways social distinctions on campus reproduced race and class meanings. This logic was so deeply embedded in common sense that, frequently, when I asked students about the race or ethnicity of a homie they had mentioned, they would answer hesitatingly and with ambivalence, as if they only noticed that the kid was a homie and didn't notice his race. This was more than simply an awkwardness about revealing race consciousness (and hence belying a race-neutral conviction); white students at Valley Groves seemed either to not take note of race or to erase racial observations from their minds as quickly as they made them.

Lived Experience, White European American Culture, and the Construction of Normative Racelessness

I suggest that the logic of race-neutrality that was a central organizing principle of social life at Valley Groves was at least partially constituted and reinforced by, on the one hand, little face-to-face association with racialized "others" and, on the other, a normative school culture predominantly derived from white European American culture but experienced as natural, commonsense, and normal.

Honors courses at Valley Groves were the most difficult and demanding and best fulfilled the academic standards required for admission into the University of California and other high-ranking universities. Entry into honors courses usually required a preliminary examination and a departmental selection process that took into account the exam score, previous grades, and school record. I followed Maria through a schedule of honors-level, college-preparatory courses. In her classes, students were all very well-mannered and disciplined in the classroom. They would arrive in class with their work done and minds ready for discussion. Pens worked furiously during lectures, and when given the impulse to speak, youths always raised their hands and waited on the teacher to call on them. The students in Maria's classes, like Maria, also tended to be active in school leadership, major sports, and other core activities of school life.

General curriculum courses filled the basic requirements for graduation from Valley Groves, but were not rigorous enough to satisfy U.C. requirements. Carli was a junior, white, middle-class girl with whom I attended some core courses. Students in Carli's history and English classes were a mixed lot; some were disciplined and attentive and others much less so. Carli's history class, for example, happened to catch a good number of counterculture students—skaters, punks, and hippies—who seemed to enjoy challenging the teacher's authority. They would talk or do other inattentive things while the teacher lectured or tried to get discussion going, or they would defy her pleas to sit in their assigned seats. Usually, the teacher would be able to restore order after no more than the second admonition. Work got done, discussions were engaged and lively, and the next day students would return with their homework completed, even if they had copied it from someone else's.

In the vocational courses I observed, the students had a commitment to their education similar to that of college-prep students. Since course work was more based on hands-on projects and not lectures, students were allowed to converse informally among each other, but always with their attention to the task at hand. They took their work seriously and frequently spent after-hours working on their projects.

Though different in academic content, rigor, and student expectations, these different course tracks shared one attribute: the students in them were predominantly, if not exclusively, white. Exceptions were Maria's advanced-level Spanish class, of which about one-third were students of color (Latino and Asian), and her honors biology and algebra classes, which were about one-fifth Asian. However, in all of her other classes—honors history and government, leadership, honors English—Maria would be one among two or three students of color. Few youth of color were in Carli's general education courses. The students in her classes, which included history, English, drama, and band, were almost entirely white, with no more than two or three students of color. And although the vocational courses tended to draw in more working-class youth and, hence, more students of color (Filipinos and Latinos, mostly), those classes were still predominantly white.

While in these classes, students of color rarely acted culturally different from the white students. They mixed easily with the white peers and friends surrounding them, speaking like them, laughing at their jokes or buffoonery, and being just as attentive or rowdy as they. Sandra, for example, was an African American girl I would see in a drama class I frequented. She was the only person of color in the class and, when in there, she spoke in standard English, used words like *dude*, and joked and gossiped with the three white girls at her assigned table. She did not reveal the Sandra I would see outside of class, hanging out with a small group of black girls with whom she used elements of Black English and changed her physical demeanor to be more performative of blackness than whiteness.[6]

Of course, Valley Groves *was* a predominantly white school, so the limited numbers of students of color in the classrooms can be expected. However, in the core courses, demographic representation was not proportional to the school demographics. I never completely ascertained just where the students of color were, except that one day, while roaming through the halls during class time, I came upon a class in which the *majority* of students were of color, African American and Latino especially. I recognized many of the youth. I had seen them clumped together in racially homogeneous groups at break and lunch, unengaged with the school mainstream. They were younger students, too—sophomores and freshmen. I wondered, but never confirmed, whether the class was one of the school's Special Education classes, designed to meet the needs of students who "show a discrepancy between ability and achievement."[7] Mounting evidence suggests that students of color get farmed into remedial classes for reasons based more on biased expectations than on merit, a topic I address in the next chapter.

Plausible explanations for the paucity of students of color at the junior and senior levels are, first, that the school was in an upward trend toward greater diversity. That would place more students of color among the newest arrivals, at the freshmen and sophomore levels. Also, one teacher told me that there was considerable attrition of students of color; many dropped out or otherwise moved elsewhere by their junior or senior year. Whatever the reasons, the results were that students of color were either starkly minoritized in some classrooms, or congregated in others where they were invisible to students in the core courses. The significance of this came across strongly in my group interview with the ten African American students. Several of them spoke at length about feelings of ostracism and racism they experienced in their encounters with white students and authorities, but their experiences were not "seen" by the white students. As one girl put it: "[The white kids] hang out in the middle of the Quad—in the center of everything—but haven't got a clue [about what's going on with the students of color.]"

When I asked white students at Valley Groves what amount of interaction they felt they had with people of color, most looked at me as though I had asked a stupid question. "None at all" or "very little," they would say. Carli commented to me in our interview that she valued the fact that one of the band members was African American, because otherwise she had virtually no opportunities to interact with youth of color.

School Cultural Life

Just as the dominant norms in classrooms were defined by white students, so were the dominant school norms outside of class. This was at least partially because most school activities were organized by the "leadership" students, who comprised the elected school officials, the elected presidents of each class, and twenty appointed officers. During my year at Valley Groves, there were thirty-five students in the leadership class, and all were white except one African American sophomore girl, an Asian American senior girl, and two Mexican American girls, one a junior and the other, Maria, a senior. The students met daily during a regular class period and used that time to plan and organize school events, create and administer policies on student activities, and evaluate their own effectiveness. They were charged with the task of designing ways to raise other students' engagement in and support for the school through various collective activities. They were also in the position of interpreting what would appeal to students while at the same time trying to constitute and model such acceptable behavior on campus as studiousness and spirited participation in extracurricular activities. On several occasions I observed the leadership teacher or students admonishing other students for not setting the right "example."

Music: Rock-Centered Eclecticism

The type of music that dominated campuswide events and special occasions tended to be eclectic, but predominantly based in sounds and songs performed by white artists for white audiences. On special days, like Oktoberfest, Homecoming, or Valentine's Day, youth were allowed to play music over loudspeakers in the Quad during lunch. Usually, as students moved into the Quad from class, the music set would open with something with a strong beat, like a rap or reggae song. Then, whoever was at the audio equipment (usually a student from the school leadership) played a range of songs that favored rock in all its transmutations: alternative rock, classic rock, and heavy metal.

This rock-centered musical eclecticism was most obvious at school dances, when the mix of music would be critical. For the Senior Ball, the organizers painstakingly put together a song list they believed everyone would enjoy. It contained a mix of alternative and classic rock, with some rap, reggae, heavy metal, and country tunes. At the Ball, however, the hired disc jockey (white male) did not play the list and drew on his own idea of what would go over with the crowd. Though the organizers were disturbed by this, the new play list seemed to make little difference to the youth on the dance floor. For the first few hours of the Ball, the DJ played a range of dance club music, like "house," disco, and some pop r & b. As youth finished their dinners and began heading to the dance floor, he varied the musical styles even more, including some non-"Gangsta" rap (the Beastie Boys, a white male rap group, was a favorite), some alternative music, reggae, disco from the seventies, and classic rock.

As the hour approached midnight, the music became thematic, partially imparting messages to frame the moment and partially leading youth through a nostalgic path back in time. One set started with "Celebrate Good Times," a song to which students sang along, shouting "GOOD

TIMES!" at the appropriate moments in the refrain. To "Staying Alive," a song by the Bee Gees that was popular when the dancers had to be toddlers, the crowd screamed in approval. The youth danced with one arm on their hips and the other jutting diagonally out then down across their bodies with index fingers extended, like John Travolta in the movie *Saturday Night Fever*. A line dance started and gathered about fifty youth to the song "YMCA" by the Village People. Youth howled as they moved around the floor in a giant snake and tried collectively to synchronize a rhythmic foot pattern.

Homecoming

The school rallies and events I attended featured predominantly white students, with one or two exceptions, and attracted audiences that were themselves overwhelmingly white. Possibly the most popular and well-attended series of school activities were those surrounding homecoming. Leadership students sought to involve the whole school in the homecoming activities, so they tried to design activities that would excite the interest and imagination of all students.

Homecoming was celebrated by a series of activities that took place throughout the week preceding the big game. Events included the nominations and elections of the Homecoming King and Queen, who were seniors, and Princes and Princesses, drawn from each of the three lower grade levels. Each weekday was also a "Theme Day," in which students were encouraged to dress according to the specified theme. In the homecoming I observed, the themes were the decades of the fifties, sixties, seventies, eighties, and nineties. At lunch, the leadership students played music from those eras and staged different contests or performances. For example, on the "fifties" day, leadership boys wore white t-shirts with the sleeves rolled up, tucked into fitted blue jeans with the bottoms cuffed. Girls tied colorful cloths around pony tails, and wore pedal pusher pants or poodle skirts. During lunch, the music of Jerry Lee Lewis, Roy Orbison, and Elvis Presley filled the air. Leadership students staged a hula-hoop contest, for which ten white girls volunteered to put their hip-swinging skills to the test. The contest quickly narrowed down to three, then two. The winner exited the stage with the hoop still gyrating around her midriff.

The day before the homecoming game there was a daytime rally, duplicated and scheduled so that the entire student body could attend in parts.

Students flocked into the gym to the driving beats and thundering bass of a heavy metal tune and found seats in different quadrants of the gym, depending on their grade level. Each grade quadrant had their respective cheerleaders to help incite enthusiasm and augment the decibel levels to proddings by the MC. Just before the official ceremony began, two big, husky white males (appearing to be seniors) dragged into the center of the auditorium a small boy (appearing to be a freshman) whose feet and legs were bound with silver duct tape. The crowd laughed and applauded. The two husky guys pumped their fists in the air to encourage the crowd, then dragged the boy off center stage. After a brief greeting, members of the student leadership committee introduced the junior varsity and varsity football players. The players came out and formed a line across the middle of the gym floor. The boys were white except for three black players on the junior varsity team and, on the varsity team, two boys with Hispanic surnames. As each player's name was called, he stepped forward to acknowledge the applause. Most did so hesitatingly, with their heads bowed and shoulders shrugged as if to express shyness or humility. Two or three boldly strutted out, trying to play up the roars of the crowd. These few stood out like dissonant notes in a harmonic chord.

Then the varsity cheerleaders bolted to center stage, leaping energetically before getting into formation for their choreographed performance. The girls were all thin, some overly so, and wore uniforms with tight bodices and short skirts that made them look even more diminutive. But their body sizes belied their strength. Their dance, driven by the music of the hard-rock group Rage Against the Machine, was gymnastic, with lots of cartwheels, flips, and pyramid constructions that were punctuated by the top girls falling trustingly into the arms of their comrades. Long, silky blonde hair parachuted out with each acrobatic stunt. The audience remained silent and attentive, with an occasional collective gasp at the girls' athletic mastery, until the performance was over. At that time, the cheerleaders took in roaring, vocal applause.

On day three of Homecoming Week, students held a parade after school. As with other afterschool events I had observed, a sizable number of parents now joined in the activities. As the parade was assembling on the basketball courts outside the gym, parents helped their teenagers with their costumes and the lineup, and some did other tasks, such as staffing a cold drink and snacks table. Younger children stayed close by moms and dads, or found each other and invented games to keep themselves busy and out of the center of things.

The parade took off from the basketball courts and wound its way through the student parking lot, across the main road running in front of the school, and onto a residential side street. Four adult males, two of whom appeared to be Mexican American, led the parade, mounted on prancing horses and wearing Mexican serapes and sombreros. The *caballeros* sat earnestly on their horses, and the front two carried large replicas of the California and United States flags. Following them were two convertibles, one of which was a white Corvette carrying the white, female city mayor. Following her was a blue mustang carrying another official. The two esteemed riders smiled broadly and waved ceremoniously to the onlookers on the sidewalks.

The music of the marching band, which followed closely behind the mayor, announced the arrival of the parade along its path. A group of eight white and one African American female dancers led the band, tossing and spinning colored flags in sync with the beat of the band's percussion section. The fifty musicians in the band, most of whom appeared to be white, with five or six exceptions, marched in tight formation. Uniformed in white t-shirts with denim jeans and athletic shoes, they paused periodically to finesse a quick turn with intricate footwork while competently sustaining musical and metrical precision.

Following the band was a truckload each of varsity and junior varsity football players, wearing their team jerseys and visor caps. They were flanked on two sides by cheerleaders, who were keeping up with the trucks on foot. Directly behind was a string of Chevy pickups carrying the school "royalty." Paper banners strung along the sides of each truck identified the class level and royal rank of each couple. Wearing casual school clothes and paper crowns, the sophomore and freshmen "Princes" and "Princesses" and the senior Homecoming "King" and "Queen" sat stately upon ornate thrones and smiled regally at their admirers. The next-to-last contingent in the parade was a group of seniors, piled high on a flat bed and hooting and cheering as if their graduation day were already here. The tail end of the parade was punctuated by a lone white preadolescent girl on a palomino horse.

The parade wound through several blocks of residences before returning to the main street and slowly making its way back to the school. Proud parents were perched on the sidewalks with their thirty-five millimeter and video cameras in hand. Community residents stepped onto their front landings to wave and cheer as the parade passed their homes. Others peered out through large pane windows with cats in arms and dogs at heel.

Reading Homecoming

As I saw it, homecoming at Valley Groves was not an event—not *only* an event, anyway—it was a process. The activities were packed with values, behaviors, assumptions, and origin stories that privileged white European American perspectives as well as gender, sexuality, and class-based norms (all of which coproduce one another). As such, they contributed to the process of constituting and reconstituting what being white and American meant.[8] For example, during lunch in the Quad, representations of fifties rock and roll were dominated by white artists, even though that was the era when African Americans still ruled rock and roll and were its greatest innovators. The "hula hoop" is derived from the "hula," a traditional Hawaiian ceremonial dance that European Americans appropriated, modified, and recoded. In short, both of those public displays gave testimony to and confirmed white domination through cultural colonization.

At the rally, the implicitly condoned display of the hog-tied freshman asserted white (male) supremacy through domination of the "weak" and demonstrated that whiteness is sustained not only through the subordination of nonwhite others, but of "other" whites as well.[9] The virtues of personal mastery and self-effacement were exemplified by the humble postures of the footballers and reinforced by the slights the audience gave to those who presented themselves with more bravado. Then, the cheerleaders' gravity-defying athletic feats demonstrated that the girls had successfully learned to subjugate their bodies and overcome nature. Their thin, bounded physiques brought to my mind reports about the ways white male constructions of "pure" and repressed womanhood historically helped bolster white patriarchal authority over white and black women and black men.[10]

Finally, the homecoming parade, with its display of the national and state flags, American cars, marching band, and school royalty was a stunning way to observe the coproduction of whiteness, American-ness, citizenship, and gendered codes of conduct. The "Mexican" horsemen heralding the parade with the California and United States flags and followed by a long trail of white youth in American vehicles tells its own story of white European domination and artfully knits together whiteness with "America." The marching band—itself an icon of white European militarism, patriotism, and ingenuity—confirmed values of discipline, competence, and mastery, and the "royalty" confirmed gender and sexuality norms. And, by virtue of who was there and who was not, the knitting together of the themes of mastery, domination, nationhood, and industry with *whiteness* was seamless. Other cultures in the school and community were not represented in the parade. There were no Filipino dancers, Asian martial artists, or African American rappers. The event was performed by whites and for whites, and, thus, little contradicted the cultural and political assumptions at play.

And what of the young girl on the blonde horse taking up the end of the parade? I saw her as a figure of the lone rider in Hollywood Westerns who heads off into the sunset, a symbol of (white) independence and individualism with her gender and youth signifying, respectively, liberalism and "we've only just begun."

In this chapter I have argued that a *race-neutral,* norm-other logic was the principal scheme by which white Valley Groves students organized their social world and, as succeeding chapters will illustrate, their identities as whites. Race neutrality was not particular to Valley Groves; several scholars have observed the same culture in other American suburban schools.[11] My main objective has been to illustrate the processes by which race neutrality was constructed and reinforced. In a word, whiteness was *hegemonic.* Raymond Williams defines hegemony as that which

> supposes the existence of something that is truly total . . . which is lived at such a depth, which saturates the society to such an extent, and which . . . even constitutes the limit of commonsense for most people under its sway. . . . [Hegemony] is the whole body of practices and expectations; our assignments of energy, our ordinary understanding of man and his world. It is a set of meanings and values which as they are experienced as practices appear as reciprocally confirming.[12]

At Valley Groves, white European-American cultural norms and expectations "saturated" practical life. White students had very little association with racialized identities or clearly defined racial and cultural difference to whiteness, making white European-American norms ubiquitous and unmarked. Meanwhile, the construction of those norms as "normal" and taken for granted was actively, if unconsciously, achieved through collective approval and reinforcement from white students and adults alike. That approval came across in a range of ways, from the mild manners of the school authorities and supervisors who continually assured students that they were "good kids," to the enthusiastic reception of school parents and neighbors to students' activities and public displays.

The argument in this chapter will come into sharper focus in the next chapter, where I present the social and cultural milieu at Clavey High. School life there was not as saturated with whiteness as it was at Valley Groves, and daily, face-to-face interaction with youth and adults of color led to very different constructions of social life for white students at Clavey.

2. Clavey High

"There aren't enough white kids here

to have many skaters."

It was my third visit to Clavey and the student activities director had invited me to sit in on his student leadership course and take a few students out of class for brief, preliminary interviews. The first student I spoke to was Maxine, an African American senior and a member of the varsity cheerleading squad. We sat facing each other on wooden chairs behind the classroom, she appearing fully composed and I feeling a little nervous doing my first interview. I asked Maxine to tell me what were the main cliques or groups that hung out together at the school. She replied confidently, "Well, there are the white groups, the black groups," the tone of her voice suggesting the list went on to include "Asian groups," "Latino groups," and so forth. She continued, "You'll see the white people hang out on the senior lawn, the blacks outside the cafeteria and the 30 and 40 buildings."

Naively assuming Maxine didn't fully understand what I was getting at, I asked if there were certain kids who were considered "popular" and, if so, what made someone popular. Maxine responded, "Well, it kinda depends on the [racial-ethnic] group. Each group has its popular people. The athletes, like the basketball players, are most popular among the blacks. I don't know who is popular in the white group, but it's like that."

What I came to grasp, after a few more preliminary interviews and observations, was that, unlike Valley Groves, where students were primarily categorized by their orientation to the mainstream and secondarily by race, at Clavey the opposite was true. Race was the primary principle of social organization. Here, whiteness was neither taken for granted nor unmarked for white European American youth.

Clavey High: A Multicultural Pie in the Sky

At the foot of the hill leading up to the high school campus is a colorful, student-produced mural depicting eight youths standing in a semicircle with their hands cross-linked behind their backs. Each figure is painted with different skin tone and type of hair to signify racial and ethnic differences. Inscribed along the mural's border is "unity" written in eight different languages, only three of which are Western European.

Directly behind this upbeat and inspiring image, however, is a tall chain-linked fence that passes the mural as it wraps around the periphery of the school. Entry onto the school grounds is permissible through a large gate that is dutifully guarded by a hefty security guard. The fence, gate, and guard, and not the mural, set the prevalent tone around Clavey High. If the mood and disciplinary style at Valley Groves was maternal, reinforcing, and nurturing, at Clavey it was paternal, authoritarian, and punitive—distinctions that other scholars have observed between predominantly white suburban and predominantly "minority" urban schools.[1]

"We teach discipline here. That's all," Clavey's dean, Mr. Richards, said to me after he commanded a group of students, who were still moving haltingly toward class long after the period bell had rung, to pick up their pace. Once a school counselor, Mr. Richards bemoaned the fact that, as dean, he had become more a "policeman" than an administrator or youth advocate. During times when students were passing between classes or on break, Mr. Richards, an African American male, and four security guards, also African American males, would roam the campus with bullhorns and whistles. Their stern admonitions and commands could always be heard well above the din of student chatter. Detention hall awaited all those late for class or acting out of line.

At lunch the school principal, Mr. Grey, joined the security team. He was a tall, big-boned, and hunched-over white man with a long, drawn face that, on occasion, contrived a smile. It seldom appeared to me that he was out among the students to join, talk informally, and connect with them, only to control them. If he wished congenial interaction, his sober, authoritarian demeanor was not particularly inviting of it. When I first talked to Mr. Grey about conducting my research at Clavey, he initially refused my access to the campus. He said, "To be honest, I'm afraid. You'll be out there talking about race and I'm afraid you'll stir up racial tension." (After a brief probationary period, I proved myself harmless and he finally consented to my field presence.) This low regard for the maturity and self-discipline of Clavey students was frequently echoed by teachers, many of whom generally referred to the youth as "disrespectful," "difficult," and "unmanageable."

School Life

Just over half of Clavey students identified themselves as black/African American, and the rest as Asian or Asian American, white, Latino, Pacific Islander, and Native American. When students were all out and about the campus during breaks, they formed a "colorful," multidimensional sea. The sea formed eddies in places, where surface currents took on a distinct, semiuniform appearance before reintegrating into the choppy, unpredictable whole. If there was one thing that unified the contours of this sea, however, it was, to borrow a descriptive term from one of my interviewees, the "drip look." Most boys wore clean oversized denim pants or sweat pants, the crotches of which sagged a quarter way to their knees. With these, they donned large and long, untucked t-shirts or hooded sweatshirts, large bulky parkas, and sparkling-clean athletic shoes. It was the style that only the "homies" wore at Valley Groves, but at Clavey it did not mark any particular group. Although it had its origin in styles worn by African American rappers, it was not confused with such. It was just the norm, the conformist style. One informant called it the "leveler" style because it made all who wore it "the same."[2]

Girls' styles, as is usually the case, were less uniform than boys', but for the most part, also stuck close to the "drip look." For casual wear, most African American and Latino girls wore loose-fit, faded blue jeans, a cotton blouse tucked in with a belt, and a lightweight jacket or an additional, heavy blouse. They wore athletic shoes or different kinds of oxfords and sandals. Asian-American girls leaned toward the "houser" look, the defining feature of which was wide-legged, bell-bottomed pants. For white girls at Clavey, the most favored style was "grunge," another baggy look, only in clothes that looked well worn—faded, torn in places—and as though they had been purchased in a thrift store. Grunge girls commonly wore two shirts, usually a short-sleeve t-shirt over a long-sleeve t-shirt, that they tucked into faded denim overalls or let hang over baggy cargo pants. With this they wore either tennis shoes, open sandals, heavy shoes, or boots with pattern-base soles, and some kind of choker around their necks. Short- to medium-length hair clipped with little plastic butterfly or bow barrettes and looking as though it had not been washed for several days was the norm.

African American girls, more than other girls at Clavey, paid attention to standard notions of feminine beauty. On occasion, they wore dresses, or skirts and blouses with pump shoes and leather jackets. Even on casual days they always paid meticulous attention to their hair and nails. A common hair style was shoulder length with bangs, chemically straightened and gelled so that the hair lay close to the scalp. For more dressy days, black girls had their hair sculpted into awe-inspiring creations of waves and curls. Nails were very long and artfully painted.

At lunch students often had a wide, if unremarkable, assortment of foods to buy. The cafeteria serviced students with assorted plastic-wrapped sandwiches and burritos, corn dogs, fresh onion rings, hamburgers, slices of pizza, and a small salad bar. Now and then the kitchen staff put out a barbecue stand and served chicken or ribs. On special occasions, like Christmas or Thanksgiving, they prepared meals like turkey with mashed potatoes and gravy. And once a month or so, students would sell food to raise funds for their class or club. Lumpia, a deep-fried Filipino egg roll, was a favorite among all youth, so Filipino students sold that often. It was one of a few items that were made in the home. Other foods that students sold included store-bought cookies, cakes, and candy.

Youth Cultures and Race

Maevis was a senior girl of European-American descent. She had pearly skin, short and straight blonde hair, blue eyes circumscribed with dark eyeliner, and a sparkling smile enhanced by lips bathed in garnet-colored lipstick. She caught my attention on my first day at Clavey when she walked into the drama class I was observing, approached a group of African American girls and boys, and affectionately plopped herself down on the lap of one of the boys. She was clearly comfortable with herself and her close association with black students at the school, and so I sought her out for an interview. I was particularly interested in her perspective on the different styles and cultures that students adhered to. Maevis explained to me,

> "[Among the white kids] there's the preppies, the stoners, and the alternatives. That's basically it. The preppies are kids from [a predominantly white, middle- to upper-middle-class neighborhood in the hills]. They'll hang out in the Gap clothes, eating their couscous and, you know, all that. They'll have the nice cars and the good upbringing. They all hang out together. Then there's the stoners, who hang out near the gym. They just basically spend the whole lunch smoking cigarettes and joints and stuff and, you know, talking about how bad they are. And then there's the alternatives, people who listen to alternative music and dress grunge and all that. I hang out with them 'cause that's what my best friends are, you know? But I'll hang out with everybody else, too."

Maevis went on to name some of the distinctions among black youth at Clavey. "There's the ghetto people, which are more gangster wannabe type of people. There's like a richer and upper class of black people who wear clothes from Macy's and hang out with each other. There's the athletes, who are all really popular and stand in the middle of the lower lawn. There's the Muslims. You've seen them on the senior lawn at lunch, praying and stuff."

From conversations with other students of different racial-ethnic identities, I learned some other terms that marked intragroup distinctions. For example, in addition to the subgroups Maevis defined among whites were "straights" (alternate word for preppies), "skaters," "hippies" (alternate for stoners), "ravers," "white rappers," and "punks." Among African American students were "rappers," "leadership," and "fashion hounds." Among Asian Americans were "newly arrived" (or, more derogatorily, "Fresh off the Boat" or "FOB"), "native," "housers," "techno," and "gangsters."

In part, the groups within each racial category were self-referential; that is, in-group distinctions played off internal differences in real or putative class backgrounds, religious affiliation, immigrant generation, subcultural identities, and levels of mainstream conformity. With respect to the white students, although Maevis's comments suggested that class background played a role in delineating different kinds of white kids, I found that in-group distinctions were less about class "origin" than class "performance."[3] I met straights, alternatives, and punks from the same neighborhoods and socioeconomic origins who carried themselves—performed—in ways that either played up or played down class background. The term by which white students differentiated themselves was, instead of "class," "mainstream," which tended to imply white, middle-class, conformist allegiances and/or performances. The straight students were the most mainstream; they were similar to the "normal" students at Valley Groves. Besides wearing Gap-type clothes, they tended to listen to classic rock and roll and mind their studies at school. "Alternative" youth, as the name implies, prided themselves on creating styles and music that challenged mainstream conventional norms, such as "grunge" clothing (second-hand, torn, faded, sometimes grimy and oddly matched), rainbow-colored hair, and atonal music. However, punks and hippies set themselves apart from alternatives, claiming that the *latter* were too mainstream.

For example, Pickles was a punk who wore ripped-up, green army fatigues, painted combat boots, and a silver-studded dog collar around her neck. She shaved her hair close to the scalp with the exception of a strip in front that spiked out about four inches from her forehead. In a conversation, she referred to the "little mainstream grunger girls." I, surprised, asked if she thought that grunge (alternative) music was mainstream. She replied, "Yeah, definitely. They're 'alternative' to the mainstream, but it's mainstream. . . . Don't [bother] with alternative music. Just assume that it's a bunch of shit."

However, despite what seemed like hard and fast distinctions between different kinds of white students, the boundaries between them were not actually that rigid. In many ways, sartorial differences between the "white" groups were not as striking as they were at Valley Groves. Grunge and punk hair styles and colors were subdued by comparison, body piercings were minimal and mostly confined to ears, and, overall, a faded, worn, and unkempt look made punks, alternatives, hippies, and some straights look quite alike. Moreover, crossing over subgroup boundaries among whites was not a big issue. As Maevis said, she hung out "with everybody else, too." And finally, several students I asked about the different subgroups among whites said that they didn't think white students were that cliquish at Clavey because they seemed to get homogenized by race. One boy told me, "There are so few whites, and *race* is so central around here that we tend to all blend together. Race sort of makes the differences between us less important."

Indeed, besides being internally referential, white and other racial-ethnic subgroups were also *externally* referential to the extent that they all marked racial difference and identity.[4] In the eyes of whites and nonwhites alike, straights, alternatives, punks, and hippies were unambivalently "white"; things like Gap clothing, Standard English, spiked hair, tie-dyed clothing, and modern rock marked whiteness and white identity.[5] Similarly, Black English, gold-plated chains and ear studs (for boys), crispy clean clothing, and underground rap music were codes for African American identity; "Ben Davis" pants, speaking Spanish or "Spanglish," long curly hair wrapped in a high pony tail (for girls), and listening to traditional Mexican and contemporary Latin music marked Chicano and Latino identity; broadly belled pants, martial arts, techno music, and certain hairstyles achievable only with thick, straight hair marked Asian American identity. Youth within those racial-ethnic groups could use the codes of their identity without sanction but outsiders could not, not without being accused of abandoning their heritage.[6]

For example, Sandra was an African American girl from a single-parent, very low-income family. When we spoke, my eyes kept fixing on a small, sterling ring that pierced the middle of her lower lip. Her jet-black hair was streaked with purple; now and then a single, tiny braid wrapped in colorful string swung into her face. She spoke quietly and softly in Standard English, which she called "proper," and for which, she said, she had been accused of "sounding white." And although she liked some rap music, her favorite was alternative. She said that her closest friends admired her for having the courage to be different. Others, however, would call her a "sell-out," implying that she had abandoned her "true" racial identity.

Gloria was a sophomore who had immigrated with her family from El Salvador seven years before our meeting. She told me, "For my race, if you start wearing a lot of gold, you're trying to be black. If you're trying to braid your hair, you'll be accused of trying to act black. I'm scared to do things 'cause they might say 'That's black!' Or if you're Latino and you listen to that, uh, you know, like Green Day—"

"You mean, like, alternative rock?" I asked.

"Yeah, that kinda thing. If you listen to that, then you wanna be white. They [Latinos] don't like that kinda stuff, the majority don't. 'Oh my god, why you listening to that music?' they'd say. And, like, one time I bought this gel and on the picture outside the bottle had a little black girl. I just got it for my hair and my friend saw it and, oh my god, she made a drama out of it.

'So! Why you trying to be black? Aren't you proud of who you are?' I didn't [buy] it 'cause I wanted to be black, I wanted it for my hair!"

White youth I spoke to referred to whites who adopted black styles and demeanors as "wannabe black" or "white rappers." In some cases, however, adopting a core style and the friends to match graduated youth beyond "wannabe" to a form of cross-racial conversion. For example, I asked Barry, a "straight" white senior, if he ever had a girlfriend who wasn't white. He replied, "I had a girlfriend who was Asian, but only in the sense of the way she looked. Her family was fully Americanized, or whatever. Didn't observe any Asian traditions or anything. . . . I considered her to be white, basically, except physically." When I pursued what he meant by "American," he said, "Mainstream . . . normal. That plain ol' nuclear family, two kids and a dog, middle class. Suburbany."

Or take the case of Jeremy, a senior male of Asian ancestry. Jeremy dressed semistraight and semialternative and hung out exclusively with white kids. One day in the school auditorium I overheard a white girl say to him, "I can't believe you're Asian. I always thought of you as white. You're *white!*"

Finally, take the case of Trish, who first caught my attention when I overheard a group of teachers talking about how "black" she looked, even though she had an entirely white European ancestry. She had pale skin, light brown hair, and crystal blue eyes, but associated almost exclusively with African Americans and had assumed and embodied every nuance of the "core" black style and demeanor for girls: from Black English and body language to the way she styled her hair and trimmed her nails. Trish told me, "A lot of my [black] friends go, 'Oh Trish, you're just black,' and I go 'No, no, no!' I don't want to seem like I'm [trying to be black]. . . . I really don't put that label on myself. But they'll say, 'Oh, Trish is black anyway.' "[7]

Class and gender played a role in lending authenticity to "cross-over" identities like Trish's. The white youth at Clavey who had *only* black friends and had fully cross-identified with African Americans, assuming their styles, language, and demeanors, were working-class youth, mostly working-class *girls*, like Trish. Poor and working-class youth growing up together in similar neighborhoods created commonalities of experience and dispositions that resulted in similar styles and ways of being. And, according to Trish, white girls seemed to mix better with black girls because white boys who hung out with African American males did so more out of a desire to appear nonracist, cool, and macho—to "get the girls." She also suggested that the desire to prove manhood through the "strong thing" led to more violence between boys. With girls, she said, relationships are based more on friendship and are less competitive.

Some students, white males in particular, played at the borders of racial distinctions in style and demeanor where they were neither marked as "wannabe" nor as cross-identified. Skaters and ravers (students who liked to attend raves, all-night underground dance parties) employed cultural practices that, in this context, typically marked "black" identity, such as listening to rap music and wearing deeply-sagged pants, but they changed or added something so as to mark difference from blackness. Skaters cut off their pants at the bottom, instead of letting them pile up at the ankle, and they wore Converse-type tennis shoes or Vans instead of Nike or Fila brand athletic models. Ravers added different nuances. Duncan, who organized a rave that I had attended, told me, "You can tell ravers from gangsters by the way they dress, by their demeanor. We all wear baggy clothes, right?—So parents think! But you find that ravers have cut-off bottoms to their jeans, they wear bigger t-shirts they have hanging out of their pants, they carry packs that's full of crap that they take everywhere." He added that, whereas gangsters maintain a hard, violent facade, ravers are peaceful and congenial.

Other things that marked whiteness on skaters and ravers were long wallet chains, dirty and torn clothes (as opposed to the meticulous cleanliness of the black kids' clothes), and the juxtaposition of hip hop style with something from alternative or punk style, such as brightly colored hair or a "retro"-looking jacket.

As may be apparent, the skater and raver styles discussed above were for males. All of the skaters when I was at Clavey were white males, and though there were girl ravers, their style was quite different from the boys'. I didn't meet any girl ravers at Clavey, but what I learned from attending the rave coproduced by Duncan was that the girls tended to wear clothes more in line with the "alternative" or "grunge" style—tight halter tops that expose the midriff, baggy, soft-cotton pants, macrame or chain chokers. Overall, white girls at Clavey did not play in the borderlands of racialized styles. They tended to go either/or: either for the "white" alternative styles or, for a few, the "black" styles, as I discussed above.[8]

The racialized character of youth styles and cultures at Clavey was such that terms like *raver, straight, gangster, houser,* or *skater* served as racial code words. Duncan's comment above came out of the context of my asking him about *racial* distinctions in styles or culture. He responded speaking about "ravers" (whites) and "gangsters" (blacks, in this context.) Similarly, when I asked other students if they observed differences in styles or cultures between whites, African Americans, Asian Americans, and such, many automatically said something like, "Oh yeah, like, *skaters* wear their pants cut off at the bottom and wear Vans instead of Nike shoes" (my emphasis). Alternatively, one day, while talking to Patti, a working-class, "alternative" girl, about the relative paucity of skaters at Clavey compared to Valley Groves, she said, "Yeah, there aren't enough white people in Clavey [City] to have many skaters."

In sum, at Clavey, style, tastes, demeanor, and association had as much, if not more, power to define racial ascription as skin color or tradition. This may be particularly true of youth for whom styles, dress, and consumption activities are a primary means by which young people symbolically negotiate and resolve the dilemmas of their identities.[9] Still, several scholars have argued that, among racial-ethnic minorities, racial-ethnic authenticity depends on the extent to which the individual's behaviors, attitudes, and activities are at "variance with those thought to be appropriate and group-specific."[10] Below, I return to more ways in which youth "perform" ascribed criteria for racial-ethnic group membership. My main point here is that, whereas at Valley Groves, clique affiliation deracialized youth, at Clavey, it racialized youth. Styles, tastes, and demeanor marked racial identity, including white identity.

School Structure, Youth Practice, and Racial Meanings

In context, the racialized organization of youth cultures was only one fabric in a wider tapestry of racial-ethnic distinctions and meanings at Clavey. Other aspects of school life were segregated and racialized as well. For example, different types of sports tended to be dominated by one racial group. Football, basketball (girls' and boys'), softball, and track were almost exclusively African American. Swimming, lacrosse, and golf teams were composed largely of whites. Asian Americans reigned over volleyball and badminton. No formal sport was dominated by Latinos. Only the girls' cross-country and soccer teams were fairly integrated. Both were close to one-third each white, Asian American, and African American.

Club activities were also self-segregated. There were, as is common, clubs designed for racial or ethnic-group concerns: the African American Student Union, the Asian Student Union, Latino Student Union, Pacific Islander Student Union, and the Inter-Tribal Student Union. There was no comparable "European American" or "white" club, with the exception of a club for Jewish students, which one youth told me some non-Jewish students went to just to be in a club with other whites. To the white students I spoke to, the idea of actually starting a white people's club on campus seemed an impossibility. One said, "There'd be a riot!," intimating that such a club would come off as an expression of white pride and would infuriate black students. All I spoke to seemed to agree that a white club would probably be interpreted in that way. Some whites were angry about that, but most felt a white club would be improper. Many believed that a "white" club could not gather for any reason other than racism.

Other kinds of clubs came together on behalf of such matters as community service, professional or academic advancement, school spirit, environmental causes, and leisure interests. These, too, tended to be homogeneous by race. Key Club, Interact, and Keywannettes were community service clubs that were exclusively Asian American; the JSA (Junior Statesmen of America) was a debate club and was all white with the exception of one or two Asian American and African American girls. Conflict Resolution and MESA, a club for minority advancement in math, engineering, and science, were predominantly African American clubs.

Curricular Structure:
Achievers Versus Nonachievers, White Versus Black

Supporting these informal, seemingly self-imposed forms of segregation among Clavey students was a multitiered, intricately differentiated academic hierarchy that was also racially defined and defining. The most intellectually rigorous classes, designed to prepare students for high-ranking universities, were the "accelerated" classes: Accelerated College Preparatory (ACP), Honors (H), and Advanced Placement (AP) on the highest rung. These classes were around 80 percent white and Asian, according to a survey carried out by one of the science teachers. Melissa was a middle-class, white, "culturally Jewish" junior I shadowed through a week of honors classes. Her core classes did not quite match this average, but were still overrepresented by white and Asian youth. Her courses were fairly close to one-third white, one-third Asian, and one-third black (give or take a few mixed-race students also).

Youth officially got into accelerated classes by merit. Different departments and the teachers within them had their own requirements for entry. Commonly, for math courses, students had to have a "B" grade or better in the course preceding the one in question (e.g., a "B" in college preparatory algebra to get into honors advanced algebra) *and* the consent of the teacher. Honors and AP humanities and social science courses required an "A" in the previous sequential course, departmental nomination, and teacher approval. Advanced Placement courses tended to also require an examination.

At the core of the curriculum were the Preparatory (P) level courses, which were the standard college-prep classes, and the Future Teachers (FTA) and Performing Arts (PA) magnet academies. Students generally elected or were assigned by their counselors to these courses, unless they were from out of the district and wanted to attend one of the magnet academies. In those cases, students were admitted by an application process. African American youth were the overwhelming majority in all of these classes. Preparatory and PA classes of thirty-five to forty students might have three to six whites, two to four Asians and a few Latinos in them. Future Teacher courses had even fewer, if any, whites and Asians.

Finally, at the lowest end of the track levels were the remedial, special education, and English as a Second Language (ESL) courses. Remedial students reportedly had learning disabilities, such as Attention Deficit Disorder; special education students had physical disabilities, such as blindness. ESL students were newly arrived immigrants, mostly from Asian countries, and ESL courses were structured to bring students up to speed in language, history, and social science. What remedial, special ed, and ESL courses had in common was that the students in them were quite marginalized and rarely, if ever, intersected with youth from other tracks. They were also all composed of students of color.

Although youth were officially assigned to accelerated, preparatory, or remedial classes by virtue of intellectual ability and career path, other criteria seemed to be in force, if implicitly. The social and intellectual atmospheres in the classrooms and the things that students and teachers alike said about the students in the different track levels suggested that behavior and, to an extent, racial ascription alone were as relevant to course admittance as were "gifts," talents, and intellectual abilities. For example, youth in the accelerated classes generally considered themselves and were considered by teachers to be industrious, controlled, and able to defer gratification. These categorizations were not without their grains of truth. Students I knew in the accelerated classes always had a lot of homework and sophisticated projects they were working on. Melissa told me, "I do nothing but work. At lunchtime, I'd love to go sit out on the lawn with my friends, but I *have* to stay in or I'd never get my homework done." Her course load included honors U.S. history, honors English, advanced algebra, third-level Spanish, and modern dance. In her classrooms, students were usually quiet and actively taking notes while the teacher lectured. Discussion, when encouraged, was orderly and orchestrated by the teacher, who acknowledged only those students who had their hands raised.

Preparatory and Performing Arts students were tagged "rowdy," "lazy," and "out of control." Here, too, there were grains of truth. Anthony was a middle-class African American senior and a basketball star at the school. Classroom discipline in Anthony's P courses was inconsistent, both across classes and within the same class on different days. Most students in his chemistry, advanced algebra, and drafting classes were attentive and respectful of the teachers, but there were a few who could be disruptive at times. His U.S. history and English classes had yet more students who disrupted class or whom the teachers frequently admonished for not paying attention or for speaking out of turn.

Performing Arts classes stepped up a level in nonconventional classroom behaviors. In Patti's history class, students gossiped and chatted among themselves constantly, whether the teacher, Mr. Edwards, was lecturing or not. Girls combed their hair and polished their nails; when Mr. Edwards begged them to focus on the lesson, they would respond to his plea long enough for him to get his rhythm back, then would resume where they left off, combing and polishing. Sometimes private, verbal spats broke out, grabbing the attention of the rest of the students and arresting the progress of the class.

Newcomer substitute teachers had a particularly difficult time with standard-level classes. One day, Mr. Edwards was not at school, and I mistakenly took the opportunity to view another class instead of his PA history class. The next day Patti told me what I had missed. Things got "out of control," as Patti put it. First, students just wouldn't acknowledge the substitute teacher and her calls to bring the class to order. They talked among each other, moved about the class, and socialized. Soon a paper-wad fight broke out, which led, as I understood it, to students tossing chairs and tables around the room. In a panic, the teacher went out to locate a security guard; she returned to find herself locked out of the room. Finally, someone set one of the garbage cans on fire, which sent all of the students fleeing from the smoke-filled room.

Remedial students were considered beyond the pale with respect to conventional academic expectations and behaviors. I met Latino and African American students in remedial classes who were there not because of intellectual incapacity but because they couldn't control themselves. In a math class I observed there was, for example, an African American boy who seemed exceptionally bright. Every time the teacher put out a question to the class, he would leap enthusiastically out of his seat with his hand shooting up in the air, begging the teacher to call on him. He always had the right answer. After class, the teacher told me that this was the boy's third year in the same remedial math course. He was believed to have Attention Deficit Disorder, but his disability clearly had no bearing on his intelligence. The teacher remorsefully told me, "He's really smart, but he can't control himself. You saw how he couldn't keep in his seat?"

The fact that the actual behavior of the students in the classrooms more or less matched the stereotypes about them should not be oversimplified into a case of "calling it what it is." There is a fine line between expectations and ascriptions of behavior and what individuals will play out. Studies of the effects of teacher expectations on performance provide strong evidence supporting the claim that teacher expectations and stereotypes about students are self-prophesying.[11] And at Clavey, the impression that the students in the P level were not as valued as those in the accelerated courses was made beyond teacher expectation alone. All of Anthony's classes were overcrowded. In two, there were not even enough chairs for students, let alone course materials. The first month of Patti's algebra class was taught by the basketball coach. Although resources were slim for all teachers at Clavey, somehow the accelerated courses managed to get by without these kinds of insults.

Given the reputations and unequal resources that the different course levels had, it is not a stretch to assume that the students in those classes behaved in "bonehead" and "rowdy" ways because that was expected of them. An indication of this came up one day in a P government class I was sitting in on. The teacher had passed around two samples of new textbooks and asked students for their opinions on them. Holding up a book with a colorful cover, a girl spoke out, "I like this one. It has nice pictures." A boy, agreeing, added, "This ain't no ACP class. We need books with pictures."

The racial demographics of the course levels and the types of expectations attached to them adds another dimension to this issue. "Lazy," "stupid," and "out of control" are stereotypes that have historically been ascribed to ethnic minorities in the United States, especially blacks and Latinos, while the virtues of self-control, industriousness, and intelligence have typically been reserved for whites and, recently, some Asians.[12] Research specifically concerned with the effects of negative stereotypes on the behaviors and academic performances of stigmatized groups has provided strong evidence supporting the claim that stereotypes affect performance in ways that confirm the stereotypes.[13] Hence, we can imagine that a kind of self-confirming "feedback loop"[14] existed between the racial compositions of the different academic levels at Clavey and the stereotypes assigned to the students at those levels.[15]

These behavioral expectations and tendencies within the tracking structure made *race* seem as if it were, in itself, a criterion for assignment to a specific track level. And in many instances it was. Some white students told me that they never asked to be put in the accelerated track; they believed they were placed there because that was where their (white) friends were. A counselor who was responsible for assigning nearly one hundred students told me that she gets pressure from white parents to have their children placed in the accelerated classes and, given the difficulty of assigning so many students, she often succumbed to the parents' wishes.

Alternatively, one night at the school site council meeting, a gathering of parents, administrators, students, and community people, an African American man and woman came to complain about the placement of their son, a new sophomore. The boy had graduated from the city's top-performing junior high school with an A average, and his parents had aspirations for him to be placed in the accelerated track. Somehow, however, upon entering school at Clavey, he was assigned to the predominantly black, less rigorous Future Teachers track. The parents, seeking understanding of how this could happen, learned that the boy's junior high counselors, who did not know the formal criteria for entry into accelerated classes, were the ones who recommended the boy to Future Teachers. Apparently the counselors made their judgment on simply the boy's racial appearance. The infuriated parents ended up lobbying for and, after a series of meetings, succeeding in instilling stricter entry requirements for accelerated courses that they hoped would ensure that accelerated students were in those classes for academic merit alone and not race privilege.[16]

What all of this boiled down to was a tracking system presumably about intellectual achievement but through which racial differences and identities, especially whiteness and blackness, were constituted. Tracking at Clavey reinforced the dichotomies of good vs. bad, smart vs. "bonehead," controlled vs. rowdy, industrious vs. lazy, and *white vs. black*, since whites were majorities in the "good" classes and African Americans the majorities in the "bad." The significance of this for the identities of white students and their views of racial others will become clear in subsequent chapters when I highlight students' discourses about race at Clavey. For the current discussion, it is worth pointing out that at Clavey there were no white or black "wannabe Asians" or "wannabe Hispanics," nor any Chicano "wannabe Asians." There were not even any white girls who went for the Latina-girl "chola" style, as there were at Valley Groves. There were only black, Asian, and Latino "wannabe whites" and white, Asian, and Latino "wannabe blacks." Some white students even told me that they tended to place Latinos toward the "black" end of the racial spectrum and Asian Americans more toward the "white" end. Despite wide racial-ethnic diversity, then, a white-black paradigm remained dominant.[17] I believe the racialized dichotomies structured by the tracking system accounted for this. Moreover, to the extent that "white" codified conformity and goodness and "black" codified nonconformity and badness, they both carried positions of prestige. Upwardly mobile students may have wanted to be associated with the former, and more rebellious and oppositional students may have wanted to be associated with the latter.[18]

Racial Spaces, Embodied Racial Meanings

Immediately outside the school cafeteria was a small patio area that, during lunch and breaks, was densely packed primarily with African American students. It was comparable to the Valley Groves Quad inasmuch as it was the hub for the school majority. Black students there were of all kinds: leadership students, "gangsters," athletes, rappers, from the "hood" and from the "hills." Nonblack students might have to pass through this area to get to the other side of campus, but few stopped, stayed, and socialized. Exceptions were a few white youth with close black friends, a group of Asians that closely gathered outside the far doors of the cafeteria, and a small group of Pacific Islander males who claimed no particular territory.

Extending between the cafeteria and the entry to the campus was a long, pastoral strip of grass and shade trees flanked on two sides by classroom buildings. This area, called the Senior Lawn, was the primary outdoor gathering place for white students. White youth with skateboards mixed with other whites holding drawing pads or reading for a class. Bleached-blonde girls in torn overalls conversed with brown-haired girls in Gap clothing. Long-haired "stoners" caught up with buzz-cut members of the debate team. Some groups of whites tended to prefer more secluded areas on campus, like the AP English and History classrooms, or a certain hard-to-get-to dugout behind the humanities building, but the Senior Lawn was generally known as the "place where the white kids hang out."

Asian and Chicano/Latino "American-born" students tended to separate themselves spatially from the "newly arrived," but within these subcategories a similar internal heterogeneity prevailed as with the black and white students. American-born Chinese, Korean, and Vietnamese students gathered largely in and around the math and science building while the "newly arrived" claimed ten tables in a corner of the cafeteria, where they conversed in their native tongues. American-born Chicanos and Latinos met together in or outside the art room, while recent immigrants, including Mexicans, Salvadoreans, and a Dominican boy, daily convened in the cafeteria, in the opposite corner from the Asian students.

Although these spaces were predominantly occupied by certain race-ethnic groups, what seemed to make the Senior Lawn the place "where the whites hang out" and the patio the place where the "blacks hang out" was not so much the racial demographics, though that was important, as the type of activity, practices, and/or expected demeanors that the occupants of the different spaces observed. Students seemed to embrace, embody, and perform the meanings assigned to them by racial ascription, sometimes becoming caricatures of the stereotypes about them.[19]

The Lawn, for example, was the domain of the "cool." I first became aware of this when, one day within my first month in the field, I was having lunch on the Lawn with Patti and a group of her friends. As I was putting a spoonful of yogurt into my mouth, a glob dropped and landed on the front of my blouse. Amused, I pointed this out to Patti and another girl who, in turn, looked drawn-faced at me as though I had just made a serious transgression. "That is not cool," Patti warned as she moved to hide me so that no one else could see my hideous mark of uncoolness.

The "cool" character of the Lawn was especially apparent on sunny days when the pleasant weather overruled the compunction to sit in a classroom and study, work on a project, or talk quietly with friends under shelter. Groups of students coagulated under trees, around benches, or on the grass under full sun to speak earnestly among themselves. Controlled laughter, as if orchestrated, trumpeted from one cell of friends and then another. The youths' bodies spoke composure, confidence, self-control and suggested a hip intellectualism. A group of white European American, African American and Asian American artists, male and female, sat and occasionally sketched portraits of willing passersby. Opposite them, across the lawn, a set of white male ravers ate slumped over their sandwiches and talked in a huddle. Nearby, draped around the large rock that adorned the center of the lawn, a clique of white girls, some with hair colored black or burgundy, caught up on the day's events with critical intensity. Pockets of Asian Americans, usually gender homogeneous, gathered in quiet discourse.

The intellectual and controlled *coolness* that characterized the regulars on the Senior Lawn seemed to be that which marked the Lawn area as "white." The term *cool*, itself, tended to carry white-racial connotations for students of color. I first observed this in a drama class one day. The white male teacher, commenting on an anecdote he had just told the class, said "You may say, 'Yeah, that's cool,' " at which point an African American girl interrupted with "No I wouldn't!" The teacher blushed, seemingly in recognition of having made an assumption that didn't have cross-cultural validity; *cool* was a term he, a white person, would use but not his black students.

Being cool, or being called "cool" was a compliment to the white youth I knew and spoke to. It meant above all else that a person was, or appeared to be, self-confident and self-assured while remaining approachable. Patti, for example, always referred to the kids she liked most as "cool" and when she became visibly self-conscious and awkward about something, she felt embarrassed for being "uncool."

However, black students had a different connotation for the term. Imani, an African American senior, explained to me in an interview that "*fresh* is a better term than *cool*. *Cool* is there, it's hip, but not great. *Fresh* is *it*. Same as *bad* or *phat*—that is just everything, perfect. *Good* is the worst. If you're good you're just terrible. . . . We say, 'He's fine' or 'all that.' We wouldn't say a guy was cool because that would mean he's just as bad as good. [We'd say,] 'Go home, you're cool, get out of here!' "

I asked what made a guy cool and she replied with an example: "Renald sometimes acts cool. He's a homie, a patna with friends, but sometimes he's too conceited, acting like he's too much." (Note that *homie* at Clavey had a different meaning than at Valley Groves. It meant someone who was a good friend or trustworthy.) Conceited, snobby, stuck up, and "full of themselves" were, in fact, terms that several students of color I spoke to used to describe what they saw as the common demeanor of the white students.[20]

The cool and intellectual Lawn culture was such that youth who were not regulars on the Senior Lawn might stop there if they were in a cool (by white students' definition) or contemplative mood. Marcel was an African American junior whom I interviewed. He was a well-known actor, dancer, and rapper on campus who frequently took the opportunity to perform spontaneously on the "Lower Lawn," a staging area between the Senior Lawn and the cafeteria patio. He had a tight set of friends with whom he always hung out in the patio area. But when we met after school for the interview, he suggested we sit under a tree on the Senior Lawn. At a point in our discussion, when we were talking about the segregated spaces on campus, he said that he sometimes liked to sit on the Lawn when he wanted to "think" about something. It was an area conducive to that. In that moment I sensed that he had suggested we talk on the Lawn because it seemed an appropriate place, given the formal, thoughtful nature of the interview.

The subdued, "cool" culture of the Senior Lawn contrasted sharply with the atmosphere just a few yards down the way, on the Lower Lawn and cafeteria patio. Once a month or so, formal spirit rallies took place on the Lower Lawn for the audience on the patio. At these events, cheerleaders strutted and danced, rap music blasted from loudspeakers, and youth engaged in raucous games or modeled "ethnic" fashions from non-Western countries. With or without planned events, however, black students sustained the values of performance, cultural production, and the body in this area. A small group of black males frequently stood at the corner of the stairs and quietly composed songs. With their heads bowed closely together, each attentively listened to the harmonies and rhythms the others were contributing to the mix. If music was audible from anywhere, somebody would be dancing, usually "freakin' " (a sexually explicit dance form), goaded by the catcalls and screams of appreciative onlookers. Boys eyed girls and shouted accolades (sometimes appreciated, sometimes not); girls eyed boys, then turned and made their assessments to each other. Youth typically spoke in Black English to each other and exercised the latest slang terms. Always the air was dense with infectious laughter, loud conversation, and shouting accompanied by the sounds of Nike shoes on pavement, palms of hands meeting, leather rustling, cellophane wraps snapping. Now and then the behaviors of students here got "out of control"—the dancing would get too sexually explicit or a tense encounter would spark a fight. At that point, the deep and resonant voice of some security guard would rise above the cacophony, and order would be restored.

The 70 building, where "the Asians" purportedly hung out was, as I mentioned earlier, the science building. This befitted the group most stereotyped for being "smart," and "good at math." As with the other spaces, the 70 building at break times had significant numbers of non-Asian students roaming around in the halls or standing in classroom doors. *Inside* those doors, however, rooms would be mostly full of Asians and Asian Americans only, busy doing school work or carrying out a club meeting. The halls there smelled of formaldehyde, propane, and other "instrumental" (as opposed to edible) odors. Chalk-inscribed mathematical formulas or question sets filled classroom blackboards. A blanket of serious studiousness and academic rigor covered the building at all times.

In short, territories at Clavey took on racial meanings in part because one racial group or another was numerically predominant, but also because certain use values of the space or practical behaviors within them simultaneously reproduced and constituted particular racialized styles or stereotypes.[21] The Lawn was marked by *whiteness*—understood in this context to refer to "coolness" (or snobbishness, self-assuredness, confidence), control, and intellectualism or the mind. The Lower Lawn and patio marked *blackness*—performative, corporeal, "out-of-control." And the 70 building marked *Asian-ness*—smart, studious, academic.

Some scholars have argued that these traits are characteristic of deep-seated cultural differences between whites, blacks, and others. Thomas Kochman, for example, asserts that black and white behaviors differ in "stance and spiritual intensity. The black mode is . . . high-keyed: animated, interpersonal, confrontational . . . heated, loud and generates affect." The white mode is "low-keyed: dispassionate, impersonal, non-challenging . . . cool, quiet, and without affect."[22] Even though these characteristics match my observations, I do not agree that they stem from inherent or essential differences between white European Americans, African Americans, and others. I see them as part social-historically constituted behavioral differences and part the playing out of the ascribed criteria one must take on when claiming a racial-ethnic identity in a racialized society like the United States. Plenty of structures within the school context at Clavey, tracking in particular, provided the respective scripts for different racial-ethnic groups to take on and perform.

On the Flip Side

It wasn't *all* "black and white" at Clavey, even though race consciousness and racial distinctiveness were certainly the dominant trends of things. When students had the opportunity to mix under conditions of equal status, "race" often became passive as youth found affinities and solidarities along other lines of identification. Two venues in particular enabled such interaction: sports (when not entirely segregated) and drama.

Murray was a white male senior with a diverse set of friends. In my interview with him, I asked him how his schooling at Clavey influenced the person he saw himself to be. He replied,

> "At Clavey? The biggest thing that has changed my views is probably football, where I was the only white kid on the team. I have very good friends from football that are of totally different races. I mean, it's a great experience. If I've learned one thing it is how to get along with other people. 'Cause it's not just races—it's dealing with people who are different from you, race or no race. . . .

You learn who a person is before you judge them. When it comes to playing football, you have a jersey on and a helmet and you can't see the color of someone's skin. You're just out there as a team of people playing. There could be females out there—I mean, as long as the job gets done, you're playing football and you're having fun with a lot of other people."

In spring 1994, my first semester at Clavey, the advanced drama class was putting final touches on a play the students had written about the dangers of unsafe sex. By the end of the school year, they were performing the play at numerous other high schools in the area to highly appreciative audiences. The class was relatively small, around fifteen active members, and very diverse: five whites, six African Americans, one Filipino, one mixed white-Asian, one mixed white-Latino, and one mixed black-Latino. On any given day in class, students' interaction appeared ideal. In my field notes, I wrote this one day:

> The students of the advanced drama class are preparing to do an improvisation. As the rest of the class sets up chairs facing the small, raised stage in the classroom, five students wait in the wings, talking among themselves while they wait for the teacher to give them instructions. Gary and Kintu are standing at a distance from me, facing each other, talking and smiling. Gary is a white senior with blonde hair that falls straight to the top of his ears then wedges into a razor cut that ends at this lower hair line. . . . Kintu is a black senior. His hair is in locks down to his shoulders. His right pant leg is tied below the knee with a checker bandana. They talk, laugh. Gary gives Kintu a friendly shove, an obvious extension of something said between them, then opens his arms, raps them around Kintu just below his shoulders and squeezes him generously.
>
> Now the students are sitting in a circle, conversing with the teacher (who is in the circle with them) about the junior prom. Bobby is a white junior with a nice face and blonde hair in a kind of surfer style. Sunny, an African American junior girl with long wavy hair, is sitting between his legs on an overstuffed chair. She is leaning back into Bobby's arms, then sits up forward to announce that she'll be going solo to the prom because she doesn't have a date. Bobby affectionately strokes her hair as if to console her.

One day the drama teacher let me talk with students during class about the intergroup harmony they found among themselves. A few students said that a type of self-selection occurred in drama class because it attracted students who were more "open," outgoing, and "weird." Another suggested that the class didn't so much attract those kinds of people as made them by forcing students to open up and "be themselves" through the creative process of acting. All agreed that the experience of working jointly on a project that "you both love and hate" and over which you "sweat, cry, laugh, get frustrated, and get happy together" created a context that stripped students of global categorizations and made them see each other as unique individuals who shared an array of interests and experiences.

Murray and these drama students all spoke to similar experiences stemming from integrated, equal-status, and joint projects. They experienced finding paths of sameness and cross-identification with peers that superseded and subordinated differences based on ascribed racial characteristics. In addition to this, integrated, equal-status projects often provided opportunities for students to discuss delicate racial issues in open and collaborative ways. For example, in the drama class one day, in my second year in the field, a white female student proposed a scene for the class to develop. The scene as she described it went like this: The curtain opens with a white girl and black boy in bed, cuddling as if they'd just had sex. They are in love and talking about having children together. They then doze off in each other's arms. In his sleep, the man starts to hear some voices saying racist things about the girl and about their relationship. He calls out from his sleep. The girl wakes him and asks what's wrong, and he says, "Nothing." They doze back off, and the girl goes through the same thing. After she screams out and tells her partner that everything is all right, the two go back to sleep, this time facing away from each other. Next, people of different races and genders come in the room, laughing and pointing at the couple. The two in bed simultaneously sit up as in a nightmare, and the stage goes black.

In the first improvisation of this, a mixed white-Latino boy did the first voice and played it like a bigot, yelling racist slurs. At one point he said to the boy, "Hey, you nappy-headed piece of black trash, what are you doing with that white girl?" When he said that, a black student in the audience called out, "Hey, don't go there. No," and insisted that he play the part of the voices. But the first boy continued and said, to the girl, "Hey slut! Why are you betraying the race with that garbage! Nigger lover!"

After the improvisation was over, students commented that the voice sounded too much like a white racist, and that wasn't right. A black girl said that it would be better if a black girl's voice was in the mind of the black boy and a white guy's in the mind of the white girl. Then, she said, the things they said would be about the kinds of dynamics that go on among members of the same race but of different genders. The author of the scene said that her initial idea was that the voice would sound more like society trying to keep the two apart. The other students came to agree with her and with taking a more subtle approach to the racism in the scene. A black girl added that at first the voice should sound like "friendly" common sense but gradually reveal itself to be "that racist shit."

In the next improvisation, two girls, one mixed Latino-black and the other mixed white-black, did the voices. Alternating each phrase, they said, first to the boy then the girl, "What are your parents going to say?" "What will people think when they see you walking down the street, a *black* man with a *white* woman?" "Black man." "White woman." "Black man." "White woman." When the scene was over, the class agreed that it was going in the right direction. The author said she would write out some other possibilities of text for the voices and bring them to class the next day.

In sum, while plenty at Clavey drove wedges and buttressed boundaries between students of different racial-ethnic identities, when youth had opportunities to interact with one another under conditions of equal status participation in joint projects, those boundaries became porous and subordinate to lines of sameness and cross–identification. Porous boundaries also allowed students to discuss racial issues openly and undefensively, hence creating opportunities for personal growth and deeper understanding of different perspectives.

School Culture: White on Black

In the previous chapter I argued that at Valley Groves, because white students were the majority and their common cultural experiences, practices, and expectations went unchallenged, white youth experienced themselves as normal. The same was not entirely true for white youth at Clavey, who were not the majority nor the cultural norm. To an extent, clothing styles, types of spirit activities, and broadcasted music reflected the diversity of backgrounds, tastes, and interests of the school's population, including white students. By and large, however, those things were overwhelmingly influenced by black, urban youth culture. I refer to the styles, music, and other meaningful practices that have risen out of urban black communities, that are linked, if remotely, to diasporic traditions, and that, in urban communities especially, mark black identity and peoplehood.[23]

The multicultural but largely African American influence on school culture owed in no small measure to the fact that school activities were organized by a fairly diverse but predominantly African American leadership body. During the first year of my research, the students in the leadership group included about eighteen African Americans, seven whites, two mixed-race white/Latinos, one Chicano, one Filipino, one foreign exchange student from Argentina, and one Chinese American, who was the student body president. Though not entirely proportional to the wider student population, the diversity of the leadership group enhanced the organizing of such events as "multicultural week" or schoolwide forums in which students expressed what they saw as the most pressing problems of the school. Most school events, however, such as the spirit rallies, school proms, and dances, were organized by and for African American students and infused with urban black style.

I have already mentioned that clothing styles at Clavey tended toward a basic hip-hop "drip look," derived from black urban styles. Morever, during breaks and lunchtime at Clavey, the ambient hum of casual conversation echoed with the sounds, words, and inflections of Black English and the most recent innovation in street slang. The types of music heard most frequently—almost exclusively—were those preferred by African American students, namely, rap and r & b. "Gangsta' Rap" was most popular among African American youth at the time, but they rarely got away with playing it because of its profanities. Rap songs by groups like Salt 'N' Pepa or the Fugees and the r & b sounds of Boyz II Men were common. Only during multicultural week, when students were supposed to celebrate the different cultures at Clavey, did some musical variety enter into the usual mix, but African American or Afro-Caribbean music still predominated. One day during multicultural week, for example, the organizers played a rap song, one r & b, a reggae tune, then an alternative rock song by Green Day. That was followed by some jazz, another r & b tune, and a rock song by the "artist formerly known as Prince," who had wide cross-over appeal.

An interesting aside: some weeks after multicultural week, Pickles (the punk rocker) told me that she had brought a punk piece for students to play during multicultural week. A white student tending to the music said that they couldn't play the tape because it wasn't "multicultural," it was "white people's music." Pickles replied, "But it's WEIRD white people's music." She still was not allowed to play her choice. I found this intriguing, both for the way "multicultural" meant "not white" in this case and for the example of how whites will define and sanction the boundaries of what is "white" with other whites.[24]

Rap and r & b also reigned at the school dances, including the Junior Prom and Senior Ball, which were quite well attended by the whole range of students. I chaperoned two Senior Balls and one Junior Prom at Clavey, and at all three, African American students ruled the dance floor. Couples danced in stylized synchronicity to slow romantic ballads, their bodies knit together at the pelvis. Then an upbeat hip-hop song would turn the dance floor into a celebration of arms, knees, torsos, hips and groins, all moving in concert with the metric pulse of the music. A few chaperoning teachers would, on occasion, join the students in dance, but others stayed at their posts along the periphery of the dance floor, prepared to separate any couple whose movements became too explicitly sexual.

About every sixth to tenth song was either a reggae, "house," or alternative rock tune. When these came on, the majority of the African American and Asian youth on the dance floor took a break, and white and some other Asian students took their place. They danced without patterned form or style, moving their bodies less to the beat than to the spiritual inspiration of the music. Some youth danced with partners of the opposite sex, some with partners of the same sex, and some without partners at all. When the tune ended, the white students returned to their tables and black students to the dance floor. I asked Patti, who I knew loved to dance, why she wasn't out on the dance floor more often. She told me, "They don't play my kind of music. I can't dance to that stuff."

Homecoming

At Clavey, homecoming was structured in a way fairly similar to homecoming at Valley Groves and included "theme days," the nominations and elections of "royalty," an indoor rally during school hours, and the big game. Apart from these similarities, the two homecomings widely diverged. The theme days had a multicultural flair: "Farmer Day," which caught the imagination of several white girls who came to school wearing pigtails, flannel shirts, and overalls; "Zestfully Clean," in which youth, mostly black, wore bathrobes, shower caps, and bathroom slippers; "Tropical Day," where leadership youth distributed leis, and some Pacific Islanders wore indigenous attire; and "Mackin' Playin' Day," in which African American youth dressed in the styles of pimps and hookers depicted in the 1970s film, *The Mack*. On that day, African American males got particularly involved, wearing their hair in modest afros under brimmed hats and donning stylish leather jackets and platform shoes.

At lunch each day of homecoming week, music, games, and other events took place on the Lower Lawn, facing away from the Senior Lawn area and toward the patio where mostly African American students hung out. Each day there was a "costume" contest. Black students in colorful dashikis, Asian girls in silk brocaded gowns, Samoan males in calf-length skirts paraded about in front of the hundred-plus youth on the patio. The winners were chosen by a vote of cheers. There were other contests and games, too, such as a pie-eating contest—gooey cream pies consumed without the aid of hands, let alone utensils—and a tag relay race.

On the "Zestfully Clean" day, just after the costume contest, three black males grabbed the microphone and began performing a three-part song, a capella. The leadership organizers tried to remove them from the staging area, but the disapproval of the crowd weakened their resolve. Eventually, the leadership students prevailed and the pie-eating took place. Not long after that, however, the boys returned, put on an instrumental rap piece on the public address system, and began another impromptu performance. One boy rapped in the microphone to the beat of the music while the other two danced. They danced the "butterfly," a dance in which the knees turn inward and outward in a movement like the opening and closing of a butterfly's wings. As the knees open, the pelvis thrusts forward, and accompanied by a particular facial attitude, the movement is undeniably sexual. Encouraged by the cheers of the crowd, the girls especially, one of the dancers took the "butterfly" movement into a low, wide-legged split climaxing with a lunge into the ground, pelvis first. As the crowd roared with enthusiasm, the music abruptly stopped, and the school dean stepped in and escorted the performers off the stage. That was the end of the day's lunchtime activities.

White youth for the most part stayed uninvolved in these activities, both as spectators and participants. The only exception occurred in my first year in the field, when a white girl of German ancestry modeled a native *lederhosen* jumper for the costume contest.

The day of the homecoming game there was a rally in the gym during lunch. The booming bass of a rap song lured students into the auditorium. As at the Valley Groves rally, youth sat according to their grade level in different quadrants of the room. The bleachers filled quickly, forcing some students to stand on the sidelines. Besides the nonblack members of the leadership class, who were scurrying about with other classmates making sure things ran smoothly, there were very few spectators who were not African American.

The rally opened with a greeting from the student body president and a soulful a capella song harmonized by three African American girls. Then the cheerleaders—one white and ten black girls—sprang out onto the floor. Their choreographed routine was fluid, rhythmic, and dancelike with movements drawn from traditional and contemporary African and African American dance forms. To the pulse of an upbeat r & b song, the girls flirted with their appreciative audience, using playful hand and eye gestures. Several boys gave in to the urge to dance in dialogue with the girls and leapt down to the gym floor. Others, boys and girls alike, stood up and danced in place until the performance was over. Finally, the varsity football players paraded out. They were all African American with the exception of two white boys and one Latino. As each boy's name and number was announced, the player bolted forward to embrace the cheers from the audience. Each took his moment in the limelight boldly and proudly, pumping a fist high in the air or performing a little dance to please the crowd and draw more applause.

At Clavey there was no homecoming parade that extended into the community, as at Valley Groves. Instead, a small procession of vehicles circled the football field during halftime at the homecoming game. For the event, the bleachers were packed with African American students; a few teachers and parents sat among them. The parade opened with a procession of convertible cars carrying the "royalty" the student body had chosen by ballot—the sophomore Duke and Duchess, junior Prince and Princess, senior King and Queen, and, topping them all, the senior "Emperor" and "Empress." All the royalty and their drivers were black. Two convertible cars and one large flatbed truck followed them, representing the sophomore, junior, and senior classes, respectively. Students had decorated the vehicles with colored crepe paper, balloons, and artfully painted paper signs with the class names on them. Clavey had no marching band, but the school jazz band supplied arousing music, and Clavey's award-winning gospel choir provided a spirited culmination to the halftime events.

In an interview with Melissa and three of her friends, all finishing their sophomore year at the time, one of the girls, Linda, complained that she was missing out on the "fun" she believed high school should be. When I asked why, she answered, "Because I don't enjoy the people. The people that dominate the football games and dominate the rallies and cheerleading and everything. The same group of people that I don't enjoy being with."

Although the negative tone of Linda's comments was not particularly representative of other white students' comments about why they didn't participate in school activities, her basic sentiment was. Youth explained that the events didn't have the kinds of music, entertainment, or general atmosphere that they enjoyed. Barry was explicit: "School is like a foreign country to me. I come here to this foreign place then go home where everything is normal again."

In this chapter I have sought to illuminate the ways that face-to-face association with differently "raced" individuals within a social structure that helped assign, constitute, and confirm the criteria ascribed to "racial" difference contributed to the construction of "white," "black," and other racial-ethnic identities at Clavey. The comparison with Valley Groves reveals the significance of this interplay between demographic context and school structures for marking and making meaningful "white" identity in particular. For whites at Valley Groves, little to no association with racialized differences within a social-cultural milieu that was self-confirming contributed to the construction of white as "norm" and a race-neutral logic of social organization. On the contrary, for white students at Clavey, white identity was not entirely the norm, nor was their logic of social organization race neutral. The "foreign" dominant cultural milieu and the logic of racial-ethnic distinction that permeated formal and informal social organization put "white" in relief, making it an identity with which to contend.[25]

Revealed in this chapter also are the ways "self" and "other" were negotiated through sometimes subtle differences in clothing styles. Part II will look more closely at that and other ways that everyday interrelational processes, conditioned by the social and structural milieus at Valley Groves and Clavey high schools, shaped the different, often multiple ways white youth reflected upon and gave meaning to their identities as whites.

part two

Identity and Culture

Identity is that by which we define ourselves, a name we call "home,"[1] even if only temporarily or strategically.[2] Stuart Hall defines cultural identities as the "points of temporary attachment to the subject positions which discursive practices construct for us."[3] As such, cultural identity formation involves, above all, a process of investment in and *identification* with the meanings attached to one's social location.

I have found that people can have very little or a lot of conscious identification with their racial identity. At the "very little" end, racial identities are no more than a social ascription with implications individuals are required to bear. At the "a lot" end, racial identity is a meaningful source of community and self-understanding, and a way of anchoring oneself in the world politically and/or spiritually. At this end of the continuum, the sense of shared characteristics and solidarities is defined or implicitly understood as a "culture" and peoplehood.

The chapters in this section explore the extent to which white youth at Valley Groves and Clavey high schools identified with white identity as part of a culture and/or peoplehood. I took several approaches to examining this among youth, from asking them outright if they could describe white culture, to engaging them in discussions about the things with which they most identified and seeing if their answers led toward something indicative of a white cultural identity. I also closely observed students' everyday activities and interactions, looking for nonverbal, performative, and/or symbolic ways that youth implicitly expressed racial meanings and identity.

Chapter 3 discusses what youth explicitly said about white culture, and chapter 4 explores the meanings of race and white culture as students performed them in their daily practices, clothing styles, tastes in music, and other consumption activities. I reveal striking differences between the two schools in how youth interpreted and performed whiteness as a cultural identity, and I discuss several ways in which the students' respective experiences of association with people of color influenced those differences.

3. Situated Meanings of "White" as a Cultural Identity

"How would you describe white American culture?" I ask Laurie. The espresso machine in the café where Laurie and I are talking is hissing, spitting, and growling, making me lean across my soup-size bowl of mocha latte to feel certain I can be heard. Laurie is a white middle-class senior and self-described "popular" girl at Valley Groves High. Medium-length sandy hair dances around her open and friendly face when she speaks. She is popular, she explains, by virtue of knowing a lot of people, being well liked, and involved in a lot of school activities. She is a member of the school council, chair of the Conflict Resolution Club, and overall coordinator for all the club activities around school.

Laurie pauses, her expression at first visibly perplexed, as if she didn't understand the question, and then reflecting that she might be drawing an absolute blank. Wondering if she heard me over the roar in the background, I awkwardly reiterate, "You know, like, what would you say white American culture is like?"

"I wouldn't be able to tell you. I don't know." She pauses and laughs nervously. "When you think about it, it's like . . . [a longer pause]. *I don't know!*"

I try to help her out by suggesting that she imagine she has met a Martian who is very interested in hearing things about what her society is like, what foods she eats, what she does for fun, that sort of thing. The perplexed look on her face barely softens, "You mean, how would I describe the society?"

"Yeah."

She thinks a bit. "I don't know! It's so *hard!* Materialistic in a sense. Lots of people care about what they look like. Stuff like that. I don't *know*. I can't!"

I then ask her what it means to her to be white. "Nothing really," she says after a moment's reflection.

"Do you have an ethnic background you are tied to?"
She replies,

"We're a bunch of everything. My great-great-grandmother is Cherokee. Whenever I fill out [questionnaires] about what's my ethnic background I write "white" because everything is so random. We have German, some family from Wales—but that means nothing to me. So, I guess not. It's not that I'm so much of something that I—or, maybe it's the way that we've been taught. Like Filipinos care about where they came from and the hardships, but whites don't. We don't even have a student club for whites. So I don't have any ties to anything. I haven't heard about anything my parents have been through except for my grandparents in wars. It's all been about people, not culture."

"Food. Food. Everybody eats different kinds of food. . . . It's an incredible bond, eating," Jessie chuckles self-consciously and continues,

"Actually, I have a whole philosophy worked up around food, the way people work around food. I've noticed, like, okay—of my Asian friends: food. You eat. You got something on the table, you eat. Okay. Like my friend Anita. She is eighth-generation Chinese on her dad's side and second on her mom's and [eating] is important to her. She eats, eats, eats. Also, Monique, who's Filipino, eats, eats, eats. *Then* all my white girlfriends go, 'Oh, I've been anorexic three times and bulimic eight times,' and deh-deh-deh-deh. And you see that in white culture—*skinny*, you know? Nice figure, okay, but you go to other parts of the world and a full-figured woman is more appreciated, you know?"

Jessie is a middle-class white senior girl who attends Clavey High. She is a talented writer and assists the English teacher in his first-year creative writing class. Like Laurie, Jessie is involved in peer mediation and conflict resolution in her school and is well-liked among white kids on campus, but unlike Laurie, she is not popular—but that is only because "popular" isn't a category of distinction in the social organization of students at Clavey. We talk for several hours in a room in the school library. The space is small and sterile but quiet, which is important, because Jessie has much to say.

"Oh wait!" Jessie interrupts as I am about to ask another question. "I have something to add." Then she continues,

"I think that white culture is much more thoroughly defined in places outside of the Bay Area, like Denver, Arizona, and places like that. Minnesota! It seems like, Minnesota especially, they've got the whole thing going on. Like beer bread . . . [inaudible moment in tape recording] the knitting and making of quilts or whatever. I don't know. It's all these different things and you're like 'Oh, okay, this is along the lines of what you can consider culture,' you know? The whole attitude of what people do and, you know, polka, parades, apple pie, and things like that. It's like 'Oh, okay, white culture, funky time!' It doesn't feel rich to you because it's not exotic but at the same time, you go home and say 'I went to a polka bar' and your friends say 'Wow, you must have been in Minnesota!' "

Laurie's and Jessie's responses to the question "What is white American culture?" represent two ends of a continuum ranging from, on the one end, a "cognitive gap"—a total inability to define "white" as a culture—and, on the other, relatively effusive distinctions between white and other American cultures. In my discussions and interviews with white students at both Valley Groves and Clavey, the young people's answers to my probes into white culture ran along that continuum, but Valley Groves youth tended to congregate predominantly around the cognitive gap end and Clavey youth around the loquacious end.

In this chapter I will compare what white students at Valley Groves and Clavey could explicitly say about "white" as an identity or culture. Interesting differences obtain between the two schools. At Valley Groves, where students had virtually no association with people who were actively marking racial-ethnic identities and cultural boundaries, white students believed they lacked culture. At Clavey, where white youth were forced into both explicit and implicit dialogues about race-ethnic distinctions, cultures, and identities, white students struggled to mark and define a white racial identity and culture. Between the two schools, three narratives of white culture were most salient: normal, European American ethnic, and postcultural.

Valley Groves:
White Means Never Having to Say You're Ethnic

Billy was a senior at Valley Groves, a popular boy active in athletics and school leadership whom I met in his advanced college placement (ACP) government class. The teacher of that course, Mr. Riley, always welcomed my participation in his class, which I appreciated because many of the school's most popular and mainstream students were enrolled in it. I interviewed Billy at his home, a small family farm near the outskirts of Rancho Nuevo. We sat at the dining room table and talked while his parents did chores outside. I asked Billy what he called himself when asked about his ethnic or racial identity. He said, "White. I just say I'm white." When I asked what that meant to him he responded, "Nothing. Means nothing, really. Color of my skin, that's about it."

Given that Billy said being white meant nothing to him but skin color, it seemed to me at the time that any further inquiry into how he might describe "white" as a culture would not bear much fruit. So I asked him what would be his first response to the question "What are you?"

"I'd say I'm an American."

"And what does being 'American' mean to you?" I asked.

"Mainly living in America, being free, having choices, being able to vote and just being here, I guess."

I then asked, "What do you think is culturally specific about American culture?"

A long "hmmmm" told me that Billy's mind was at work. Then he asked, "Like, what's American culture?"

"Uh-huh."

"Hmmmm," he sang again. Then, after a fairly long pause, he added, "I don't really know, cause it's like [pause] . . . just [pause] . . . I'm not sure! I don't know!

For Laurie, Billy, and most white students I spoke to at Valley Groves, especially the more mainstream students, "white" was an empty cultural category. When explicitly asked to describe white American culture or, simply, "American" culture, they fell into what I call a cognitive gap. The cognitive gap, I believe, is little more than what Gramsci called "common-sense" and Bourdieu "doxa"—that which goes without saying because it comes without saying. It is that which is so embedded in the hegemonic that it is taken for granted, not reflected upon because it is experienced as "natural" or "normal." In this respect, it is understandable that youth who were most identified with and integrated into the mainstream culture would be least reflective about that culture.

And, indeed, the youth at Valley Groves I spoke to who positioned them-selves outside the mainstream had a little more ease in responding to ques-tions about white American culture. Carli was a self-made rebel whose style and allegiances were not easy to pin down—semihippie, semialternative, semipunk, semigeek. She lived alone with her mom in an apartment house not far from school, in a "middle-lower"-class part of town, as Carli called it. Carli had this to say when I asked her what it meant to be "American":

"I think—I've thought about this lately, being American. I used to hate it because I'd think, man, I shouldn't even be here, you know? This isn't even my country, you know? But it is. I was—you know, I was born here. I think it's just a dreaming country. It's for the dreamers, because really we came over here for—I like why we came here. I don't like what we did when we came here. It was wrong. But I like why we came here. We came here for something new. I mean lots of dreams, lots of goals, lots of happiness, lots of expectations, lots of excitement for a new—and I love that. That's why I love excitement for new things, for change. So I love being an American because I am a direct— uh—I don't know what to say. [I try to help: "Descendant?"] Yeah, descendant of that dream. So I'm glad that I'm here for that reason. So I'm proud of being an American, even though I feel like you don't have much of a culture because I think the cultures come with origin, and really our origin is just a bunch of politics [chuckle]."

Carli then said, "But . . ." with enough pause to suggest that she was wanting me to break in, so I did. "You know, that's an interesting point 'cause, well, you originated here. I mean, you know, at least in this corporeal form." Carli laughed with me at my insinuation that she may have appeared in some other corporeal form elsewhere, an idea I don't know *how* or *why* came into my head. I rearticulated the point by saying, "I mean, your parents are from here and their parents, so, like, there's an origin here."
     "Yeah," Carli chimed in.
     "So why doesn't it feel like you have an origin here?"
     She replied,

"Why doesn't it feel like an origin? I think because this generation is so lazy, I think. 'Cause our—it seems like American culture is television. And that's why I feel like I don't have [cutting herself off]—I'm just not happy with our, with my culture right now. I don't like living in the houses we live in. I don't like going by the systems that we go by. I don't like the patriarchalness of our system. I don't. I don't think it's—I don't think it originated that way. I like to go—I want to go back. I want to study ancient, ancient, ancient things, and maybe—[cutting herself off]. I don't know where purity comes in. I want to find that. I mean I'm sure, you know, medieval wasn't pure. I'm sure—[cutting herself off]. I don't know. I can't say what this is—but that's why I don't like it.

I don't like this culture. I want to go back to what was before, because this culture to me is television, television."

"And what does 'television' mean?" I asked.

"Just escape, craziness. Your brain doesn't have to think. Everything's there for you. You don't have to think and you don't have to figure it out. You don't have to contemplate it. You just see it. Go to sleep. I hate that."

In Carli's narrative, although she doesn't explicitly refer to "white" American culture, she implies this when she asserts that *we* did wrong when *we* came here. In context, her "we" is implicitly referring to white Europeans and their various acts of domination. She acknowledges, with ambivalence, her ancestral link with those white Europeans. And she is critical of the contemporary "American" culture she sees those ancestors largely responsible for: types of houses, patriarchy, impurity, escapist television. She also suggests that white American culture is *not* a culture because it has no "origin."

Carli's response differed from Laurie's in that it was not stunted by a cognitive gap. She had reflected on and could talk about some of the common practices, habits, or characteristics of white American culture. This difference, I believe, was attributable to the fact that Carli was more countercultural than Laurie in her style, self-image, and political views. She positioned herself outside the mainstream, and from there she could more easily objectify it. However, Carli and Laurie did share a certain perspective on white American culture—that it somehow had no origin or, as Laurie put it, no "ties to anything."

The idea that being white meant that you had no origin or ties to a past was widespread among all the white youth I spoke to at Valley Groves. Mara was a middle-class senior honors student who was active in leadership and a star athlete. She was Mormon and described herself as "conservative" politically, but her views on affirmative action were not set in stone. We talked in a small conference room on campus, and quite quickly after preliminary introductions I told her a true story about a census taker who recently had come to my house. The census taker introduced herself and then asked, without any prompting, "What are you?" I asked Mara, if she had met that census taker, what would have been her first response to the question "What are you?"

"Like a race?" Mara asked.

"Could be a racial category . . ." I replied, trying not to influence her response. "I'd have to answer 'Very white.' I am, yeah. I am 100 percent white. Whenever I hear that 'What are you?' I think either of race or religion. But race usually first and religion second."

Her answer struck me because, over at Clavey, white youth referred to suburban whites as "very white" to suggest their shelteredness, lack of interaction with people of color, and naivete about racial issues, if not explicit racism. Mara, however, used the phrase unabashedly and matter-of-factly to express how she viewed herself. Also, on the consent form I gave Mara for her and a parent to sign for this interview, I included a section where I asked students to name the racial category with which they identify. Mara noted that she had a mix of European backgrounds and wrote "pretty much white" on the form. So I asked her if being white meant having a European mix.

Mara replied, "I just think that there's not much . . . I don't really think of myself as European. I think of myself as a white American girl. I *wish* I had a little more uniqueness to me, I mean, I don't know . . . [inaudible tape] I don't really go back to my roots, though I know I have family and where they come from but they're all white races."

"You don't have any heartfelt devotion to your European past?" I asked.

"Not really. We've done a lot of genealogy work in church. That's how I know where everybody is from and I appreciate that as my background, but my family has lived here for generations, so I don't really draw on that."

In sum, to Mara, the more distant you were from your ancestors, the more white you became.

One day I asked Mr. Riley if he knew any conservative students to whom he could introduce me. He suggested Jonathon, a senior in his government class who was an outspoken conservative Republican and a big fan of Rush Limbaugh. Jonathon was an athlete and very active in school leadership. He and I met in an empty classroom during his study period, a time more easy to negotiate than taking him away from one of his many extracurricular activities during lunch or after school.

I told Jonathon about the census taker who came to my house and asked him how he would have responded to "What are you?"

"Like in what context?" Jonathan asked.

Once again hoping not to influence the first response, I said, "Well, traditionally census takers count people and place them in broad categories of race, class, gender, religion. This census taker seemed to be curious about what people call themselves, how they categorize themselves without any particular prompting, like without saying, 'What race, or gender, or nationality are you?' "

"Uh huh," Jonathon uttered, as if hoping for a little more prompting.

"So what comes to mind first, how would you categorize yourself?"

"I'm . . . white, if anyone asks me. I'm a white boy. I have—you know?"

"Yeah?"

"I have no minority standing," Jonathon continued. "Any scholarships or anything like that, just out of bounds for me. All that kinda stuff. I'm just white. I come from like some—I think I come . . . primarily from Sweden, Germany, whatever, you know, but those European cultures have probably been mixed in so much that I'm just white."

"Right. You don't have any—there's no strong pull toward your European ancestry?" I asked.

"Well, I know for a fact [that I have] ancestors from Sweden, the ones that I've heard about. But we've lived in America for a long time. . . . [My last name] is a German name, but it's not. It's my dad's, it was his step-dad's name and it has no ties to us. I think [my ancestry is] a lot of, kind of Norwegian, Sweden, those kind of cultures."

"Yes?"

"Pretty much white," he concluded.

Matt was another boy I met in Mr. Riley's class. I was interested in talking to him because he made comments in class that suggested to me that he was fairly liberal on issues concerning race. He lived with both of his parents, who had working-class jobs and a house near campus.

"What does being white mean to you?" I asked Matt after we had spent some time getting acquainted and talking about the different types of kids at school.

"I feel like an American. But I guess I'm kind of jealous because I don't have this kind of ethnic background that I can claim and get college scholarships and stuff. You never see the young white American scholarship foundation, which I think they should have. . . . I guess because the so-called minorities have a lot of ethnic heritage, I don't think white people really have that. Not a strong racial background. They're just kinda there."

To sum up these responses white youth at Valley Groves gave to questions regarding white identity as an identification with a "culture": Billy, Laurie, Carli, Mara, Jonathon, and Matt represented a wide swathe of different types of white students at Valley Groves: mainstream/alternative, liberal/conservative, middle-class/working-class, male/female. Yet they all had fairly similar definitions of white identity and culture. Most, especially the more mainstream white students, experienced a cognitive gap when asked to describe white American culture, and when asked to define what being "white" meant to them, they all said that it meant you had no culture, specifically no ties to some kind of European ancestry or heritage. Moreover, this understanding did not particularly disturb them, with the exception that some believed that *having* an ancestry entitled people to special treatment when it came to college scholarships and admissions. Another exception was Carli, who dreamed of going "back" to a more "pure" time.

I expected white youth to be somewhat more concerned over not having an ethnic ancestry. There is considerable research claiming that multigenerational European Americans who, through the melting pot, have lost all semblance of their ancestral culture will retain symbolic attachments to a European ancestry because it makes them feel unique and gives them a sense of belonging to a community.[1] Besides Carli, the only youth I talked to at Valley Groves who felt some attachment to an "ethnic" past were first-generation European immigrants who *were* still tied to a non-American culture. But even for Carli, her desires for a "past" were not driven by a longing for "meaning" as much as freedom from the aspects of American culture she disliked—patriarchy, consumerism, and television.

Another commonality in youth's constructions of what "white" meant was the us-them formulation white/majority versus ethnic/minority. This is most evident in Jonathon's and Matt's narratives, where Jonathon said he had "no minority standing," and Matt said that "so-called minorities have a lot of ethnic heritage" and whites do not. In other conversations with white students at Valley Groves, they tended not to distinguish much between the different peoples that comprise U.S. minorities. Blacks, Latinos, Asians, Filipinos were all alike in certain respects: they all had culture, "close family ties," uniqueness, and certain advantages over whites because of their "standing." A Filipino girl I interviewed corroborated this observation without direct solicitation. I had asked her what stereotypes she thought the white students had of different racial-ethnic groups, and she replied, "The white kids don't really stereotype, like, specific groups. Just generally . . . *minorities.*"

Clavey High: Situated Renderings of White Culture

Jessie was referred to me through two sources: Eric, one of the more radical, critical-minded students I met at Clavey and with whom I became friends, and Barry, a conservative Republican whom we will hear more from shortly. Both described Jessie as articulate and smart and respected her insights into their school experience. I started my interview with her by asking her why she chose to attend Clavey High School. She said that she had gone to a predominantly white middle school and wanted a "better shot at being an individual, a better shot at having a balanced collection of minority friends and being able to know more about other people and, hence, to know more about myself."

I asked her what caused her to believe that a racial-ethnic balance of friends would be a good thing for her. She said that she had never really felt that she had a culture, that she could "identify [her]self as a culture." However, during the preceding summer she had lived for a week on an Apache reservation. She said, "It was an incredible experience to me. They were very open about the importance of their culture and I was able to participate in a sunrise ceremony. [The Apache culture] was absolutely intriguing to me and that [experience] was one of the most powerfully wholly cultural experiences I've ever had. It really changed how I felt about having something like that."

Another factor that contributed to her desire to know more about her culture was not only that she felt she might be missing out on something meaningful but also that not having a clear identity made her susceptible to self-hatred as a white person. "You cannot love yourself and hate your culture," Jessie said. "A lot of African American activists have said that. I don't think that [culture] is at the root of everything, but I do think that it's important to have some respect for that facet of who you are because you see it every time you look in the mirror."

These concerns, raised largely from her experiences of close association with people who had culturally bounded self-identities and, to an extent, negative ideas about white people, inspired Jessie to explore just what white American culture was. The extent to which she could articulate traits she believed to be of white culture—negative obsession with food, skinny figures, quilts, polka, and beer bread, to name just a few—was exceptional among the white students I spoke to at Clavey, but not too far off the spectrum. Every white kid I spoke to at Clavey had *something* to say about white American culture, even if that something was that they took white culture for granted. As Eric told me, "I think I'm too immersed in [white culture] to be able . . . It's probably a lot of things I take for granted, I'm sure of that."

Overall, the term most descriptive of the ways the youth I spoke to at Clavey dealt with the question of white culture would be "pained." Youth were aware of the difficulty in defining white culture and identity and struggled to make sense of that. Linda, Sera, Melissa, and Ann were four close friends who were finishing their sophomore year when we first met to talk. All three were in high-tracked courses and had aspirations to attend universities after high school. Sera, Melissa, and Ann described themselves as "alternative" and wore the understated clothes and hair that went with that identity. I didn't learn explicitly from Linda, an orthodox Jew, where she placed herself in the spectrum of youth styles and tastes, but she tended to dress semistraight and semialternative.

We met at Linda's place, a single-family house not far from Clavey in a predominantly white, high-middle-income neighborhood. We sat in the den. Melissa and Linda spread out on opposite ends of a large, overstuffed sofa, and Sera, Ann, and I alternately sat or stretched out on the floor. Between us was a bag of cookies I had brought. About thirty minutes into our discussion, in which we made introductions and talked casually about the girls' experiences at Clavey, I asked, "What is white American culture?"

Linda spoke up first. "White American cu'—I mean, like—just the three people in this room. White? I consider myself Jewish. I don't know what this 'white' is." She looked at Ann and asked, "If someone asked you, would you say you're Lutheran or you're white?"

"Well, I'm white," Ann replied. "But I don't know about my white heritage."

Speaking over Ann's last words, Linda broke in, "Like, *white*. So I'm, like, *white?*"

"Yeah, I'm white," Ann repeated with a slight tone of defiance.

"That has nothing to do with me," Linda said.

Then Ann continued, "So like why do we say color, I mean, okay [she points to me], you're tan. We should have a tan group." Pointing to her bare arm she said, "I'm white now—no—*this* [pointing to paper] is white. Am I white? [pointing again to her arm] No."

Linda: "To me, like African Americans, when they have the AASU [African American Student Union], their race in a way is different than say 'white' because 'white' is so general. African Americans have . . . fewer divisions [among them] than we have. They're more one, and we're more different."

Sera, who until now had been lying on the floor with her eyes closed, suddenly came to life and said, "I think it's the opposite. We've grown up—we don't know but, TV is our culture, everything about us is our culture so we don't think of it as special or significant. Africa has so many different cultures and they combine as Africa. And [then people] say 'I'm African American'—half the people [identified as such] have no connection to Africa."

"That's what I'm saying!" said Linda, enthusiastically, "So many white people don't—[cutting herself off]. Either you're religious and you know your ancestry, you know your culture, your background."

Melissa then chimed into the discussion, "I know my background but I'm not religious."

Linda, defensively: "I'm saying *or* you know whatever, or you don't. You're not religious and you're just a part of the color. I know so many African American people who don't know anything about Africa."

Ann again: "Why do people have a label? African American, European American or whatever. We are American, period, that's it. Yes, I'm European. I'm glad I know my European history . . . but we're *American*."

"We shouldn't have any labels," said Sera. "It shouldn't be like us and them, it should be *we*." Ann, agreeing, said, "We are of the human race" as Sera kept talking, "Why do we have labels? What's the purpose of saying you belong to this group—already saying you have this difference?"

"Remember the day we had to wear labels? 'I am proud to be   ?' You wore, 'I am proud to be a virgin!' " Ann said, directing this to Sera.

"I'm proud to be a human being."

"But most of them had a culture!"

Sera replied, "It's good to be proud of who you are, but . . ."

"But that's like a blockade!" Ann said, exuberantly finishing Sera's sentence.

"I'm white and I'm proud, like 'Oh my god!' " Sera said, in a tone indicating that to say such a thing would be impossible without severe sanction.

"I have a question," continued Ann. "I want to discuss this—Why are white people racist and other cultures aren't? Why? Why, like about the label 'I am proud to be white'—'Oh my god she's a racist!' [But] 'I'm proud to be Asian'—'Oh wow, that's so *cool*!' "

Returning to the conversation, Linda replied, "I don't know; to me, when I hear people say, I am proud to be white versus I am proud to be Asian, there is a big difference because people don't understand how to be white."

"But why?" asked Ann.

"White is American," asserted Sera. "White culture and American culture are the same thing."

Ann: "But why are white people only American, why aren't they European American?"

In quick succession, Sera: "They are." Ann: "No they're not."

"Whatever . . . to say, like, 'I'm white' is nothing, white isn't considered culture because it's American. We all have the American culture born within us."

Cutting Sera off, "Why because you're white does that equal not having a culture?" Ann asked.

Linda: "It *does* if you—It's so divided within the white race. White is more general than anything else. That's why I'm saying to say 'I'm proud to be white' doesn't mean anything to me. I don't think you would say 'I'm glad to be white.' You'd say, I'm proud to be me. I'm proud to be liberal. I'm proud to be a democrat—I don't know. I don't think anyone says 'I'm proud to be white.' I think people say 'I'm proud to be black' easily. It's like they're a group together, it's like we're . . ." ["not," interrupts Ann]. " 'We [African Americans] are here to fight against everyone else. I'm so proud to be African American, we have our ties, we have our connection'—but really they don't. Some of them don't even know their background. It's just the whole, like, I've got to watch out for my fellow—whatever."

"Which is good, but not to an extreme," added Sera.

At this point, I put one of my own thoughts into the mix, "I know, when I hear 'I'm proud to be white' I immediately think, ooh, that sounds really racist." This elicited responses from everyone simultaneously, "Yeah!" "It's weird!" "Slave-owners!" "We're so evil!"

Ann, persisting with the hard questions, asked, "How come? Why do they think that? They think that *we* did it. We didn't do it. Our ancestors did it. That's behind us. We are not like that."

Linda, in a tone of disgust, "The word *ignorant* comes to mind. It's the same thing as like saying, 'Well, you're German; you persecuted my people.' Like, I have to forget that, you know what I mean?"

Ann: "But people don't understand that not all our ancestors did that."

Sera: "None of my ancestors were slave owners, but if [somebody's ancestor] was I wouldn't be, well, 'You must be a racist.' "

Linda added, "We're living in a different world. A different society. We can't look back and drag on and judge people from their ancestors."

For no obvious reason, except that the topic seemed to be spent, with Linda's comment the subject changed to the fat content of the cookies we were heartily chowing down. ("Ah-ha!" Jessie might say. "White culture—*skinny*, you know?") Still curious, however, about what the girls' responses would be to questions about their ethnicity as opposed to racial identity, I asked what they said when people asked them what their ethnicity was and how they felt about their "ethnic" heritage.

Both Ann and Sera simultaneously replied, "I'm white." And Linda said, "I say 'white' because that's the closest thing. But I don't *relate* to white. I am white, I guess, but there's no . . ."

Ann, cutting Linda off, "I guess white is basically European. Like, it's basically asking, 'Are your ancestors from Europe?' "

I have presented this conversation at length in order to do justice to the complexities and confusions Ann, Sera, Melissa, and Linda dealt with when confronted with the question of what is white culture. They had no ready answers, and that fact seemed to enflame, not diminish, the emotional charge of the topic. Numerous themes emerge in the discussion: white as an arbitrary ascription, as heterogeneous, as "American," as an amorphous amalgamation without community, without culture, without pride in itself. The tension between "white" as an impersonal social ascription and as a personal, cultural category with which one can identify runs throughout, too. This is best summed up in Linda's final comment: "I say I'm white . . . but I don't relate to 'white.' " And, finally, the ways the racial-ethnic identities and behaviors of nonwhite students help the girls think about their whiteness are evident.

Similar struggles and themes emerged in my interview with Barry, with some added twists. Barry was introduced to me by a student who described him as "the only Republican in the school." I was thrilled to meet a more conservative student since I had met several at Valley Groves but none at Clavey. At least, not one who was admittedly conservative. I had been on campus for most of the year and had never seen Barry, a thin, medium-height, dark-blonde boy. I came to learn that he didn't hang out much in the public spaces. At lunch and during breaks he stayed in classrooms to work or talk to friends and did not participate in school activities.

Barry and I started our conversation on the topic of his politics. He said that he wasn't the *only* Republican on campus, but he was the most vocal and the most "extreme." By that he meant that he was actively involved in Republican politics, something his mother and he shared. We then got into talking about school life at Clavey High and eventually came to the subject of white American culture because, in the course of our conversation, Barry had mentioned "suburbany kids" who dressed "normal," and "Asians" who were "plain ol' Americans" whom he "considered to be white." I asked him to define the terms *white, American,* and *normal.*

He said, "Let's start with the 'white' and 'American' thing. When I mentioned about the Asians who are white, they generally are people whose families have been in America for five or six generations or whatever and they don't have—don't take on a lot of the Asian traditions and Asian cultural things. You ask them about Chinese new year and they have less idea about it than you do. They've adopted the American culture rather than hanging on to the old world culture. You know?"

"And then, there is some sort of equation for you between what is white culture and what is American culture?" I asked.

"I suppose, yeah."

"And how would you describe that? What is American culture? And maybe that gets us back to 'normal'?"

"Yeah, normal to me," Barry replied. "I guess just that plain old nuclear family, kinda—you know. Two kids and a dog. House in the suburbs or somewhere near the suburbs. One or both of the parents work, I guess. Middle class."

"Are there cultural things in terms of clothing and food and stuff like that?"

Laughing as though the question felt a little awkward to answer, Barry said, "I suppose" then paused to think. "The clothing's just, you know, normal clothes. Not anything cultural, not extremely grunge, not extremely formal all the time. Food I guess just not any—no culture dominates. You know? The family will have Chinese food every once in a while but they won't every night or anything."

Barry seemed to be a little self-conscious and unsure of himself as he spoke, so I added, "One reason I ask this is because it can be very difficult to describe white American culture."

With a sound of relief as if he had been taken off the hook, Barry replied "Describe that, yeah!"

"Why do you think it is difficult to describe what white American culture is?" I asked.

"I guess it seems so—[I'm] so used to seeing it that it's hard to pick out what things it is that makes it what it is, you know? It's like it's so much easier to pick out the differences in someone else's culture than to pick out the characteristics of your own."

Of all the students I spoke to at Clavey, Barry came the closest to falling into a cognitive gap on the question of white culture. His responses also resonated the most with the responses from several Valley Groves students, such as Jonathon (who was also a Republican) and Billy (who was not), for whom *white, American, middle-class,* and *normal* were closely connected if not synonymous. Moreover, his definition of "normal" matched closely with the ways "normal" was defined at Valley Groves—as basically mainstream conventional.

At the same time, however, Barry was more racially conscious and reflective of whiteness than most whites I spoke to at Valley Groves. He understood that the reason he struggled to talk about white culture was because he was "so used to seeing it" and took it for granted. He pointed out that, because white American culture is hard to "pick out," he relied on "the differences in someone else's culture" to illuminate his own. Finally, Barry was mindful of the race–class dimensions of that which is considered "normal." Elsewhere in our conversation he revealed a fairly sophisticated understanding of the links between the constructions of class and racial difference:

"I think [tastes, interest, behaviors] have mostly to do with the situation you're in. I think a lot of the black families—maybe their parents were teenagers when they were born or they come from broken families or poor families, they're on welfare, public assistance. Maybe they come from abusive families or bad situations. And a lot of the white kids don't. And I think that if you put a white kid in the same situation as a black student and a black student in the same situation as a white student, they would come out following the stereo-type. I don't think it's a racial thing, I think it's more the situation that you're in. And it's just that black people tend to be in a bad situation that multiplies down the line. So everyone stays where they've always been."

Although Barry's description of the black families was somewhat stereo-typical, he spoke to ways that racialized distinctions are often *class* distinc-tions, the differences between people living in concentrated poverty and those not.[2] Putting that aside momentarily, the point I wish to put across here is that, overall, Barry, like Sera, Ann, Melissa, and Linda, floundered a little bit when challenged to discuss white American culture, but rose well to the task. Common themes that came up for all of them were "white" as heterogeneous, middle-class, eclectic, American, normal, and taken-for-granted.

Coming to Terms with the Past

So far, I have focused on the extent to which white students at Clavey reflected upon whiteness as "cultural" in the sense of it being bounded by certain shared practices, habits, or assumptions. The above discourses also reflect what youth had to say about the cultural origins of white people. Interestingly, whites at Clavey, much like whites at Valley Groves, defined "white" as having "ancestors from Europe," but no ties there. Or as Eric said, "We don't have lengthy traditions. A lot has been lost in the good ol' melting pot."

However, Clavey whites had very different responses to their fuzzy cul-tural history than did their counterparts at Valley Groves, for whom having no cultural ties was a matter of fact that caused no apparent distress. At Clavey, the informal culture of the school impressed on youth the impor-tance of knowing your racial-ethnic background. As one white student, Tina, put it, "I think [knowing your ancestry] is important to anybody you ask. Everybody wants to know who they are, where they come from. It's a major part of being [at this school.]" Hence, at Clavey, the lack of an origin story was a charged issue for Clavey whites I spoke to. For Jessie, for exam-ple, her self-perceived lack of identity made her susceptible to low self-esteem in the face of groups who not only found pride in their heritage but looked at her and saw the history of white oppression.

There were two different ways in which Clavey students resolved their discomfort over having no clearly defined ancestry. One way was the "ethnic option"[3] or "symbolic ethnicity."[4] Those terms refer to the ways that multigenerational white Americans, in the absence of ethnic community and cultural practices such as language, will choose an ethnicity and embrace it largely in name only for the purpose of providing meaning and a sense of community. Jessie chose one kind of ethnic option—defining "white" as a cultural community with traditions that, although "funky," gave her a sense of roots. Barry chose another type of ethnic option. I asked him if being at Clavey or living in Clavey City caused him to think about his background. He responded, "It's made me think about it a lot more. You'll see on my [consent] form that I'm German and my grandparents are extremely German. My grandmother grew up in a family of immigrants, learned all the German traditions. I found that I would ask her about them more mostly because of the Asian kids. I really respect the way that they carry out all those traditions *here,* and I'm really interested by that. And I sort of found myself being more interested in what a German family would do, culturally."

I asked, "Do you feel that your German ancestry is a part of you—more than just an interest—something that you carry with you, that gives you something meaningful?" He responded,

> "I don't know. I didn't realize how many German traditions my family followed until I went there and noticed, 'gee!' And I was there with a group of students and we'd go through the town and we'd see churches and things and they'd say how interesting that was and I'd think, 'Well, we do that. We do things that way. My church service is like that.' I didn't realize how much of it I had until I saw how much of it other people don't. ['And at home?' I interjected.] I discovered my family's diet's pretty different because my family eats red meat seven times a week sometimes. We eat a lot of pork and beef and I discovered that a lot of people don't. [Laughs] A lot of potatoes, too! I guess that's very different. I've discovered, too, my parents are both very heavy drinkers. Not to the point where it bothers me that much, but I've also noticed that people seem to have more fun at my house than at other houses. At my house there's the nightly cocktail hour, dinner conversation can get kind of loud."

With that last comment, Barry laughed out loud and added, "My family seems to laugh more than other families do."

Barry's association with Asians inspired him to reflect on his own cultural background, just as Jessie's experience on the Apache reservation caused her to reflect on hers. In doing so, Barry looked to the types of foods and manners of his family culture to represent his ethnic culture. This is most common among European Americans who have lost touch with traditional communities and cultural practices.[5] And the family can represent the ethnic culture regardless of whether or not family practices actually originate from European traditions.[6] For example, we can imagine that parents who drink a lot and get loud at dinner are probably randomly distributed across the whole population of white (and other) people, yet Barry has attributed that to his parents' German ancestry.

Another way in which youth resolved the issue of having no clear ties to an ancestry was through adopting a romantic or postcultural notion of the self.[7] By "postcultural" I mean a self-concept that dismisses all relevance of and indebtedness to the past. It is a decidedly present- or future-oriented identity that emphasizes innovation and genius, as opposed to an ethnic identity, which is past-oriented and emphasizes tradition and continuity.[8] Linda touched on the postcultural when she said, "We're living in a different world [from slavery times.] A different society. We can't look back and drag on and judge people from their ancestors."

Murray was a white Jewish senior and the first person I interviewed at Clavey. He caught my attention at a student-faculty meeting about multicultural education where he was the only white student and one of the most outspoken on behalf of greater representation in the school curriculum of all the different cultures at Clavey. In our interview, Murray told me that he was the only white male on the football team and, at home, had an adopted black brother. For these reasons, he was very aware and intolerant of racial-ethnic injustices and "realized what white means," especially with respect to white privilege. He added, however, that "in terms of my background and everything, I have no clue and I'm glad about that."

"Why are you glad?" I asked. Murray replied,

"Because . . . I don't believe in tearing about the past. Guaranteed, relatives of mine were in the Holocaust, but does that mean that I should be upset about that? No, I should realize that happened, but there was a holocaust here against Native Americans, a lot worse than in Germany, but no one ever talks about that. It's happened in a lot of societies because there's always going to be a dominant race. But I don't think that white means that I should know everything about my whole past, my whole heritage, just as I don't think any race should because I don't think that's important. What's important is being able to get your own life on your own track. Being able to direct your life not for what your ancestors did . . . but to do the best thing for you for where you want to go. . . . What happens is if you harp on the past and believe this door is closed because of what happened four hundred years ago, then doors keep closing for you because of what you believe."

Daniel, whose father was Portuguese, gave a response similar to Murray's, but with a bit of ethnic option mixed in. Daniel was a sophomore when we first met. Of all the students I came to know, he had the strongest antiracist principles—so strong that he did not reduce a vicious attack on him in the bathroom by two black boys in his sophomore year to a "racial" incident nor make it into an excuse to stereotype, fear, or dislike all black people. I asked him if, given the semidark complexion he inherited from his father, he considered himself white or Latino. He said,

"People have suggested I am a person of color or mixed. There was a lot of pressure in junior high to have ethnicity, be a minority so you could claim stuff. Then I decided, no, I'm European American. I mean, that's what I am. Ancestry doesn't matter. I mean, things have changed. People look back in the past and judge you for it, and I don't think that's right. Sure, people enslaved people. At one time every race had slaves. I think you need to move on and see what's going on now. History is important but you have to work on getting together now and don't use that to divide."

"Are there any things you're proud of or ashamed of for being white?" I asked.

"None of that stuff comes up. I don't think of myself as a white person. If I'm talking to someone I don't think, 'Oh god I'm a white person' and all these things go through my head. I don't hold any of that stuff. I'm proud of my Portuguese culture. I think everybody needs to look back to their ancestry and be proud of it, but not to a point where you're using it to dictate or make decisions."

Daniel felt ancestry did not matter; "now" (which, to him, owed little to the past) mattered most. In the now, he was simply himself, without racial baggage. At the same time, ancestry *did* matter; it was a source of pride. Though logically contradictory, the co-occurrence of postcultural and cultural, or "symbolic," identities arose in several other discussions with students. Often, the postcultural identity was attached to a particular us-them relationship and the symbolic identity to another. For example, recall that Barry said that he became interested in his German ancestry through his relations with Asians and respect for the way they continued their Asian cultural practices here in the United States. Later in our conversation, the topic shifted to African Americans, and Barry said,

> "In the black American culture I sort of get this feeling that it's fashionable to be black and try and separate yourself from white society. There's a whole thing about how minorities should be able to get tax cuts and black people are saying 'Let's try to get paid back from slavery.' And I'm just sort of like 'That was a long time ago.' And this whole—I don't understand the whole concept of trying to tie themselves with the African heritage thing, because, you know, you're not African. I mean, unless your family immigrated or something from a much later date but for the most part you're American. That's all you are, you know? Your culture over there is gone. It's too many generations to dig back for it now. It seems like people are trying to separate themselves just to be different. Not for any real purpose."

When thinking about black efforts to revive a cultural ancestry, Barry's thoughts about the value of ancestry became hardened and dismissive, and by virtue of saying that black ancestry is too far gone to have meaning now, he implies the same should be true of whites, who for the most part, also have long-gone ancestries. Yet, earlier in the conversation, when thinking about Asian Americans, Barry spoke enthusiastically about his amusement and intrigue in discovering traces of his distant German ancestry in his current practices. Overall, when students at Clavey thought about or embraced a symbolic ethnicity, the stimulus came from their relationships with Asians, Native Americans, and, to a lesser extent, Latinos. When they spoke from a postcultural identity, the stimulus was their relationships with African Americans.

To sum up all the responses white youth at Clavey gave to the question of white "cultural" identity: First, somewhat like their counterparts at Valley Groves, most white youth at Clavey found it difficult to describe white American culture, but none fell entirely into a cognitive gap and some could say quite a lot. Themes or characteristics of white culture that youth expressed included heterogeneous, middle-class, commercial/consumerist, American, normal, and taken-for-granted. Second, unlike whites at Valley

Groves, white youth at Clavey were not content to believe that whiteness was a culturally empty category. They struggled to make sense of it and to resolve that struggle. One resolution was an ethnic option, finding some sense of pride and continuity with either white American culture or with a European ancestry, and another resolution was a postcultural identity that dismissed the contemporary significance of ethnic identity and the past. Third, for Clavey students, "minorities" were not a homogeneous mass but were composed heterogeneously of African Americans, Asian Americans, Latinos, Native Americans, and other racial-ethnic groups. The images of or beliefs about a specific people influenced what white youth thought about their own whiteness and, in that regard, defined what it meant to be "white." Finally, all in all, white students at Clavey were not particularly uniform—not between themselves nor within themselves—on their reflections upon white as a cultural identity.

White Culture: Normal, Euro-American, Postcultural

The variations in white students' reflections on white culture, both among Clavey students and between Clavey and Valley Groves students, begin to make sense if we look at some of the roots of the normal, European American, and postcultural narratives and the contexts that make one more salient than another. While different in character, the three narratives all stem from the particular experience and history of white European Americans as a colonial power and the national majority. First, in any nation, not only the United States, the citizens who are members of the dominant culture will not have a collective definition beyond the national identity nor a sense of having a culture.[9] Only those cultures that are different from and marginal to the national norm will be marked as "cultures." In the United States, white culture is co-constructed with American culture and, by virtue of saturating everyday life, is taken for granted and culturally invisible. Only African Americans, Latinos, Asian Americans, and other minorities are represented as having culture.

However, national cultures are not "normal" and cultureless; they are composed of values, mores, laws, and epistemologies that have definable cultural origin. The culture of the United States is mulatto and becoming more diverse all the time. Still, at its core lie values, practices, and types of knowledge that stem from the cultures brought here by early English and other western European immigrants.[10] Whites may try to tease out some of those core features or vestigial European practices from American culture, or otherwise appropriate and adopt as their own something from American culture generally. What is teased out or appropriated becomes material for constructing a symbolic ethnic identity.

The postcultural identity takes another direction, but is a part of the same European colonial history. It encapsulates some of the more rigorous tenets of Western Enlightened thought, particularly of the romantic and modern varieties.[11] These include the value of individual responsibility and self-determination, the belief that the present holds no debt to the past, and a self-concept that is grounded in the present and looking ahead.[12] It is an identity that first marked the "primitive" from the "civilized" and now, in postmodernity, marks the "cultural" from those who are beyond culture, postcultural.[13]

Three social processes conditioned which narrative—the normal, symbolic ethnic, or postcultural—was most salient and when: different types and proximities of interracial association; the ways racial-ethnic differences were structured by school practices; and the ways youth defined their relationships to people of color. The unconscious construction of white as norm was most prevalent at Valley Groves because whites there had little to no association with racial difference and found their social-cultural milieu to confirm their normalness. With little to put white culture in relief such that whites could see it and name it, white youth at Valley Groves could not define white culture and fell into a cognitive gap when asked. Lack of challenge to a "normal" self-concept also kept the identity fairly stable, providing a self-narrative that was as grounding as any bounded cultural identity. This accounts, I believe, for the relatively uniform voice in which white students at Valley Groves spoke about their identities and for the confidence that made them impervious to feelings of loss or remorse for not having cultural ties and community.

In contrast, white youth at Clavey were in close association with marked racial-ethnic differences and, hence, frequently challenged to define white culture and identity. For this reason, at Clavey, more whites investigated their "ethnic" pasts or adopted postcultural identities. However, even they were not immune to the co-construction of white culture as American culture or other ways white is posed as the norm in the wider society. Barry was an extreme example of this: he explicitly defined white culture as "normal" and "American" and described school as a "foreign country" to him. He would go to school, then go home where everything was "normal again." In Barry's case, however, although he went to a minority-white school and lived in a minority-white city, he told me that the neighborhood in which he lived was predominantly middle-class and white. He also made it clear to me that he isolated himself from interactions at school. This meant that Barry's social world was much like that of white students at Valley Groves—confirming of the construction of white as American and normal.

Nonetheless, as I pointed out earlier, fully integrated whites at Clavey also, at times, unconsciously implicated themselves as "normal." This occurred, I believe, because normative whiteness was reinforced through institutionalized practices at Clavey High. In the preceding chapter I discussed at length the racial meanings constituted through the tracking structure. I argued that accelerated students, who were for the majority middle-class white and Asian American, were marked as the most normatively well-behaved in the school, whereas lower-tracked students, who were predominantly black and Latino, were marked as intellectually and behaviorally flawed. In short, white and, in this case, Asian American students were positioned as the standards by which other students were judged.

Multicultural practices at Clavey similarly constituted white students as the norm and standard by positioning them as cultureless. There was no integrated multicultural curriculum at Clavey, only a "world cultures" class for all sophomores, which was basically a world history course. Although different teachers taught the course differently, the standard textbook was markedly Eurocentric. In the first chapter, titled "Dawn of Civilization," the opening page featured a picture of the ancient English monument Stonehenge. By my interpretation, the page implied that humankind originated in England, and I wondered if students reading the book didn't get the same message.

Beyond this course, there were two main, formal multicultural events a year: the "cultural assemblies" and "multicultural week." For cultural assemblies, students gathered in shifts in the school auditorium to view a production created and performed by one of the ethnic clubs on campus—African American Student Union, Asian Student Union, Latino Student Union, and the Inter-Tribal Student Union. A common assembly featured performances illustrative of the history, arts, and folk cultures of the particular racial-ethnic group, including ceremonial dances and rituals, live music and song, poetry readings, and slide shows. Multicultural week was a week of activities in which each day focused on celebrating a particular aspect of the different cultures of the students. For example, on a day devoted to traditional and national clothing styles, students held a fashion show in which African American youth in dashikis, Chinese girls in brocade gowns, and Mexican American students in ceremonial dance costumes paraded before youth gathered outside of the cafeteria.

These events were valued by all, particularly students of color, who told me that they enjoyed having the opportunity to teach others about their cultures and perhaps dispel negative stereotypes about them. However, I suggest that because multicultural events were not integrated into the core of school life and did not include white students, they constituted students of color as marginal to the (white) norm. Moreover, by making students of color more culturally visible, the events made whiteness culturally invisible.[14] When white students spoke about the assemblies, they usually expressed enthusiastic appreciation for "the chance to learn about so many cultures." But learning about other cultures merely gave them more references by which to define what they were not. As well, when they spoke in this way, it was as if "cultures" were like books—objective things that existed outside the self but could be consumed to pleasure the self. In my conversation with Ann, Sera, Melissa, and Linda, I asked them how they thought their experience at Clavey would influence their adulthood:

> Ann: I think it's going to be a very positive thing. [Melissa interjects: Yeah.] Because it teaches us how to deal with different kinds of people. . . .
> Sera: Yeah, you learn more about others. . . . It's a positive experience.
> Melissa: Yeah, you gain street smarts. You gain stuff. . . .

Greater knowledge of other cultures was something Ann, Sera, and Melissa appreciated because it gave them tools to enhance their sociability, but it did not make them reflect on their sociocultural location as whites. When other white students at Clavey spoke to me about the value of the multicultural events, they made similar kinds of statements and inferences. Overall, multicultural events, as "add-on" school practices in which white students could pleasurably gaze upon racial-ethnic others without putting themselves on the line, reinforced a sense of whiteness as center and standard (cultureless) and racial-ethnic others (by virtue of having culture to display) as different and marginal to that.

Furthermore, no white students I spoke to questioned why there was not a white American cultural assembly. Granted, to most this was untenable, largely because it might be taken as a white-supremacist act. As I mentioned earlier, when I talked to students about school clubs for whites only, they categorically dismissed the idea. One said, "There'd be a riot!"; another said, "It wouldn't be right. It would be taken all wrong." But it was also untenable because, as another student put it, "White is all around. It doesn't need special attention." The idea that white culture doesn't need special attention (read: white is the norm and standard) seemed to be another message multicultural events gave to white students. As if for the eyes of whites only, multiculturalism at Clavey gave white students new references to add to their mental cache of exotic others while further obscuring the invisible power of white culture.

Institutional practices at school, then, reinforced the notion of white as norm for white students at Clavey. However, unlike their counterparts at Valley Groves, Clavey whites were not safely grounded in an undefined, normative identity. Cultural identities were not entirely for show at Clavey: they were an important grounding for students of color and a rallying point for political organizing at school. From schoolwide forums to special principal-student advisory committees, students of color at Clavey demanded that classroom curricula and school activities reflect their backgrounds and help them learn more about their ancestries. In these forums, culture was represented by students and adults alike as something like a genetic code that, once deciphered, carried all the wisdom necessary to know who you were, how you got here, and where you were going.[15] Clavey whites could not escape from these discourses and dialogues and were compelled by them to explore the value of cultural identity for themselves. The two foremost ways they did that were through the symbolic ethnic and/or postcultural perspectives.

Which leads to the third and final point about the different uses and saliences of the normal, symbolic ethnic, and postcultural identities at the two schools. Just *how* students defined white identity and culture in a given moment depended on feelings and sentiments associated with how they defined racial-ethnic difference at that time.[16] A "me-you" or "us-them" relationship was shaped by the types of interracial association white students had and how that relationship was structured. At Valley Groves, because white students had little to no direct association with students of color, they often confronted what it meant to be white not from direct challenge but from choices they had to make when asked to tick off their race or ethnicity on educational tests and application forms. It was an impersonal relationship to racial-ethnic others that, at the time of this research, was imbued with abstractions generated from public debates about the California anti–affirmative action bill, Proposition 209. Those debates, from which such notions as "reverse discrimination" arose, contributed to white youth viewing culture as a type of currency that "minorities" had and they, as whites, did not. This made some white students, like Jonathon, Matt, and others, resentful, believing that their lack of cultural currency threatened their future prospects for college and scholarships. Overall, this impersonal relationship made the dualism "majority-minority" the most salient us-them construct among whites at Valley Groves.

At Clavey, on the other hand, white youth had personal relationships with youth of different racial-ethnic groups and saw wide differences between minority groups *and* within them. One of the things Clavey whites said they appreciated most about their experiences at Clavey High was how they learned to differentiate between different types of people within racial-ethnic groups, to see differences based on class, on academic orientation, on whether someone was a gangster to be avoided or harmless.[17] I, too, noticed that, in casual discourse, white students at Clavey tended to make clear distinctions between different types of African American, Asian, and Latino students. That was true, at least, until white students were called upon (by me, for instance) to categorize themselves or a particular racial-ethnic group, or if something in the discussion placed them on the defensive. At such times, whites at Clavey glossed over internal differences among groups of people and perceived them as homogeneous.[18]

In those categorizing and defining moments, the feelings and sentiments associated with a different racialized relation, be it white / Asian, white / Latino, or white / African American, gave rise to different thoughts about what was white culture. In the minds of the white students I spoke to, Asian, Native American, or Latino students were more legitimately "culturally" different to whites than African Americans. At Clavey, there were many recent immigrants from China, Korea, Vietnam, and other Asian nations, as well as from Mexico and Latin America, all of whom spoke in native languages and wore native fashions. This strongly marked the cultural differences of immigrants, but it also benefited American-born, multigenerational Asian Americans and Latinos by providing "proof," if you will, of origin and continuity. Association with these youth raised feelings and curiosities among white youth about their own cultural backgrounds and sparked interests in rescuing something from European or European American cultures.

African American students, in whom white youth saw no vestiges of African culture, were defined by white students less by cultural differences and more by power differences, particularly by white domination, past and present. This tension was not merely in the imaginations of white students; it was frequently made and remade through common debates and conflicts that came up between whites and blacks in the classrooms. Slavery and white oppression against blacks in the past was a common, if not prevalent, theme in classrooms at Clavey and in other situations where white and black youth dialogued with each other. In predominantly black classrooms, especially, the slightest invocation of white domination would spark a riotous discussion. From what I observed of these discussions, African American youth saw slavery as a painful issue, and they intuitively believed it impacted their lives today. Whites could only see that slavery was something "in the past" that no longer existed, and they believed the preoccupation with slavery was misguided and unproductive.[19] Moreover, whites frequently heard or interpreted grievances about slavery in personal terms, as if blacks were charging that "Your people enslaved us." White youth who knew for certain that their ancestors were not slaveowners got indignant about the accusation. And even if there were slaveowners in their background, they did not feel they should take responsibility for someone else's behavior.

In short, for white students at Clavey, racial-ethnic difference between whites and blacks was not experienced as cultural as much as social-structural and as a contest over interpretations of the past. Some have argued that white denial of the significance of the past is a defensive mechanism designed to exonerate whites from taking responsibility for the legacies of white oppression.[20] I believe that may be partially or sometimes true, but I more firmly believe that, at least for the white students I came to know at Clavey, dismissal of the relevance of the past stemmed from the postcultural characteristics of white European American epistemology. Debates about slavery and white oppression *triggered* the postcultural response in some whites, largely because it was counterintuitive for them to understand how the past had a bearing on the present.

This chapter has examined what white youth at Valley Groves and Clavey high schools could say about whiteness as a culture. I argued that the ability to define, let alone say anything about, white culture was situational. It was shaped by the types of interracial association the youth were most familiar with and how they experienced and defined a particular white-other relationship. Overall, both sets of youth did not have a lot to say about white culture. However, the spoken word is not the only way to "say" something. In chapter 4 I examine the indirect and symbolic ways that white youth at Valley Groves and Clavey explored and culturally expressed their identities as whites.

4. Doing Identity in Style

American youth are engaged in popular culture at a level of intimacy that surpasses that of any other age group. On the one hand, the very categories of "youth" and "teenager," and the styles, music, and behaviors we have come to take for granted as the natural properties of adolescence are, in large measure, constructs of the popular culture marketing industry.[1] Youth, on the other hand, have come to drive that industry with a continuous stream of cultural productivity and innovation. Possibly at the core of this relationship is the particular social location young people occupy. If adults define identities around their occupation, parenting, and/or civic responsibilities and political affiliations, youth today, who have limited if any access to those spheres, explore and define who they are through their leisure activities.[2] Such things as music, clothing, hair styles, body piercing, sports, and street language are the principal tools by which young people can claim personal power and mark a multiplicity of identities, including peer group, gender, class, and racial identities.[3]

This chapter examines the indirect and implicit meanings of race and racial identity that white youth conveyed through the types of music they listened to, the clothes they wore, the ways they spoke and carried their bodies, and the free-time activities they pursued. Given that the meanings inscribed in cultural practices are registered more by feelings than discourse and are inherently slippery, unstable, and multivocal, interpreting them is always a dubious process. While doing this research, I immersed myself in the different music and leisure activities of the youth in order to, at least, expand my frame of reference with the students and, at best, give me insights into what the students' practices meant to them. I listened religiously to the local classic and alternative rock, rap, and r & b radio stations; watched MTV; bought and listened extensively to the CDs of the most popular rock and rap artists; attended major school dances; went to underground alternative and punk rock concerts; and even attended a rave that some Clavey students produced. Two students, Pickles and Eric, were generous enough to compile ninety-minute cassettes of their favorite music—a mix of punk rock styles from Pickles and an eclectic mix from head-banger to surf music from Eric—and to keep me informed of bands to see that were coming through town. And, ultimately, I listened very closely to what students said about why they liked the things they liked or did the things they did.

In what follows, I argue that youth cultures of white students at Valley Groves were nearly devoid of "racial" meanings per se. Whites adopted certain cultural forms associated with African American people and identity, but because of the students' distance from a black community, those cultural forms did not signify black identity or identification with black people, but instead putative qualities of *blackness*. At Clavey, the same cultural forms that Valley Groves youth freely sampled were charged with racial-identity meanings and usually used selectively by whites to signify African American identity in some way or another. Meanwhile, Clavey whites attributed their own musical tastes to their interests and experiences as whites. I conclude the chapter with a discussion of some of the everyday inter- and inner-relational processes at play in the construction of white racial identities, tastes, interests, and styles.

Valley Groves: Acting Cool, Being Tough

PP: *What's your favorite music?*
Billy: *Rock and roll, modern rock. I listen to some country. I'm not really into rap. . . . I like the beat of rock and, yeah, I like upbeat songs, so some country is kind of boring and slow. . . . Rap to me is just talk. I just never got into it. The guys just talk, I guess. That's something that just never appealed to me.*

PP: *What music do you listen to?*
Laurie: *It depends. I didn't listen to the radio for a long time so I listened to what Dad listened to. I just got the Eagles'* Hell Freezes Over *CD and the new Pearl Jam. [I like] random stuff. My sister has an 80s CD and I bring that to work with the soundtrack to* Forrest Gump. *I don't really like classical and jazz because they play that here [in the coffee shop where she works] and I*

get sick of it. I don't listen to too much rap, just a few songs that I like when I want to get revved up for a game or something. I mostly like older stuff and modern rock.

PP: *What about classic rock appeals to you?*

Howie: *I don't know. I just—friends listen to it and like, you know, you hear it and you like it and so then you decide to start listening to more and more of it.*

PP: *And do you like modern rock or not as much as classic rock?*

Howie: *Yeah, pretty much. I mean, it doesn't really matter. If I like the song, I like the song. That's how it is with most music. It's not like one classification. If I like the song, it doesn't matter what kind of music it is. I mean, I like some rap songs, but it doesn't mean I like rap.*

In chapter 1 I introduced youth cultures at Valley Groves and some of the meanings attached to them. To summarize briefly: the main clique cultures were popular, skaters/smokers, hicks, homies and the "normal" kids. The overarching organizing principle behind clique membership was a norm-other semiotic code, with "norm" being those who more or less conformed to mainstream expectations of the school and wider society (the popular and normal kids) and "other" being those who stood outside of those parameters in one way or another (the smoker/skaters, hicks, and homies). Racial distinctions did not enter into clique differentiation largely because all of the cliques, except homies, were predominantly white, and even homies were not exclusive of white students. Through becoming "popular" or "smoker" or "homie," clique members subordinated the salience of racial-group membership to clique membership. Overall, then, being popular or a skater did not simultaneously mark one as "white," as it did at Clavey, nor did being a "homie" mark one as "black" or "wannabe" black.

When I asked mainstream white youth, like Billy, Laurie, and Howie above, what kinds of music they liked and why, they tended to have similar answers. They named some form of rock and roll (classic or modern) first, then usually also named other kinds of music they liked, including some country, rap, and r & b. Most of the time they could not say more about why they liked what they liked than "I like the beat" or "It's what I always listen to." This is to be expected of musical tastes, especially, which tend to be embodied kinetically and emotionally and, hence, unconsciously. Usually, conscious framing of musical and other cultural practices comes with the drawing of sharp identity boundaries.[4] For example, the students at Valley Groves who could best tell me why they liked a certain kind of music tended to be those who identified themselves outside of the mainstream, such as punks and hippies. Jeffrey, for example, was the most radical-looking punk rocker at Valley Groves. He wore torn-up army fatigues, studded neck and wrist wraps, and three-inch hair spikes. He told me that he always felt out of place, not "normal," and like a "loser" until he got into punk music. He said, "I used to eat out of garbage cans. That's not normal. Kids would beat me up. . . . I was fucked up until one day a guy turned me on to punk music. . . . Punks don't give a damn about what people think. Fuck them. That really spoke to me in here [placing his hand over his heart]." Jeffrey went on to describe punk as the voice of outcast people and everything else as "crap."

Most students I spoke to, however, were not like Jeffrey. They liked a range of music for reasons they claimed were largely aesthetic and otherwise unconscious. This was even true of some rap songs. Several students said they liked to listen to rap whenever they needed to "get going in the morning" or to get energized for a game or other school event. Others liked to dance to it. School leadership students tended to play rap at the beginning of lunchtime events or rallies because it got people "revved up."

In short, in all of these accounts of likes and dislikes, no students as much as suggested that race or racial identity had anything to do with their preferences in music and other types of popular cultural consumption. However, race did enter indirectly and implicitly in some of their discourse and practices. This was especially true of the meanings white students assigned to popular cultural forms derived from African American and Latino urban culture. Some of the things Matt told me in our conversation best illuminate this. I asked him what his favorite music was, and he said, "I just got through a rap stage, but I guess now I'm going back to easy listening stuff. I'm all rapped out."

"How long were you into rap?" I asked.

"About two months. I borrowed a CD from a friend. It was pretty cool. Made me feel tough listening to it. That's why. I was listening to a lot of alternative, but I got tired of all the screaming, the heavy metal screaming. Too much."

"So, it sounds like you're sampling around," I remarked.

"Yeah, not country though, I won't take country," Matt said.

"What about rap made you feel tough?"

"I found in all the rap songs they always talked about themselves, cruising down the street, and I just imagined that was me while I was driving. It just felt cool. That's what, I guess, is the attraction to that kind of music."

Matt liked to listen to rap because it made him feel like he was "cool" and "tough." In fact, he got very similar types of feelings when, at times, he mimicked the "homie" or hip-hop style in clothing. He told me, "Sometimes I like to dress like a homie, but a conservative one. I can never find the right sized pants to get them baggy like that. I don't know how they do it. Sometimes if I'm in a bad mood I'll wear all black or something. I tried on my black jacket today but it just didn't feel good so I put on this one. If I wake up and I'm in a bad mood and I want to act tough, I'll dress like a homie. Then I'll look at freshmen and give them the evil eye."

Interestingly, freshmen white males wore more hip-hop fashion than any other age or peer group, beside homies. My sense was that wearing hip-hop clothes was a way for freshmen to try elevating their status toward the more cool and composed upperclassmen, or at least to fend off preying seniors like Matt.

"Cool," "tough," and "gangster" were recurrent themes in white students' discourse around hip-hop music and styles. Billy, for example, told me that the homie style was "to look tough, give the impression you are from the city." Mara called it the "tough guy image." Laurie told me that the white kids who were into the "rap scene" were after the "gang-banger, cool kind of thing." And Matt, too, went on to elaborate on the underlying meanings behind the homie look. I asked what impression the kids wearing the style gave him and he answered, "I think they're trying to say they're tough or bad. When I see them I think—Can I say bad words?" he asked.

"Yeah, sure."

"I say, What the hell is your problem, man? Can't you dress like everyone else? They just look kinda like freaks. I don't see why they have to do it. It just makes them look menacing."

"Do you know any of those kids, their history?" I asked.

"Yeah, I've been in class with some of them. Homie guys are always loud, goof-offs in class. If somebody says something to them they got tough, shoved them, cussed at them."

"And are these guys white? Black? Latino?"

"Well, I'm talking about some white guys I know. . . . It's like they're pretend black guys, trying to fill the role of what is missing [at school.]"

Matt's words, "pretend black guys," evoke, as I see it, the core of what is behind the meanings youth ascribed to hip-hop cultural forms appropriated by white youth. To listen to rap and don "homie" styles did not suggest that youth identified with black people or wanted to be black; they wanted characteristics of *blackness*, namely to be "cool," "tough," or hip.[5]

When I asked white youth to tell what some of the stereotypes were of black people or black culture, they all said pretty much the same thing. "Tough" was the most common response, followed by "street-smart" or other associations with inner-city life. Billy, for example, told me that "the main stereotypes to me [of black people] are that they are from the inner city, tough." Inner-city life, with its exalted gang violence, was both feared and revered by youth. When I was sitting one afternoon outside a coffee shop and talking with a group of four girls and one boy, they told me how they preferred Valley Groves to other high schools in the area because the other schools had too many "gang-bangers." Jolie, a Valley Groves sophomore, told me: "Valley Groves is cool, everyone gets along. But [the other high schools are] full of gang-bangers. It sucks." Shortly following this conversation we all went into the nearby Payless Shoe Source to browse. While roaming down an isle, Jolie picked up a shoe and cooed, "I want this shoe. I like that name 'Eastside'; it sounds gangster." In other words, while Jolie was happy to have a safe distance from "gangsters," the romantic appeal of urban gangster life remained compelling to her.

The association of "cool" with blackness came out more spontaneously, as in an informal conversation I had with a senior white male at lunch one day. This self-described "sheltered" young man told me that he "admired blacks." He was intrigued by their "difference" (presumably from whites). "[They have] dry hair; have to wear caps," he said. But most of all he loved the way they spoke: "Really cool."

Often, coolness and toughness at Valley Groves were captured not only in hip-hop clothing but also in popularized elements from Black English and slang as well as particular body gestures derived from rap performance. Students used slang terms like "fresh," "Y'know wha' I'm sayin'?," and grammatical constructions of the verb "to be" as in "you be messin' with me" with an air of cocky self-satisfaction.[6] In my notes one day I wrote down this exchange.

Carli has just come into the classroom. She is looking again like a meticulously composed bricolage. She's wearing her usual (unusual) blue, Levi hat which today has a pink pin on it that says "Sexism is a social disease." Baggy belled blue jeans, Latin American–style hooded tunic jacket, white t-shirt with "peace" written in a zillion languages, Birkenstock sandals. She spies Mark across the room, breaks her slow shuffle into a swaying, wide-leg strut, and as she approaches Mark, lifts her right hand high, slams it down on his out-stretched palm and beams, "*Whatsup!*" They exchange a few words outside of my hearing range until Carli swings around and I hear, "Y'know wha' I'm sayin?" I have never heard her use those expressions before.

I intuitively felt at the moment of witnessing this exchange that Carli was punctuating her presence with urban black slang and body language to impress Mark, a meticulously styled punk-rock enthusiast with a slick and confident—cool—veneer, whom I knew Carli admired. I observed perfor-mances of blackness like this several other times by other white students, and at another time by an African American female student in a drama class. The girl was asked to improvise a scene with a white boy, and the only direction they had was that she had to make him leave his chair. The girl leapt up from her seat, ran up to the boy and said "*Duude!* We gotta get outta here. They're comin'! We'll get busted!" As the girl continued to coax the boy into getting up, using these types of verbal incentives, she snapped her fingers in front of her face and bobbed her head from side to side, a mannerism common among and indicative of urban black females. At another time she thrust the backside of her right hand toward the boy and then folded both hands high across her chest in a way often seen in rap performance. As an African American girl, she did not seem to be trying to invoke an image of a black person per se, but rather an image of an urban, sassy, and tough (black) person, and to that end, she performed types of blackness to invoke their associative qualities.

In short, at Valley Groves, rap music, hip-hop clothing, and other cultural forms and practices originating from black youth cultures and identities were not linked to black *identity* or identification, but linked to stereotypical or putative qualities of *blackness*. To explain this in terms of semiotics, the black cultural forms served not as symbols, but as icons. Icons "convey an idea by virtue of its very close reproduction of the actual object or event."[7] They invoke conscious and unconscious sentiments by way of representing an image or utterance that evokes feelings, ideas, and associations with that image. People worship religious icons like the Virgin Mary not because they want to become the Virgin Mary, but because they want the qualities associated with her—holiness, virtue, purity.

Besides the associations of toughness and coolness, however, blackness also tends to evoke a type of masculinity.[8] Hence, most often the white students at Valley Groves who deployed the associative meanings of blackness in certain styles and physical demeanors were boys. Girls seeking a cool and tough persona tended to look elsewhere, and Latina "*chola*" or gang-banging style best suited them. Key elements of the style included long, dark, curly hair drawn back and wrapped with a colored bandanna on the top of the head, super-baggy "Ben Davis" pants, mud-colored lipstick, and dark eye makeup. There was a small group of girls at Valley Groves, whom I heard referred to as "gangster chicks," who all wore this style. I knew some of them to be from white Northern European backgrounds, although that was not easy to discern by appearances. Carli told me that she wore her hair and eye makeup like that for a while. She didn't associate it with *cholas* until I pointed it out to her in the interview. She said that she liked the style because she thought it made her look attractive and less "nerdy."

Clavey: Youth Cultures and White Cultural Community

Kirsten and Cindi were two close friends. Kirsten's parents were both white European American and Cindi's mother was white and father third-generation Chinese. Both girls were "alternative." They commonly wore work pants and two t-shirts—a long-sleeved one under a short sleeved one—and colored their hair. At the time of this interview, Kirsten's hair was dyed jet black and Cindi's was dyed ivory blonde. They both struck me as fairly shy, so I suggested that the two of them, together, meet with me for an interview. In the course of our conversation, the topic of self-segregation around campus came up. Cindi said, "Outside of class it's very different. Like, in class, you can be friends with anybody and you hang out with them in class, but once you get outside of class it changes and different races tend to stick to their own races."

"And why do you think that is?" I asked. Kirsten replied,

"There's a lot of peer pressure at Clavey. Not so much that's really noticeable like, 'Oh come on, I know you want to do those drugs.' Not like that, but it's an under-thing [undercurrent]. Like today in my drama class our teacher was talking and we were doing pantomime stuff and the teacher was like, 'Come on you guys, just get up. No one's gonna think that you look stupid and no one's going to criticize you.' Then I thought about how I sometimes thought that in class, like if I got up, people would be like, 'What the heck is she doing?' So I think that, regardless of if they say there's no peer pressure, there still is that feeling of being accepted. . . . And even people who say they don't care what people think, maybe they don't as much as some others, but I think everybody does to a certain little percent."

Cindi added, "I think there is also the factor that some people feel like they may not have very much in common with someone from a different race, which in some ways is true. Because you have different music tastes, different styles of clothes. Also, like, what your friends think."

"Or, like, different things that you do on the weekends, things like that," Kirsten chimed in.

"Yeah, so I think that's something that separates the different races."

Kirsten pointed out that there was outside "peer pressure" at school, referring to the sanctions that came with crossing racial boundaries and not sticking with your kind. As I argued previously, unless white students at Clavey identified with African American students, wanted to mimic a black person, or were trying to relate to an African American friend, they tended not to listen to rap, speak in black slang or Ebonics, gesticulate in ways that mimic gestures associated with African American youth, or wear hip-hop styles beyond the generalized style most males wore at school. Those practices tended to signify black identity and/or identification, not merely a "tough" or "cool" person of whatever race-ethnicity. The only whites who seemed to adopt black urban styles to appropriate from them some of the meanings associated with blackness were white male skaters and ravers, but even they altered the look such that it was not mistaken to signify black identity.

Cindi's comment, however, added another dimension to the question of why some youth consumed or participated in certain kinds of cultural activities and other youth in others. Besides external sanctions, there was also an *internal* force that influenced the types of cultural forms and activities students preferred: different "tastes" and ways of thinking. As our conversation continued, this perspective kept coming up.

"That leads to my next question—What kind of music do you like to listen to?" I asked.

"Alternative, [the local alternative radio station], punk, stuff like that," said Kirsten.

"I've been trying to figure out alternative rock," I said, as an opening toward engaging Cindi and Kirsten in a discussion of the music and its meanings for them. But Kirsten had more to say.

"I also like other music, like, I like country. I don't know why. We kind of ride horses and I went to horse camp and so they play country music and it grows on you. I also like opera and classical. And I like easy listening because when I was little every day my dad would take me to school and back, and for seven years in elementary school my dad was always listening to easy listening, so now when any song comes on I just know it, like all eighties songs. So that sort of grew on me too. I like almost everything. I don't know. Rap is sort of like. . . ."

"It depends on some kinds of rap," Cindi broke in. "Like I really don't like [when it's] degrading to women with all kinds of swearing and stuff. That just turns me off. But then sometimes I like rap, it just really depends."

I asked Cindi what other kinds of music she liked. She responded, "Same as Kirsten except the country. It's kinds of interesting because my musical preferences have just changed. In elementary school and, well, more like early junior high I listened to rap and r & b."

"Yeah, so did I," Kirsten piped in.

Cindi, continuing, ". . . and then in ninth grade I was into this oldies kick. . . . I'd listen with Mom and we'd both be singing. Then by tenth grade I started listening to [the alternative radio station] and alternative music and I kind of stopped listening to rap and r & b. I still listen to it mainly because my brother listens to it."

"He blasts it in his room so you can hear it straight through to Cindi's room," explained Kirsten.

"A lot of people say that they listened to a lot more rap in elementary school. Why do you think that is?" I asked.

"Yeah, I don't know why," answered Kirsten. "It seems like everyone, regardless of if they're black or white or Asian, I think everyone in our school listened to [the local rap and r & b radio station]. . . . Just, like, everyone listened to that. But then I think when you are little you don't really . . . have too much of an identity of yourself sort of. As you get older and mature more you discover what your 'true being' [laugh] is. So then people's musical tastes change."

Kirsten laughed self-mockingly when she said that we discover our "true being" as we mature. The term possibly felt awkward to her, but the implication was not. The "true being" she discovered was, among other things, "white" and, thus, predisposed toward particular tastes in music. The idea that something inherent to one's racial background and experiences made one predisposed to certain types of popular culture was a prominent notion among whites I spoke to at Clavey. It had caught my attention in one of my earliest interviews, a group interview with Patti, Daniel, and a boy named Riley. We were talking about the ways musical tastes define your friends and communities when Daniel commented that he used to listen to rap in elementary school, but as he got older he found his "true interests," which were in classic rock and some classical music.[9]

In my conversation with Jessie, she spoke quite eloquently about why she liked certain kinds of music over others and touched on many things that were representative of other students I spoke to, so I have quoted her at length:

"Okay, for me, rap was always hard for me to listen to because I associate that with Clavey. . . . We have rallies every Friday and they always play rap, like constantly, you know? The prom, they played rap constantly. I mean, I can have r & b but rap still bothers me. Particularly the gangster rap. If there is one form of music I could ban it would be gangster rap. I can't even—just— ugh. I've listened to very, very hard core metal before, like I was a little angry junior high school person, and that's sort of how I identify people who listen to angry music—is that they must be angry. 'Cause music is something that reaches into the core of who you are and sort of flushes out your subconscious. . . . Like in the tenth grade I went to Down on the Green and that's where metal bands play. And it [was] not even hard metal—it was, like, Metallica, Guns & Roses—and it was such a community formed around this rage. . . . It was head-bangers and those people. I used to be one of those people, you know, and it was like a bond that formed between all those people and that's why I really respect the fact of how music can drive everyone together and you just sort of felt like you knew everyone intimately, like these thousands and thousands of people crammed into this stadium, thrashing around and enacting their emotions, and it was, like—Yeah, good! Good people, get out there and be angry, you know?

"My white friends who go here seem more likely—particularly I can think of several people offhand—seem more likely to listen to a broad array of music, jazz, all different kinds of music. . . . Like I love writing and when I'm writing, I will listen to emotional music. I will listen to classical piano. I will listen to Nine Inch Nails. I will listen to things that have more powerful emotion, any given sort, depending on how I'm writing. And I have a lot of friends who are like me in that respect—and some who are even more so, who have like an incredible awareness of music they listen to, particularly the ones who are closer to my age and have more time to sort of dabble in different musical venues. They go to a rock concert and they're immediately—bam!— upstairs with the jazz or who knows, they'll be in with the other kinds of music, whereas a lot of people I know who are into rap, that's what they listen to. Rap is it. I'm usually completely surprised when I hear a black person talking about listening to something other than rap. I'm like, 'Whoa, okay, that's cool. Whatever you want to listen to.' But it's surprising to me when I hear my mind doing that, like, 'Oh, okay. That's interesting! I generally make that stereotype!' Too bad, but it's based on what you see. . . ."

Jessie and I talked for several minutes about different heavy metal and alternative rock groups, the ones she liked and not and where some of the fine lines were between heavy metal, alternative, and punk rock. Then I said, "Earlier, you were talking about rage and how heavy metal kind of spoke to you and your rage. Rap expresses a kind of rage, too. What's the difference in terms of the kinds of rage? What was the quality of the rage, or the message of the rage in metal that spoke to you, and how does that differ for you from rap?" Jessie replied,

"For me, it's the association thing. I think it's cultural and it's economic and it's all of those things locked into the evocative qualities of rock. It's the fact that what I'm angry at has something to do with what's at school. There's a completely different sound to it. I mean it's like death metal—it's metallic. It's well named, you know? It's this horrible sound. It'll be like this churning, horrible, pounding sound and you're like, 'Whoa, that's really angry.' . . . It's like the inflection of the voice and the thunder in the music and just the whole— It's completely different to actually go to a concert and experience this than it is to listen to it while you're in your bedroom. And just the power of it is stronger to me than the power of rap which is droning to me, and it's like the words—because I listen to the words—and the words of the gangster rap, which is the most angry rap they have, is offensive."

"I'm still wondering, what do you think is going on in the different types of music that it ends up that it's mostly blacks listening to rap and whites listening mostly to punk, metal, alternative?" I asked.

"Well, there certainly are more black musicians that perform rap than white musicians and the black musicians are more respected, and they certainly have more white bands that perform alternative, which is interesting. I think that the issues that rap speaks to are usually considered black issues, like you know more of the problems experienced in the sort of lower-middle-class culture, and the urban area, whereas alternative— I'm not sure what alternative speaks to. It has no focus really. It's like you can have all different sort of bands and they all do different kinds of things, but the alternative music I favor sort of has more of the themes running along its track that I deal with. I don't deal a whole lot in somebody shooting my best friend or, you know, the different issues that are really spoken to by the raps that I've heard, and the alternative that I listen to really talks more about—I don't know. Being in love. I don't know. I have to listen to it more carefully next time but the music certainly speaks to the different issues of the two different cultures."

A message that pervades Jessie's discourse and that she explicitly states in her last line is that different popular cultural forms speak to the different life experiences of racialized groups. This was the most common explanation youth of all racial-ethnic backgrounds gave for why different groups seemed to prefer different types of music and leisure activities. Anthony, for example, said that black culture differs from white because of "the way we brought up, the way we raised. How we think about society." Johnetta told me that the thing that most differentiated whites and blacks was "experiences. There are definitely different experiences between the two groups. There are white kids that hang out with black kids and they're practically black, except physically . . . because they've been in the same neighborhood, had the same stuff going on."

Jessie's narrative also indicates the many *ways* that experiences shaped identification with popular cultural forms. Three main ways might be codified *tastes*, *homologies*, and *constitutive activities*. All of these amounted to feelings of affective resonance and identification with popular culture. The first, tastes, refers to aesthetic preferences that are inscribed in what feels natural, true, or right and constituted either through learning practices or from regular exposure to the cultural form. They are often expressed as "distastes, disgust provoked by horror or visceral intolerance ('sick-making'), of the tastes of others."[10] And to the extent that exposure to certain forms is conditioned by the material conditions of existence, different tastes will tend to reflect different social locations, such as class and race or ethnicity.[11]

Jessie spoke of her visceral intolerance to rap. "Ugh," she said, in disgust. And she described the "thunder in the music" and "inflection of the voice" of metal music as that which viscerally resonated as truth to her as opposed to the types of offensive words and sounds that came from rap music. Earlier, Kirsten, too, spoke to tastes, specifically with respect to the ways her tastes for country and easy listening were constituted through regular exposure. She talked about liking country music because she associated it with riding horses and going to horse camp. She also spoke of developing an affinity for easy listening music because for seven years her dad played easy listening in the car while taking her to elementary school. In short, she liked what she liked because it hit upon something that felt familiar to her.

The second form of resonance, homology, specifically refers to types of parallels youth made between the cultural form or practice and their concerns, interests, and experiences as whites. British sociologist Paul Willis argues in his study of "motor-bike" boys, for example, that the bikers listened to Elvis Presley and Buddy Holly because that music celebrated masculinity and, in that way, validated the boys' own masculinity and their commitment to be demonstrative about it.[12]

Recall from the previous chapter that when Clavey whites talked about white culture, they tended to define it as middle-class, heterogeneous, and meaningless, among other things. When I spoke to them about the appeal of the music they listened to, those themes recurred. Class associations with racial differences came up frequently. Jessie, for example, explicitly asserted that part of the "evocative quality" of music was the "economic," meaning that which was attendant to class-based life experience. Black music spoke to issues and problems experienced in "the sort of lower-middle-class culture," and she stopped just short of saying that alternative music spoke more to middle-middle- or upper-middle-class issues, but still strongly asserted that "music certainly speaks to the different issues of the two different cultures."

At a point in my conversation with Kirsten and Cindi, they also invoked a homology between their class-based experience as whites and their preferences for certain kinds of music. Kirsten said, "I think punk is more of a 'I don't get along with my parents' kind of music. And I think rap is more of like 'Let's go kill someone' music."

Cindi agreed. "I think also I can kind of relate to punk rock or whatever you want to call it rather than to rap because I think they [express a] simpler anger. It's just kind of like 'Oh, I broke up with my girlfriend' or 'I had a fight with my parents,' something like that. Usually rap has more to do with killing and gangs—stuff that doesn't really relate to me, because I don't necessarily see a murder every day or something."

For Cindi and Kirsten, punk rock (and we were talking here about American, softcore punk,[13] the rougher edge of alternative music) is about a "simpler anger" and benign concerns befitting youth from more privileged social (and geographical) locations. Black music, on the other hand, addresses the types of violence imagined to be quotidian in an impoverished ghetto. These types of comments by Jessie, Kirsten, and Cindi in which white and black tastes were attributed to "economic" or class differences between white and African American people were echoed by many students I spoke to. They point to the ways race and class are fused in such a way that the one social category implicates the other.[14]

In addition to parallels between class experience and musical preferences, Jessie's narrative also suggested a parallel between the heterogeneity of whites as a people and their heterogeneous or eclectic tastes. Most whites I spoke to, when I asked them to define white culture, told me that it was too heterogeneous to define. Daniel encapsulated this in our interview. He said, "White society is more scattered [than African American society]. It's more diverse, I think, like you have all the different cliques and tastes. Of the African Americans at school there are a few that are different, but you don't see as many of them who are willing to try new things." Similarly, when whites spoke about their or other whites' musical tastes, they tended to say their tastes were eclectic. Jessie indicated this when she talked about how she and whites she knew tended to listen to all kinds of music, but rap listeners (read: black youth) listened only to rap. She also asserted that alternative music (white people's music) was quite heterogeneous in itself.

White students at Clavey did have eclectic tastes, as did the white students at Valley Groves. Actually, so did many of the students of color I spoke to.[15] Of significance was that whites at Valley Groves did not define their eclecticism as something particular to whites, but white students at Clavey did. Eclecticism was, in this sense, a cultural trait of whiteness and definer of white identity for Clavey whites.

The third homology, meaninglessness, was not as explicit as the others but implied when Jessie said that she wasn't sure what alternative music spoke to and that it had no focus. I gleaned from her comment that alternative music did not speak "messages." Many other whites I spoke to, whether they listened to punk, alternative, or classic rock, told me that their music didn't have messages, and that's what they liked about it. Lyrics to some songs would be nonsensical, even bizarre. In my interview with Kirsten and Cindi, the former said, "A lot of songs, alternative and stuff, make absolutely no sense. They are just words fit together. And people say that, 'Oh if you look at it and analyze it you can find meaning!'" Cindi added, "But not songs like this one where this lady doesn't put jam on her toast, she puts vaseline. Yeah! Like I put vaseline on my toast!" Meaninglessness was also implied by comparisons whites made between "black" music, which they believed tended to deal with heavy life and death issues, and "their" music, which was about more banal things like breaking up with your boyfriend or fighting with your parents.

Students of color I spoke to also commented on the meaninglessness of white music. Winston was an Asian American junior whom I met while participating on a student-principal advisory committee on race at Clavey. I asked him what he thought about different kinds of music. He said, "Slow [songs] are about love. I guess it's easy to write about that, about romance. Rock—I don't understand. [It will be] talking about melons or something. The titles of the songs and the band names are confusing. I don't understand it. Love, I can relate to that. Whether you have a boyfriend or girlfriend, you can relate to that. But rock is kinda confusing to me. I don't get it. Why are you writing about melons?"

The "meaninglessness" of white as a culture and identity came across in other ways besides students' discourses. It was particularly salient in public performances of student art, especially performance art. During my first year in the field, there was an evening dance performance of works choreographed by the school's talented modern dance instructor and some of the students themselves. The show opened with a modern dance piece featuring the twenty-five members of the class of advanced-level dancers. This was followed by an eight-person, hip-hop dance number, a modern dance duet, and then a solo ballet performance. Up to this point in the production, the dancers were predominantly African American. An Asian American girl and two white girls participated in the first piece, and one white girl was in the hip-hop piece. Except for the hip-hop dance number, which was upbeat and playful, the performances were all quite sober and dramatic. This was especially true of the solo, which, danced to a soulful blues tune, evoked feelings of grief, loss, and hardship. Following this piece was a performance of a markedly different tone, with markedly different-looking students than were in the previous pieces. The curtain opened on five white girls and one white boy, all wearing either overalls or cargo pants with t-shirts on top and flannel shirts tied around their waists. At that time, the flannel shirt worn as such was a marker of "alternative" music fans. But the musical accompaniment was not alternative rock, but something you might hear at a country barn dance. The dancers' movements were consciously clumsy and over-exaggerated, as they drew on forms derived from European American folk dancing, '60s pop, and '90s hip-hop. They seemed, at once, to parody and mock traditional white European American music and styles of dancing while also saying "white people can't dance." A few times, a dancer stepped forward with a posture of seriousness or self-importance, but was gazed upon by the others as if to say "Who does s/he think s/he is?" Then the dancer would inevitably fall on his or her face or otherwise lose composure as the rest laughed knowingly and mockingly. Throughout the dance, any attempt to bring seriousness or meaningfulness into the scene was similarly ridiculed and squashed.

When I watched improvisations in the drama classes, similar dynamics pertained. The African American and other students of color in the class would do issues-oriented skits dealing with love, lost love, violence, and police abuse, and the white kids would do something silly, nonsensical, and comparatively meaningless. Not that the students of color never did works with humor or self-parody, because they often did; but, still, their humor revolved around "serious" themes whereas the white kids tended to eschew any theme at all and do something more abstract. This "meaningless" cultural aesthetic, I propose, was a way of acknowledging, if not celebrating and validating, the meaningless of white culture and identity generally.

Finally, Jessie's narrative highlighted a third way by which experience shaped identification with popular cultural forms—through constitutive activities. As a constitutive activity, experience is not something outside of culture that is then found reflected in it or resonating out of it, but the cultural activity itself. Music, live music especially but not solely, plays a particularly powerful role in constituting identities because of its impact on the body and on creating "affective alliances."[16] Music appeals to what is in the body—the sociohistorical embodiments of class, gender, race-ethnicity, and other social identities—while also embodying new motions and meanings.[17] This is a basis for gut-level types of resonances with certain music. At the same time, music brings people together in emotional alliances and a shared cultural logic that is both aesthetic and ethical.[18]

Jessie spoke elegantly about these constitutive processes in a couple of ways. She talked about how "music . . . reaches into the core of who you are and sort of flushes out your subconscious." Other youth used similar terms when describing the appeal of their music, saying it touched their "soul" and the "deepest reaches of the emotions." These are individual, emotional responses, but responses that are also physical—evoked through the visceral sensations of the sounds, rhythms, pulse, and temporal order of the music on the body.[19] They are also emotional responses that are inherently collective by virtue of emanating from and being shared with others outside of the self. Jessie spoke to this collective, community-making experience. She talked about a particular head-banger concert she went to and how "a community was formed around this rage." "Thrashing around" and "enacting emotions" made her feel bonded with the others and as if she knew everybody "intimately."

Later in the conversation, Jessie also mentioned that black musicians tend to perform rap and white musicians alternative rock, suggesting the importance of seeing something of herself in the bodies of the music makers and in their audience. The experience of sameness and self-recognition that is in the eye as well as in the body is another piece of the process of identification with music and a musical community. Ever since Elvis brought (black) rock and roll to white people, the music industry has profited by this particular phenomenon.[20] And if we take this phenomenon as a given, then it is no wonder that the experience of a punk rock concert or a rave, in which white youth predominantly participate, would constitute a *white* musical "We."[21] In short, I suggest, the racialized identity of many Clavey whites was constituted through the process of creating affective alliances with particular music audiences that, for the majority, were white. Simon Frith writes, "Pop music is not popular because it reflects something or authentically articulates some sort of popular tastes or experience, but because it creates our understanding of what 'popularity' is, because it places us in the social world in a particular way."[22] If, in Frith's statement, we replace the words *pop* and *popular* with "white," and *popularity* with "whiteness," then my point is well encapsulated. It would read: White music is not white because it reflects something or authentically articulates some sort of white tastes or experiences, but because it creates our understanding of what "whiteness" is, because it places us in the social world in a particular way.

In summary, racialized social and cultural spaces at Clavey High were marked by boundaries that, when crossed, placed youth within territories by which others claimed a group identity. This was even true of white students, who adopted popular cultural forms as their own and imbued them with meaningful racial content. They defined their identification with cultural forms and practices with respect to their particular experiences and interests as white people, experiences drawn from habituated tastes, expectations, and associations; their social class location; the perceived heterogeneity of whites; and even the perceived meaninglessness of white culture. All of these things they saw reflected in or resonating from the music and other cultural practices with which they identified. Finally, the experiences of the cultural activities themselves, shared predominantly with other whites and bonding participants through merged bodies, souls, and hearts, constituted white collective identities and a sense of shared culture.[23]

"Us–Them Dialogues" and the "Multiracial Self"

I have implied throughout this chapter that differing types and proximities of association with racialized difference played a significant role in influencing the different meanings white students attached to their cultural practices at the two schools. I will now look more closely at some of the ways different proximities of association shaped everyday inter- and inner-relational processes of identity formation at the schools, processes I call the "us–them dialogue" and the "multiracial self."

In the last chapter I touched on one aspect of what I am here calling the "us-them dialogue." I wrote of the ways that white students' definitions of themselves depended on how they defined racial-ethnic others in a given social context. Valley Groves whites tended to categorize people of color under the broad category of "minorities" and, hence, defined themselves as the "majority." White students at Clavey, contrarily, tended to specify distinct types of racial-ethnic people, such as "Asian," "black," or "Latino," and how they saw themselves as "white" depended on the feelings, associations, and definitions they had of each particular racialized "other."

The material I have presented in this chapter reveals the "dialogical" character of this us-them relationship. How the out-group defines itself has implications for how in-group members define themselves. A "give and take" and "clash and testing of divergent interpretations"[24] occurs between the two groups. White people, by virtue of being members of the dominant culture, tend to have more power of self-determination and to impose identities on others. However, in everyday practice in some contexts, power relations in the us-them dialogue can be diffused, if not inverted.

At Valley Groves and Clavey, the ways students of color defined themselves had a significant bearing on how whites defined themselves, and vice versa. At Valley Groves, the cultural "dialogue" that white students had with students of color was not particularly racial. As I argued in chapter 1, a color-blind, race-neutral logic and discourse pervaded the school culture. This was reinforced by the fact that Filipino, Latino, and black students who had strong racial-ethnic identities were small in numbers and tended not to interact with the school mainstream. Meanwhile, white students' friends and acquaintances of color tended not to assert racialized distinctions from their white friends, neither verbally nor culturally. In the case of the African American students at Valley Groves, although they saw themselves as "black" and felt the sting of discriminatory and racist attitudes and behaviors toward them (I elaborate on this in part 3), they did not assert a distinct black culture. Most African American youth at Valley Groves spoke in Standard English, especially when in the company of white youth, and wore clothes and hairstyles similar to white students. Black girls did not even apply gels to sleek their hair, a prevalent practice among urban black females.

In my group interview with members of the Black Student Union, I asked the students if they felt at all "out of place," as if their interests, tastes, and desires were different from the majority white students at Valley Groves. All but one, Ron, a boy who was possibly the most "at risk" of doing poorly in school and getting into fights, looked blankly at me and shook their heads, no. Later on, I referred to a news article I read in which a black student in a suburban school commented that whites looked down on black students but turned around and glorified black urban culture. The students said, "Not here." "That's not here." When I asked about the white students who wore oversized clothes and listened to rap music, one of the girls quickly and excitedly responded, "That's just the thing we're talking about! All black people don't listen to rap and dress alike!" I validated what must have sounded like an overly stereotypical representation on my part of black students and restated my question, asking if there were not white students who were tagged "wannabe black" or black students tagged "wannabe white" because of the ways they acted or dressed. The students again looked blankly at me, with several saying, "No."

In short, at Valley Groves, white youth and adults framed the race-neutral terms of discourse, and students of color did not challenge that. With no clearly defined and asserted "black," "Latino," or Filipino cultural identities, white students had no terms for defining "white" cultural identity. Lack of such also meant that the meanings whites attached to the consumption of rap, hip-hop clothing, elements of Black English or slang were not influenced by the meanings black students gave to those forms, but rather by the meanings they picked up from the media and popular culture. Once incorporated into the popular culture, the meanings of cultural forms become interpreted through the dominant culture's perception of the meanings and significance of the form.[25] In this respect, media diffusion of cultural forms tends to *defuse* those meanings that might challenge the dominant culture and rearticulate them into safe, marketable commodities. Selling black males as the "biggest, baddest, streetest guys in the world"[26] has proved to be a profitable way to sell rap and hip-hop culture to white audiences.[27] I suggest that Valley Groves students translated these media-relayed images of black men and black culture into "tough," "urban," and "cool" and adopted them in order to imbue themselves with those qualities. To make meaning of racialized popular cultures, white students at Valley Groves dialogued with and took clues from the popular culture industry, and not students of color.

A very different us-them dynamic and dialogue took place at Clavey High. Most students of color there had strong racial-ethnic identities and these were clearly asserted, not only in the cultural assemblies, but in the everyday life of school. And given that black students were the school majority, black cultural production was in many ways the crowning characteristic of school life. Black English was the norm for casual discourse among African Americans, and new slang terms, new hairstyles, new shoe brands, new rap artists, new hand/head/body gestures—all of which marked black culture and identity—were in constant, crackling production. When whites tried to adopt practices associated with black identity, they had to do so "naturally" or be scoffed at.

Imani, an African American girl who was liked by a diverse range of students, spoke at length about certain kinds of us-them dialogues between black and white students at Clavey, and in the process clearly articulated a strong black cultural identity.

> "[Black youth] have always been initiating different types of things, whether good or bad. We like to be different. We don't like anybody copying off of us and we always like to be different. When people do copy us, we change it as fast as we possibly can. That's why street language changes all of the time. In our music, like rap, the butterfly [dance] came out, and then everybody started doing it, so we changed to another dance called the tootsie roll. . . . We are not known for breaking through in medical stuff or technology, and we have to break through somewhere. So we've been noticed for breaking through with different trends and different things that go on."

I asked Imani what she thought about whites who assumed black styles. She replied,

> "Some of them try too hard. And that's not a stereotype. They try too hard. Some people try to overaccommodate, like, 'I like black people and only black people.' And then they act stupid and ghetto and make us look like we're stupid. They'll be listening to rap music and trying to wear clothes that we wear and overdo it. You are completely overdoing it! Just be who you are! And that's why sometimes we don't like white people because it's, like, you're making me look bad. You're trying to be me, but you're getting only the surface."

"What do you think is the impulse for whites to do that?" I asked.

"They try to overaccommodate. Or they feel bad that we're structurally lower and so they try to be like that so they can relate to their friends more. But you don't relate to your friends that way. You relate to them for who they are. Like, we wear braids, certain types of clothes, talk a certain way, and if you've never done that and decide to start, just stop. You can tell when someone is being fake with you, trying too hard, lying to you. So when whites do that, we know they're trying to be something that they're not. If that's truly what you are, we can sense that, too. If that's how someone talks anyway, we can tell that."

Imani's comments indicate some of the unspoken negotiations and dialogues that occur between African Americans and whites trying to claim cultural space. Her discourse also points to the strength of her own black cultural identity, an identity that was fairly common among African American students at Clavey. I propose that white students' experience of and relationship to the strongly asserted racial-ethnic identities of African American and other students of color had several implications for the meanings whites ascribed to popular cultural forms and their own identities as whites. First, the marking and naming of racial-ethnic cultural boundaries put white culture and identity in relief. As Zora Neale Hurston once wrote, "I feel most colored when I am thrown up against a sharp white background."[28] Similarly, white youth at Clavey felt most white when thrown up against a black background. They could witness cultures, practices, and life experiences that were different from theirs and, in that way, illuminated their own. And whites witnessed how other groups saw them, what practices *others* called "white," and what meanings others attached to those practices. Through these processes, identity dialogues went on, if symbolically, in which whites responded to external ascriptions by either adopting them or exercising self-determination and defining whiteness in their own terms, with respect to their interests and experiences as whites.

But this in itself doesn't explain why *popular* culture—musical tastes, clothing styles, things that tend to be constantly changing—and not more traditional, slower-moving notions of culture—like religious practices, language, even culinary practices—were the terms by which cultural identities were negotiated. This is where, I believe, African American youth played a particularly powerful role. It was they who defined the terms by which identities at Clavey would be articulated. On the one hand, identity politics, multiculturalism, and nationalistic tendencies among some urban blacks have tended to essentialize culture, to assert intrinsic cultural differences between racial groups.[29] On the other hand, through popular culture, African Americans have claimed cultural space within a dominant culture that denies them. As Imani's comments testify to, music, style, and the body as a "canvas of representation"[30] have been principal elements of black culture and a means of status attainment in a society that locks African Americans out of traditional forms of status.[31] In short, black youth at Clavey brought their identity investments in style, music, and demeanor into the racial dialogue at school and forced whites to speak in the same language.

Once speaking in terms of popular culture, white youth may have found that not only could they, too, claim a cultural identity, but also that their identity symbolically solved contradictions and problems in their lived experience.[32] Participation in a subgroup culture, whether as a lone aficionado or an active clique member, may have given white youth an identity and sense of meaningful community that an explicit "white" identity could not provide. Music spoke their stories; tastes and interests were their referent. They could experience solidarity and give each other visceral validation for their experience as white people, without invoking "white" as the basis of that solidarity. Moreover, they did not need to extend their solidarity to *all* whites, and thus implicate themselves with white practices and ideologies they disapproved of. Solidarity was limited to *select* whites, without emphasizing whiteness per se.

In sum, at both Valley Groves and Clavey, the cultural identities of white, black, and other students of color were dialogically shaped with respect to one another, if indirectly in some cases. At Valley Groves the white majority made dominant a race-neutral cultural discourse, which, in turn, affected the extent to which students of color claimed cultural space, which, in turn, affected how whites defined themselves and their consumption of black (and Latino) music and styles. At Clavey the majority "minority" population made dominant a discourse of racial-ethnic distinction in which popular culture was the language of choice. To participate in the identity dialogues, white youth took up the language of popular culture themselves and found meaningful investments in doing so.

Multiracial self

The preceding discussion of the us–them dialectic, particularly as it pertained to white students at Clavey High, also illuminates the processes by which the multiracial self is constructed and played out. By the "multiracial self," I refer, basically, to the interdependent nature of racial-ethnic identities and the many ways that the self and "other" are one and the same. There are at least four interrelated facets of the multiracial self. The first is evident in the us–them dialogue. The self only knows who he/she is because of who the other is; the racial self and other are two sides of the same coin. From another perspective, it might be said that the self is "populated" by racial others: whites carry the "eyes" of blacks, Asians, Latinos, and others in their views of themselves. In the third facet of the multiracial self, the other *is* the self, projected outward. And, finally, to the extent racial identities are constructed around "cultural" characteristics, individuals will have cross-cultural competencies and fluencies that, in effect, make them bi- or multicultural, even if they predominantly identify with only one set of cultural ascriptions.

The interconnectedness that white youth at both Valley Groves and Clavey had with blacks and other racial-ethnic groups was articulated very differently at the two sites. At Valley Groves, because white students had little face-to-face association with racialized others, the us–them dialogue predominantly took place between whites and the popular culture industry. Still, a white-other interdependency was there. As I argued earlier, white students at Valley Groves tended to view themselves as "normal." While this benefited them in many ways, it also made them feel as if they lacked something in character. They had no "uniqueness," as Mara put it. Carli made similar comments when I asked her what she thought was the appeal of city life to Valley Groves students. She said,

> "I think a lot of people don't like being bored. . . . People, I guess, like the party scene. Like the party life, inner city, constant noise, constant movement. . . . Being bored just isn't cool. . . . Maybe because country life—or other than city life—is simple, the smartest thing would be the more complicated. The city is more complicated. There's so much more going on, so much more to think about, so much more to learn. [I used to] want to live in the city because it seemed like they knew so much more, you know, they were so much more street smart. You know, street smart was cool, and I felt dumb

because I lived in the farm lands. . . . That's probably why, cuz it's the smarter way to be and also the tougher."

Carli spoke to the boredom of suburban life and how it lacked street smarts, toughness, and coolness. Feeling uncool might be particularly plaguing to teenage youth, for whom "coolness" is a defining feature of their identities as "teenagers."[33] However, by embodying the "tough," "cool," and "street smart" meanings associated with urban black and Latino cultures, whites at Valley Groves were able to bolster a more "colorful" view of themselves. At the same time, their consumption of tough and cool commodities benefited the culture industry and the artists who produced and disseminated those images of "cool" otherness.[34]

At Clavey, where students were in daily, up-close association with a range of different youth asserting different racial-ethnic identities, the interdependent quality of racial-ethnic identities was vivid. All youth worked together, each group defining who they were with respect to how others viewed them and how they viewed themselves. Each and every perspective was integral to constructing the "whole," the complete mosaic of individual group identities and cultures. In this respect, whites were "populated" by blacks, Latinos, Asians, and others. Whites carried those groups' perceptions of them around with them all of the time.

This interdependency and multiracialness also revealed itself in the ways white youth interpreted and *evaluated* their own cultural practices, that is, how they determined the relative heaviness, violence, meaninglessness, and so on of their popular cultural preferences. For example, recall that in Kirsten and Cindi's discourse they claimed that alternative music spoke to a "simpler anger" than rap music, and Jessie said that rap was "droning" and offensive to her, but the anger expressed in the "inflection" and "thunder" of heavy metal was not. Many students I spoke to, regardless of their racial-ethnic identity, claimed that the "other" music was violent and offensive. Marcel, a black rap artist, told me that he couldn't listen to punk rock because it was "loud" and "violent," and I heard similar criticism of punk and heavy metal from other rap enthusiasts. Conversely, Pickles, a punk rocker, told me that punk appealed to her deeply felt intolerance for and anger about mainstream superficiality. She didn't like rap music because it was "too violent." Having attended a few punk concerts myself and seen musicians spit on audience members and kids in the mosh pit draw blood from smashing into each other, I asked her about the violence in punk rock. She said, "[Punks] act so tough on stage, but it's a very fine line between parody and reality. The [mosh] dancing is like trying to beat up a person, but you're not. Like, this guy wrote [in a recent punk fanzine] about how people threw stuff at him at a show. He got scared that he'd be hit, but then he realized they were missing him on purpose. There's more comedy in [punk]. With rap it's not. They're seriously trying to be tough. I don't like that attitude."

Listening to Pickles' and other students' comments, I came to believe that all students who listened to angry and violent music did so because they had angry and violent feelings that the music either purged, constituted, or expressed for them. The issue was just how comfortable youth were with those feelings. Youth could define and believe that their music was less, not so much, or not at all violent *if* there was something out there that was *more*. Without that something else, their music would have to stand alone as, plainly, angry and violent. Youth were therefore dependent on the measurable difference of the music of the other to evaluate their own in acceptable terms. An alternative interpretation with the same implications would be that, to the extent youth were uncomfortable with their own violent feelings, they projected those feelings onto the music of others. They could then listen to their own thrashing, loud, screaming-profanities music with the confidence that it was okay, healthy, and benign; the "bad" stuff was elsewhere.

Finally, the racialized cultural practices of white youth—again, especially at Clavey—illustrate multiracialness in terms of the extent to which youth had personal interests and competencies that, in their context, were racialized "other" and, therefore, put aside, ignored, or dismissed. Some of the cultural distinctions assigned to or adopted by different groups at Clavey included the following: black students speak Ebonics, listen to rap, dress certain ways, play basketball (boys), braid their hair; white students speak Standard English, listen to rock, dress certain ways, play lacrosse (boys), let their hair go grunge. These distinctions to an extent *forbade* black youth from speaking Standard English, listening to rock, or playing lacrosse, and white youth from speaking Ebonics, listening to rap, and playing basketball. Still, those competencies were available to all youth. African American youth *could* speak in Standard English, enjoy rock music, and dress grunge, just as white youth *could* speak in Ebonics, enjoy rap, braid their hair, and gesticulate in ways that were signatures of black identity. These competencies would come to the surface on occasions, often for strategic purposes, such as when mimicking or trying to relate to a person of a particular racial-ethnic ascription. For example, during my interview with Linda, Ann, Sera, and Melissa, Ann started telling me about how some black girls harassed her one day for wearing pink shoes. She told this story illustratively, snapping her fingers once in front of her face and then waving her index finger in counterpoint to the sideways bob of the head as her voice reached for the inflection in the girls' voices as they told her, "Uh-uh, girl. *Oh* no." The story ended with Ann folding her arms high across her chest, tilting her head slightly to her right shoulder, and putting on a face of indignation.

At times, African American students performed the whiteness in them. In my first semester at Clavey, I had the opportunity to go on a small tour around the Bay Area with the advanced drama class as they performed a play they collaboratively authored. The cast of the play comprised several African Americans, a few white students, one Filipino girl, and three mixed-race (one Asian-white, two Latino-white) students. Most of the schools the group went to were predominantly African American. In these performances, the black cast members were relaxed and they spoke their lines in Black English, making ample use of current slang terms and body gestures. The nonblack members also played up current black-urban slang terms and aspects of Black English.

One day, the performance group ventured out of the city and into the suburbs, to an all-white private school. In the play, one of the black actors played a womanizing, drug-consuming, HIV-positive gangster type. Previous to this engagement, he had always improvised his signature monologue, speaking at a fast clip and peppering it with profanities, street lingo, and gestures that usually brought on howls of laughter from the predominantly black audiences. At the all-white school, however, he spoke his lines clearly, slowly, and verbatim from the written text, with a few lewd remarks but much less profanity and street lingo. Similarly, another African American actor made some switches in her text from black slang to white slang. For example, in a moment in the play she usually said the line, "I was kickin' it with my patnas." In the suburban performance, she said, "I was hanging out with my friends."

Medria Connolly, an African American woman, wrote, "The white girl in me broadens my social repertoire. She allows me to move across a wider range of cultural experiences. In this regard, I consider myself bicultural."[35] In the ways I described above, white youth at Clavey were similarly bi- or multicultural; for the most part they kept their black and other cultural competencies shelved until the right time or place arrived to bring them forward. But there were also many youth who kept their multiculturalness out on the surface. There were those who had bi- or multiracial ancestry, but there were also youth who had fairly monoracial backgrounds (I should emphasis *fairly* since a vast number of Americans are presumed to have racially mixed blood) but identified with both whites and blacks. There was Johnetta, a middle-class black girl who wore her hair in braids, listened mostly to classic rock, and had close friends who were black, Asian, and white. Tanisha, a working-class black girl who liked alternative music and incorporated the grunge clothing style with black style. She had close black and white friends and code-switched from Black to Standard English depending on who she was with. And there was Trish, whom I wrote about in chapter 2. She was white but adopted every nuance of black female style and demeanor and hung out mostly with black girls, though she had white friends, too. She told me during our interview that although she preferred listening to rap and r & b and had a style that was admittedly very "black," she felt she could identify with "both sides," whites and blacks. It was a quality about herself she had grown to feel proud of because on occasion she had been in the position of mediating disputes between white and African American students.

In summary, the concept of the multiracial self that I have elaborated here encapsulates the many ways that racial difference and sameness are interdependent, one and the same, and, in the final analysis, arbitrary. Overall, in this chapter and the preceding chapter, I have sought to illustrate how different types and structures of association with racialized difference influenced the meanings youth gave to their everyday experiences of people of color and to their cultural identities as whites. The fact that more identity-making processes and dynamics seemed to be going on at Clavey than Valley Groves speaks to the relational character of racial identity formation: the closer and more diverse the relational context, the more racially populated, multiple, and complex the self becomes. The next two chapters leave behind the question of cultural identity and observe the nuances, complexities, and contradictions of white racial identity formation when white youth reflect on white identity as a *social* identity.

part three

Identity and Group Position

White youth at Valley Groves and Clavey had considerable difficulty reflecting on and defining white identity as an identity tied to a meaningful cultural community. They had little difficulty, however, understanding that being white meant that you stood in a particular sociopolitical relationship to African Americans, Latinos, Asians, and other "nonwhite" racial and ethnic groups. From public discourses distributed through the media and popular culture to direct experience of being both positively and negatively stereotyped "white," young white people everywhere learn that being white carries significant historical and contemporary political implications. The chapters in this section examine how white students at Valley Groves and Clavey high schools experienced and interpreted their social location as whites, drawing on representations and definitions of white identity coming from within white communities and without.

Herbert Blumer argues that racial prejudice and hierarchies are not the outcome of individual feelings and pathologies of whites, but of whites defining a group position that is based on claims of superiority and entitlement.[1] He asserts that this sense of group position is constructed largely through collective, intragroup public discourse and that all whites, whether or not individuals agree with the group position, must come to terms with it. I found Blumer's theory of a "sense of group position" to fit quite well with the ways white students came to define their social location as whites, with some important differences. In the 1950s, when Blumer wrote "Racial Prejudice as a Sense of Group Position," the world was considerably different than it is today. Then, a black–white paradigm was the only paradigm of race relations, and whites had considerable control over defining whiteness with little resistance from blacks. Today, our racial hierarchy is multitiered and people of color have a much louder voice in defining what whiteness means. Moreover, whites can no longer claim categorical superiority and entitlement without being strongly sanctioned by people of color as well as other whites.

In the next two chapters, I argue that, for white youth at Valley Groves and Clavey High, defining a sense of group position was about *making* sense of their group position out of the different, sometimes contradictory, experiences, claims, discourses, and stigmas voiced both among whites and between whites and people of color. Different types and structures of interracial association influenced the number and content of "us-them" constructs as well as the ways whiteness intersected or fused with differently positioned parts of the self, such as gender.

These chapters also illustrate how the demographic character of a community conditions the ways larger political discourses and events are interpreted. Social structures and discourses "limit" how people make sense of race and race relations, but, at the same time, communities and the experiences people have of racial-ethnic difference in their communities influence how social structures are interpreted and acted upon. Chapter 5 looks at how a big media event, the Million Man March, was interpreted by white students at both Valley Groves and Clavey high schools and gave rise to different definitions of the social location of whites. Chapter 6 closely examines what youth said about the social and political implications of being white.

5. The Million Man March

It was October 17, 1995, the day after an estimated 400,000 to 1,000,000 black men marched on Washington, D.C. for a "Day of Atonement," a day of self-reflection for black men and commitment to improving their communities and families. The widely publicized and covered event, which was called by Nation of Islam Minister Louis Farrakhan, was one of the largest gatherings in history on the Mall and possibly one of the most controversial. The self-affirming and self-empowering messages of the March were tainted by the reputation of Louis Farrakhan, whom many saw as sexist, antiwhite, and anti-Semite. Not two weeks before the March he publicly called Jews "bloodsuckers."

I had gotten up early on this morning to make it to Mr. Edwards's first period sophomore history class at Clavey High, then take the thirty-minute drive over to Valley Groves to sit in on Mrs. Washington's and Mr. Riley's junior honors and senior ACP government classes, respectively, then return to Clavey for Mr. Hansen's senior ACP government course. I couldn't miss the opportunity to see how white students who were more or less similarly placed, academically, in the two schools (Mr. Edwards's class was not an exact match with Mrs. Washington's class, but was the best I could do) and who watched the same evening news and read the same dailies interpreted and responded to the Million Man March. The March had the attention of the local and national media, which daily ran stories about it, its leadership, organizing strategies, mission, and expected turnout for more than a week before the event took place. I wondered how the March, which put "race" squarely in the spotlight, made white students at Valley Groves and Clavey think about the significance of race and their own whiteness, and if there were any differences between the two sites in how they did—if they did.

Valley Groves: "Isn't that racist?"

Mrs. Washington was a thirty-something white woman with an always-ready smile who commuted from Clavey City to teach history at Valley Groves. She had brought news articles about the Million Man March to class and prepared questions to stimulate discussion about the March and its significance. In her two previous classes, the students were not "tuned into the fact of the March," she said, and so little discussion got off the ground. This class, however, was an honors class. Students had been taught about the civil rights struggle and Martin Luther King's March on Washington, so she expected a little more response from students. There were thirty students in the class. Most were white, one girl was Filipino, one boy was African American, and two students appeared to be Latino or mixed-race.

"What happened yesterday?" Mrs. Washington asked.

After a moment of dead silence, the Filipino girl answered, "The Million Man March."

"Who else heard about that?" probed the teacher.

More silence. Then someone said, "A guy was speaking and a bunch of people went to hear him."

The Filipino girl chimed in again with a slight tone of exasperation, "It was a call for black men to come together for unity."

"Isn't that racist? Singling out black people?" a white girl asked in response.

A boy with somewhat dark features, possibly Latino or mixed-race, replied, "I think whites overreact when minorities get together."

"I'm not overreacting!" the girl shot back. "To me it's a form of racism. When groups do that, even if positive, I think it's racist."

This opened a brief flurry of responses with the first boy asserting that the March was open to everybody but whites just didn't go, another girl saying that Louis Farrakhan has a reputation for being racist, and another asking just how many African Americans *really* attended the March. The organizers had estimated over a million, but the papers reported 400,000. This latter point really grabbed students' interest.

"The organizers must have pumped up the numbers. The media count must be right, they're not biased. It would be hard for all the media to change the numbers so radically and with the same count!"

Mrs. Washington, trying to redirect the discussion back to the issues of the March itself, asked students if they would have gone. A girl asked what the cause of the March was, and a handful of students responded simultaneously. They were split between those who believed the men marched to hear Farrakhan speak and those who believed they marched for causes relevant to the black community. Among the latter students, their ideas about what those causes were ranged from problack/antiwhite protest to a demonstration for black unity and welfare.

"Why go to Washington, D.C?" the teacher asked, trying to refresh students' minds of history.

"Because that's where there was that other march. The one in *Forrest Gump.*"

Mrs. Washington nodded, "Right. Martin Luther King's March on Washington. What could happen as a result of this march?" she asked.

"Riots," someone replied.

"Could be positive," added another. "Like blacks could take on their own factories, businesses . . ."

"They are!" a boy interrupted. "Look at the NFL!"

"All right," Mrs. Washington intervened, and trying to redirect the discussion, asked, "What might be important about this March?"

The African American male in the class, who until now had remained quiet, responded, "Because it is the first time it's ever happened."

Mrs. Washington nodded, looking around the room for more comments or responses. Quiet. Without any summaries or final comments of her own, she proceeded on with the day's lesson.

The day of the Million Man March, Mr. Riley told students in his ACP government class that an anticipated million black men, called by Louis Farrakhan, were marching in Washington, D.C., and he asked them to be prepared to talk about it today. Riley, a white male in his forties known for his liberal politics, opened the class asking students what their reaction was to the March. In this class, all but three of the twenty-eight students were white. The students of color included two Filipino girls and Maria, the mixed white-Mexican girl I introduced in chapter 1.

"His speech wasn't as racist as everyone thought," a white boy called out.

"The organizers said that over a million black men showed up, but the papers said only 400,000," a white girl said. "I saw an interview with Farrakhan on TV and he sees himself as a messenger." She added something that

I didn't entirely hear, but it had something to do with Farrakhan being against the United States having a black president.

"I'd like to know what the real count was," a different student interjected.

Order broke down for a moment as a few students likened Farrakhan, in a picture of him in front of the crowd in D.C., to Hitler surrounded by his S.S. guards, and others debated how crowds get counted. "The government makes the official count, so they must be accurate," someone said.

The teacher suggested that students were paying too much attention to Farrakhan and that they were losing sight of the messages of the March— the black family, black on black crime, and drugs and violence in black communities.

Several students then spoke out simultaneously, affirming that a focus on family and self-help was a positive, important direction for African Americans to be taking. Then, a white girl who hadn't yet spoken said, "The purpose is great, but women were excluded. I read that someone in the March shouted 'Women go home.' If a purpose was the family, well, men alone don't make families."

Someone else added, "Yeah, and what about white men? They need to improve their relationships to their families, too."

At this point the teacher tried to supply some context and information to help students see the objectives of the March that he himself saw as important. He pointed out that Rosa Parks spoke, wearing a colorful shawl to symbolize interracial unity. He repeated what he understood to be the main issues of the March and said that there were more fifteen- to twenty-four-year-old African Americans in prison than in universities. This, he suggested, indicated that the need to deal with crime among African Americans was acute. (For a moment I thought, and hoped, that Mr. Riley might go further, might point out possible foul play in our criminal justice system by virtue of the disparities in the number of arrests and convictions of black men compared to white perpetrators of the same crimes, but he didn't.) Then Mr. Riley asked students, "What are the differences between the Nation of Islam and the KKK or neo-Nazis?"

"I read the *Autobiography of Malcolm X* and I think I understand what is the Nation of Islam," the first girl responded. "They are a lot different from the neo-Nazis. For one thing, Islam is a religious belief. They believe in the purity of the person and things. They've done good things for the black community, rehabilitating blacks."

Jonathon then raised his hand and asked for clarification about the Nation of Islam. He said that he understood that the objective of the Nation of Islam was not harming other people, just racial separation.

The girl responded, "Yeah. They aren't as violent or hateful as Nazis, they just want to be separate."

"Well, that's racist," somebody called out, causing a murmur of agreement around class. A white male then said, "They have some good goals, good for black Americans, but if it gets larger, we'll be looking at another Hitler. [Indicating toward the teacher] You yourself said that Hitler started out doing good things."

Clavey High: "No one should feel threatened."

On the day after the Million Man March, there were twenty-three students present in Mr. Edwards's sophomore history class for performing arts magnet students. Fourteen were African American, seven were white, one was Filipino, and another Asian American. While Mr. Edwards, a white man in his forties, was preparing a video monitor to show Jesse Jackson's speech at the assembly of black men in front of the nation's capitol, he asked how many students had watched the March on TV the day before. Three African American girls raised their hands, one saying that she stayed home especially to watch it. She asked if they could watch Farrakhan's speech, too. "People assumed he would say something racist, but he didn't. Why can't people be nice to him?" she asked.

"People's afraid 'cause we risin' up," replied another one of the girls. Then she added that the estimate the media gave of the march, 400,000, was too small. "There's racism there."

While the video of Jesse Jackson's speech was running, several students were writing and reading. A couple of African American girls searched out all the fine-looking men they could spy among the crowd. As Jackson's speech approached conclusion, Jackson got a chant going of "Keep hope alive!" that moved several African American students in the classroom to join in. One girl appeared to be in tears.

"See? He give a positive message. It not racist at all. He include all races," the first African American girl put out to the class. Others agreed and pointed out all the negative publicity about the March that drummed up fears about Farrakhan leading the event and possibly saying something anti-white or anti-Semitic. An African American boy, the first male to speak up, complained that even now the media were claiming that the March was racist because only black people were invited.

"So what?" a girl chimed in. "It's about time!"

"Yeah, it not always only blacks be muggin' people, playin' loud music . . . ," the boy agreed.

By now a lot of students were speaking out, contributing to the discussion while others carried on in private conversation. A girl said something that I missed, something to do with "chicken teriyaki" used in the context of referring to or identifying a Vietnamese family that lived in her neighborhood. A white girl, the first white person to speak, said, "I have a good friend in this class who you just offended." This started a verbal brawl of sorts, with a number of black girls attacking the white girl for "trippin' off what people sayin'." They claimed that "chicken teriyaki" was not the same thing as "nigger" or "bitch." It was just food. "You can talk about my fried chicken, I don't care!" Another scolded the girl for getting into other people's business. She encouraged the Asian, a boy, to speak up for himself and she said to the white girl, "Don't be so sensitive or you'll crack!" With all eyes on him, the Asian boy said that he wasn't offended, "It's just food."

A black student, who until now had been quiet, admonished the class for being rude and talking when the teacher was trying to get a discussion going. The mood of the class started to move on when a white boy raised his hand and said he had something he'd like to say. "The people in this class always claim that they are not prejudiced, but then go and say prejudiced things about other people. It's not right to blame a whole race for the prejudices of a few." The boy continued, "If someone here says something negative about white people, I don't say I hate all black people 'cause of that. I may not like that person, but I like black people in general." And then, as if to show that not all whites were afraid of or against the March, he concluded by saying, "I supported the March and loved Jesse Jackson's speech."

Mr. Hansen's AP government class had thirty seniors in it, including roughly ten whites, eight Asian Americans, seven African Americans, one East Indian, and a few mixed-race students. In this class there were students I have already introduced: Melissa, Linda, and Kirsten. After what seemed like a ritualistic summarizing of the discussions from the day before, Mr. Hansen brought up the Million Man March. Hansen, a stocky and balding white man, said that the news reports looked pretty positive to him and he asked, "What do you think is the potential outcome of the March?" An Asian student raised his hand and said he thought African American males would go back to their families, workplaces, and communities and better their lives.

An African American boy then raised his hand and said, "I'm not certain. We have a debate on it in my house. I support the March, just not Farrakhan. He seems to stand for separatism, and I don't agree with that. Doesn't that promote racism?"

"No one should feel threatened. Farrakhan organized the march to do good," replied an African American girl I will call Meisha.

Melissa was called on next. "I supported the March, but as a Jewish person—that leader has said openly anti-Semitic things. So I think of course Jews would feel threatened. No one knew just what he would say. I'm really glad that it came out okay."

Kirsten turned to Meisha and asked, "What if it was a Jewish leader who had said antiblack things, wouldn't you feel threatened?"

"Or if Mark Fuhrman[1] were in charge of a huge March—wouldn't you be offended? I think the March was a great idea, but that man is a complete anti-Semitic," Linda added.

A white Jewish boy, Brian, shot back at the girls, accusing them of minimizing the purpose of the March because of the personal views of one person. "This wasn't a million Muslim men marching. There were all walks of life."

"That's *not* what I'm saying!" "I didn't say that!" Melissa and Linda cried out simultaneously.

Meisha agreed with Brian. She said that there were a lot of intelligent men in the March who would not be swayed by the ignorant ideas of one man. "Most of the men were there for the black community. Are you threatened because a million black men came together? Or because you think they came to listen to Farrakhan? There were other presenters at the March that shouldn't be condemned because of Farrakhan."

Directing his words to Melissa, Brian said, "You're not looking at the event as a whole. What threatens you if one man is speaking to a million?"

"Many leaders have taken their power out of control," Melissa responded.

"Every race knows that. I completely supported the concept of the March and felt it had to go on. I was afraid of what might happen but not enough to not support the March."

Jim, a white, non-Jewish boy who hadn't yet spoken broke in, "I never heard him say that he never liked Jews. What actual threat do you feel? Physical harm?"

"Powerful leaders in control can do terrible things. Slavery. Holocaust. I believe he's capable of arousing violence against Jewish people, Asian people."

"He's not a violent person. He's trying to raise people up," Jim replied to Melissa.

In apparent response to this last comment, Dawana, an African American girl who had not spoken yet, called out, "He puts others down to raise up blacks, black Muslims particularly."

Then Brian, still addressing the girls who expressed concern about anti-Semitism, said, "You have to understand where Farrakhan is coming from. Black oppression in the U.S. is much greater than Jewish oppression in the U.S. He comes from that."

Seemingly in response, the African American boy who first got the conversation going said, "People will get frightened by any group organizing."

Then Dawana said to Brian, "I'm so tired of society being blamed for people committing violence or what else. The truth is, you gotta be black or Muslim to be okay by Farrakhan. I understand he was oppressed—that's no excuse."

"The March was not about Farrakhan," Meisha cut in. "We're losing touch with the purpose of the March. The purpose was to unify the black community. No one should be threatened by that."

This whole conversation was going on without any intervention by the teacher, except to call on people with their hands raised. He next called on an Asian American girl. The girl said that she believed we are always going to have racism if people continue to come together only in their communities and to promote the idea of different societies within the country. People need to come together, she said, "although I know we are not at that stage yet."

"We *do* all need to come together," Jim responded. "But before that, each group has to be prepared to come together." He gave an example of how the United States is "holding up" certain countries in order to maintain world peace. "That can't be," he said. Then he added that the worst problems in the black community stem from problems concerning black males. "Black men are on the bottom peg of the ladder. They need to come together to address their problems, better themselves and their communities."

Responding to Linda's question earlier about how the African American students might feel if Mark Fuhrman held a massive rally, an African American boy who had not yet spoken said that he could understand how Jewish people might feel threatened or fearful. He would if he were in their position. This provoked Kirsten to turn to Meisha and ask, "Can't you see how people might feel threatened before the March began?"

"No," Meisha replied flatly.

Mayhem momentarily erupted as multiple separate arguments broke out about Farrakhan, the positive purposes of the March, the Nation of Islam. The teacher restored order by saying it was time to wrap the discussion up with one last question. He called on an Asian girl who hadn't spoken. She said, "I felt it was a good idea to bring black men together and all that, but it was the *manner* people came together that worried me. I was worried about my friends. In the past, after these kinds of things, people were beat up. That could have happened again."

Summing up some of the differences that most stood out for me in the ways the white students in Washington's and Riley's classes (Valley Groves) and Edwards's and Hansen's classes (Clavey) interpreted the March and, ultimately, the significance of race and their own group position: At Valley Groves, students were, overall, either not very informed about the March or just not very interested. This was less true of Mr. Riley's students, but he had also told students to read up about the March in advance of class that day. In Mrs. Washington's class, some students seemed not even to know that the event took place. Contrarily, at Clavey students were very aware of the March. This was most true of black students, which might be expected, but also true of the white and other nonblack students; it was also true of the younger, sophomore whites in the low-tracked class and the older white students in the high-tracked class. In both classes at Clavey, discussion went on without intervention by the teacher to keep things going, whereas at Valley Groves the teacher's probings were necessary to move discussion along.

However, even between the more informed whites at Valley Groves and the white students at Clavey, youth differed widely in their understanding of the issues and concerns behind the March. The white students at Valley Groves tended to be unable to grasp why a million black men would want to march on Washington, and what they did understand was filtered through their commonsense logic of race-neutrality. That logic told them that the racial exclusivity of the March was "racist," and Farrakhan, who by their knowledge promoted separatism, was himself a "racist." Moreover, to the extent that they understood that some of the issues of the March were about the "black family" and lifting up black communities, they read those concerns through the ideologies of "family values" and personal responsibility. Students seemed to be unaware of the particular issues threatening many African American families, such as the absence of men, and assumed that the family issue was a universal, race-neutral problem about men "improving their relationships to their families," something, one boy commented, white men needed to do, too. And to the extent white students could muster up some support for the March, they did so because it seemed like an effort by African American men to take personal responsibility for the problems in their families and communities. Black men pulling themselves up by their own bootstraps.

At Clavey the issues of the March were taken for granted; at least it seemed that way because nobody spelled them out explicitly and the need to do so never came up. White students in Mr. Edwards's class were less engaged in the conversation than those in Mr. Hansen's class, which I believe was a function of both being younger and outnumbered by African American students in the class. Socioeconomic class may have played a role, too, as I will discuss shortly. Nonetheless, in both classes, white students expressed support for the March and interpreted the relevance of it through awareness of the particular issues and problems that African Americans face as a racially oppressed group—a "race matters" as opposed to a race-neutral commonsense. A few of the white males in Mr. Hansen's class stressed that point most assertively, raising the history of black oppression and the subordinated social-economic location of African American males as an important backdrop for understanding the motives of the March. When one white boy, Jim, applauded black men for coming together to address their problems, his comment was not in the spirit of supporting personal responsibility as much as supporting black resistance to the forces that keep African Americans down, "on the bottom peg of the ladder."

The biggest reservation expressed by white students came from some of the girls in the class, several of whom were Jewish. They expressed concern that Farrakhan was going to say something anti-Semitic before the large crowd, and, as at Valley Groves, references to Hitler emerged in those discussions. However, whereas at Valley Groves, students' concerns were based on public opinion alone and focused on Farrakhan as a "separatist," at Clavey, concerns were focused on Farrakhan's anti-Semitism and based on firsthand knowledge of recent anti-Semitic statements he had, indeed, made. Moreover, the girls at Clavey still supported the March *despite* their reservations and were all the more supportive once the threat of anti-Semitism was no longer a threat. Melissa, who was the first to raise fears of anti-Semitism to the class, told me in a later interview that she believed the opportunity for black unity was a necessary one and for that reason she supported the March. For white students at Clavey, something negative could have happened but didn't; for Valley Groves whites, the fear was that the worst was yet to come.

It's worth noting that, in Mr. Hansen's class at Clavey, whether one supported the March wholeheartedly or with reservations was not drawn along racial lines. Several African American students were, like several whites, concerned about Farrakhan's anti-Semitism and separatism ("Doesn't that promote racism?" a black boy asked), and several whites were the strongest of all in defending him. At one point, Dawana, an African American girl in the class, berated Brian, a white boy, for blaming "society"—by which she meant racial oppression—for Farrakhan's beliefs and practices. Usually it is whites admonishing blacks and other oppressed groups for "blaming society" for their problems.

Another interesting difference I found between the two sets of students was the degree of concern about the official count of who attended the March. The subject came up only once at Clavey, when an African American student in Mr. Edwards's class accused the media of being "racist" for undercounting the organizers' assessment of the number of people who attended the March. Her implication, I believe, was that the media misrepresented the count as a means of social control—to make the March and the issues raised there appear marginal, things that were not and *should* not be of concern to most blacks. At Valley Groves, students in both classes were virtually obsessed about the count and from the opposite perspective. They assumed that the official count, which they believed was made either by the government or the press, had to be the "true" count. The organizers had to be the ones tampering with the numbers for their own gratification. In effect, the *organizers* were the "racists," by virtue of misrepresenting the numbers, possibly in order to stir up the involvement of other blacks in the presumed separatist intentions of the March.

In one of my later interviews with Melissa, I told her some of my observations of how white students at Valley Groves responded to the Million Man March, particularly how little they seemed to know about it and how they struggled to feel supportive of it. She asked me, "Are there many black people at that school?" Melissa seemed intuitively to know that association with black people would make a difference in how one interpreted the March. She said, "The March was more real, more hands-on here. Like, I knew a lot of people who were going. They're really nice people—some of them were my teachers." Valley Groves students, on the other hand, did not have that "hands-on" experience and relied principally on their race-neutral common sense and the media, both of which they took as truths in the absence of any opinions or information challenging them. Mr. Riley himself told me after class that his students had "no real sense of the magnitude of the hardships in the black community." He had showed *Mississippi Burning* to the class to give students a sense of that, and they were "incredulous," he said.

The significance of there being few African American students at Valley Groves to help raise awareness of the Million Man March and its purposes extended beyond the impact of that on white students. The black students I spoke to at Valley Groves were not much more aware of the March and its messages than the white students. In my focus interview with ten African American students, all members of the Black Student Union, they were fairly ho-hum about the March, saying it was "just there," and they didn't pay a lot of attention to it. Several said that their teachers didn't talk about it in class, and only one girl commented that "teachers are scared to bring stuff up like that because they're afraid what the blacks will say." She added that one white in her class said, "Why not have a Million White Man March?" "They don't get it," she scoffed. Then one of the black males commented, "Maybe if we lived in a black community it would make more of a difference [on our understanding of the event.]"

Juxtaposing the different responses to the March reveals a lot about the influences different proximities of association can have on how youth will interpret and understand racial events, issues, and politics. Although more subtly, the different ways youth interpreted the significance of their own whiteness also comes across. For the white students at Valley Groves, whiteness was absent from the discussion. Only once, in Mrs. Washington's class, did a student objectify whites; he stated that "whites overreact when minorities get together." Other than that, students' own racialness remained invisible and neutral, and the implications of whiteness—of white racism for why a million black men might need to march, of the interests of the white media in underrepresenting the numbers—remained silent.[2] At best (or worst), whites—at least those in the discussion—were implicitly constructed as egalitarian and nonracist; *they*, the March organizers and participants, were the "racists" for drawing attention to their black racialness and, by implication, the students' white racialness.

At Clavey, whiteness, of both the institutional and personal kind, was all but invisible. In both classes, black *and* white students in one way or another raised issues of white racism, the history of white oppression, white duplicity in the media, white fears of black resistance, white fears of blackness. And when white students spoke in both Edwards's and Hansen's classes, they knew their voice was racially placed and codified—they spoke as "white" people addressing "black" students or "Asian" students or other "whites."

However, they did not all uniformly situate their whiteness; socioeconomic and gender differences inflected how students experienced their whiteness and constructed it in the moment. The students in Mr. Edwards's class were predominantly middle- and working-class and poor students. Black students, who were the majority of the class, were moved and charged up by the video and the March itself and spoke firmly and unswervingly in support of the event. White and Asian students stayed quiet. My sense was that they felt eclipsed by the energy of the African American students and possibly a little intimidated to speak out, whether in support or opposition. White and Asian students had told me in other contexts that this was often the case for them. Yet, two whites did speak out, and it seemed to me that they spoke less in response to the discussion about the March than to the implications black students made about whiteness in their comments. The first girl spoke indirectly, claiming that a comment offended someone *else* in the room, an Asian boy. She received a verbal flogging for that from several African American students who, in a sense, were trying to teach her a lesson about how to get racially thick skin. The second white speaker, the boy, also spoke cautiously and indirectly, asking the black students in the room to not prejudge all whites because of the actions of others. In short, the white students in Mr. Edwards's class experienced themselves as *raced* and in much the same way that racial minorities in the United States experience it, by being silenced, sanctioned, and stereotyped.[3]

Mr. Hansen's class was fairly evenly distributed among whites, blacks, and Asians, and most students were middle- to upper-middle-class. For whatever reasons, be they the comfort and confidence afforded the students by relative economic stability and/or academic success, or the diversity and safety in numbers each group enjoyed, white-black polarization in opinion did not occur and students across racial-ethnic groups felt relatively at ease about being somewhat ambivalent about the March. Interestingly, in this class the strongest racial tension occurred *intra*racially, between white boys and white girls. Brian and Jim spoke proudly from their positions of unconditional support for the March and each raised big-picture considerations, namely, the sociohistorical oppression of black people, and why the event was important and necessary. They were not threatened by Farrakhan or the March in general. Melissa, Linda, and Kirsten expressed reservations about the March because of fears about what Farrakhan might stir up, and the boys tried to make them look ignorant, if not racist, for that.

That dynamic between the white middle-class boys and girls in Mr. Hansen's class speaks to the ways whites will sanction or correct one another in the effort to define white identity. It also speaks to gendered differences in the experience of race and white racialness, differences that have to do with differing degrees of *distance* middle-class boys can take from racial issues than middle-class girls can. In my interviews with middle-class white boys, many of them spoke in ways and said things that I never heard from girls; namely, they spoke unequivocally about racial injustice and its roots in a long history of racial oppression. White boys also said things like "I don't think of myself as white." The ability of white males to not think of themselves as white in a racially charged context and to say the "right" things about race attests to their privilege as males, be it the privilege of self-confidence, of not being race-sexually harassed (something that white girls did face), of feeling they can and will defend themselves if harassed or assaulted, or of knowing, consciously or unconsciously, that in the wider society, white men dominate. As Bobo and Hutchings assert, "The more secure the relative power, economic and status advantages of the dominant group, the less alienated and threatened they will feel."[4]

White girls at Clavey, on the other hand, had various gender-based insecurities, fears, and defenses that made their experience of race more complex, multiple, and nuanced. One of these sprang from their sexual-objectification as girls. Kirsten and Cindi told me that sexual harrassment around school was worse than racial harrassment, and that it came from both white boys and boys of color. Some told me that they played down their femininity in baggy, unisex clothing in order to not draw too much attention to themselves. And when called names like "white bitch," a term used by both African American girls and boys, white girls felt the sting of a double-edged, race-gender stigma, and were deeply disturbed by that. I suggest that, all in all, these experiences made white girls feel less self-assured and more physically and emotionally vulnerable than white boys, and more sensitive all around to potential "threatening" situations. Although the debate between the white boys and white girls in Mr. Hansen's class focused on Farrakhan as a threat to Jews, beneath that discussion, I believe, were gendered differences in the degrees to which girls and boys could distance themselves from that and other potential threats based on categorical distinctions.

I asked Melissa her opinion on why the boys came down so hard on her in class and she said, "Oh, god. Yeah, I couldn't believe—one of those guys I've known my whole life. . . . I don't—I think you have this extreme sensitivity towards black people, and I think they really just feel the need to be extra nice, extra considerate towards black people and the black community, and they're, like, 'whatever the black community asks from the American society, they should receive because they haven't in the past.' Also, though, I think they are lacking some sense of an understanding of the whole issue." Melissa's explanation differs somewhat from mine, except that I might argue that a relative position of power affords white boys the ability to be "extra nice," and not understanding the whole issue grants them equanimity of voice.

6. The Social Implications

of White Identity

What does it mean to you to be white?

Are there advantages and / or disadvantages to being white?

When I asked white students at Valley Groves and Clavey high schools these and other such questions, they responded very differently than when I asked the question, "What is white culture?" As I argued in chapter 3, this question tended to stump most white students at both schools. They had no ready answers, and few, especially at Valley Groves, had even thought about the question before I put it to them. However, questions like the two above seemed to touch on students' experiences of being labeled "white" and to bring forth a sense of white identity as a social identity, as a racial–social location positioned in particular relationships to other racialized groups. To those questions, white students had much to say.

This is not surprising given that the United States is a racially hierarchical nation and racial politics rivet the attention of not only the legislative bodies but also the mass media and entertainment industries. From where one stands on affirmative action to whether or not one believes O.J. Simpson was guilty of murdering Nicole Brown Simpson and Ron Goldman, there is no getting around the issues of race, racial location, and racial interests. What most piqued my interest while doing this research, however, was not that white students had answers to questions of their social identities, but that they had different answers in different relational contexts. Different experiences of people of color conditioned the ways white students made sense of their social location as whites, and the closer the association with racialized others, the more complex, multiple, and contradictory white identities became.

In this chapter I will argue that at predominantly white Valley Groves, white students' "sense of group position" was strongly influenced by neo-conservative articulations of the social position of whites. Namely, white students felt it was they, not people of color, who were the disadvantaged: they were stigmatized as "racists" and discriminated against when seeking spots in college, scholarships, and jobs. At multiracial Clavey, white students' social identities were more messy, situational, and contradictory. They felt they carried the unfair mantle of the "oppressor," while acknowledging that they were also unfairly privileged as whites. Their ways of dealing with this dual awareness ranged from beliefs in radical political change to racist articulations of the inferiority of African American and other underprivileged groups. And underneath it all, including their avid egalitarianism, some felt that their experience at Clavey taught them that they were, indeed, racist.

Valley Groves: "Racist" Stigmas and Declining Status

I noticed Howie in my first days in the field. I would see him hanging out with his friends at lunch under the senior tree in the Quad. He reminded me of a friend of mine in high school, a hefty wrestler whose popularity stemmed as much from his easy sociability as his athletic prowess. Howie was not a wrestler but a varsity football and baseball player who was also active in school leadership. I managed to approach him one day before a student council meeting to ask him if he would be willing to be interviewed. He agreed, and a few days later we met after school and talked sitting on a picnic table between two of the halls on campus.

Howie came from a comfortably middle-class home and was looking forward to attending the Naval Academy after high school to study engineering. We had already talked quite a bit about his hobbies (sports, of course), musical tastes (classic rock, mostly), and perceptions of other kinds of kids at school when I asked him what it meant to him to be white.

"It doesn't mean much to me. I mean, sometimes it bugs me being white, because everybody thinks of you—you know—I just don't like being part of the group that, like—it seems like nobody likes white people."

I asked if there were any racial tensions around Valley Groves. He said no, but that there was just a lot of "unawareness." He added,

"Like 'cause, growing up in Rancho Nuevo and Valley Groves, you don't run into a lot of Mexicans and blacks, and a lot of people feel uncomfortable. I mean, sometimes I'd have to say if I am the only white person around, I feel uncomfortable, but just because you haven't been exposed to it. I mean, I wouldn't say I'm racist at all, but [because of differences], you know, that's how it is. You feel uncomfortable. But I mean, it's not that I'm afraid of them. It's just that I think they look at me and they say, 'He's a racist,' you know? That's what I'm always afraid of, what they think of me, you know? And that's not how I am. That's one thing I'm always [worried] about."

"And you believe they think that 'cause you're white?" I asked.

"Yeah, that's the feeling I get. I mean I don't know if that's wrong to think that or it's normal. I don't think of myself as racist at all."

Several other students I had spoken to before this meeting with Howie told me that, although they did not consider themselves racist, they none-theless felt uncomfortable in the presence of a lot of African Americans. They had no concrete explanations for it; no one told me stories of being explicitly harassed or victimized. Some said that they would be uncomfortable because they wouldn't know how to act, others expressed concerns like Howie's, that they might be taken to be a racist or otherwise treated racially. Jonathon, for example, told me that one time, at a track meet in which he was the only white guy in a race, he felt that his black competitors thought that, because he was white, he didn't have a chance against them. No one said this directly to him; Jonathon just sensed it was true.

In my conversation with Laurie, she said something that agreed with Howie's belief that whites were not "liked" and somewhat confirmed his comment that whites at Valley Groves were "unaware." Laurie and I were talking about student clubs and she said that it might be good for whites to form a club at Valley Groves because "maybe there is something we went through. Or maybe there's something we'd figure out. I had a conversation or discussion in a class once about how a lot of the history shows America as great and right, and like most America was whites before, I guess. That actu-ally counted a long time ago. And maybe that's not true. Maybe we need to find out about our mistakes so that it doesn't happen again, so maybe we will understand why these other groups don't think highly of us. I don't know."

Although Laurie suggested that she did not know why "groups don't think highly" of whites, the thing that seemed most to give white students I spoke to the feeling they were disliked was their belief that blacks saw all whites as racist. Like Howie, many students made a point in our conversations to tell me that they were not racists. By this, they usually meant that they believed in equal rights for all people, did not look down on African Americans or other minorities categorically, and/or did not speak racial slurs or tell racist jokes. Usually, however, the fear of being tagged "racist" was not expressed explicitly. It was implicit in the efforts Valley Groves youth made to dissociate themselves from anything or anybody that may have racist implications. The students' color-blind ethic told them that to *see* racial difference and/or identify it was racist, so getting them to talk about race or identify people racially was always like pulling teeth. Often students used the terms "African American" instead of "black" and "Caucasian" instead of "white," presumably because they seemed less like racial and more like ethnic terms. For example, one time Carli was trying to tell me a racist joke she had heard, a joke that impressed her because it was actually more derogatory toward whites than blacks. She said, "I heard a joke once. It went, there was a little African Amer—[cutting herself off]— actually it should be *black* but I hate saying *black*. Sometimes I say it but I don't like it. It sounds like things are all just race."

Moreover, it seemed to me that students were often projecting "racist" out onto others. At Valley Groves the students who most carried those projections were the "hicks." Carli called them "totally racially young," and others brought them up whenever I asked if there were any racial tensions around school. Jonathon said, "There have been problems. A couple of years ago we had a big group of hicks that would wear Confederate flags and stuff. And even though they were outnumbered, the black kids at school would get really upset about it. And there were problems with that. But those people have left, and I think that everything is a little bit milder now."

Laurie similarly said that hicks brandishing Confederate flags or making racial slurs had caused some racial tensions. She added, "I talked to two black girls who said that they felt a lot of racist tensions at our school. There probably is, but I don't have any friends who talk about it or care. I guess it's more, like, the cowboys. They say the cowboys don't like the blacks."

I tried but never managed to talk with a hick to hear his or her response to the accusation that hicks were racists,[1] but the African American students I spoke to told me that it was not the hicks alone who were "racists." They experienced forms of racism from everybody at Valley Groves, not only the white students but white teachers and administrators as well. The offenses ranged from blatant racial slurs and stereotyping in everyday interactions to hurtful insensitivities expressed in the classroom. For example, an African American boy, Derek, told me of a time in his history class when students were watching a slide show about Jim Crow in the South. A slide of a lynched black boy went up on the screen and a white boy laughed and said, "He looks like Sammy Davis Jr.!" Derek said to me, "Can you believe that?" with a look that simultaneously expressed disbelief and pain. Another black boy told me that in his first year at Valley Groves he learned that he was on a special list of students that administrators were supposed to watch out for. He had no idea how he got on that list, except by virtue of being black.

In the time I spent at Valley Groves, I never personally witnessed this kind of blatant racism (only the "color-blind," power-evasive kind), but I was convinced by the African American students that it was alive and well at the school. And while the hicks may have been perpetrators of some of it, they may have unfairly carried the burden of it all so that other whites could see themselves as nonracist.

To come back to my conversation with Howie, I was interested in the extent to which he grasped certain types of structural or institutional racism. I asked him if he thought he, as a white person, or white people in general had any particular advantages in the society over people of color. He replied,

"I think so. I think affirmative action helps [minorities], but I think, like, SAT-wise, that type of thing, [white] students have an opportunity to take [classes]. If you're more well off, richer, you can take classes. I know I took a class [laughs]! My parents wanted to pay the money, so I took classes in SAT, and I know a lot of students don't have the opportunity to do that. And, I don't think that's right, that you can judge a test where people can get help and help their way through it to get good scores. I don't know. What else? Do you mean like schoolwise? [I nod.] Academically, if you grew up in a bad neighborhood, I don't know. It seems like it would be harder 'cause maybe you have to work. If you're less [well] off, you have to work and then do school. I think that'd be a disadvantage. But I think everybody, like, black or white . . . [doesn't finish sentence]. Maybe there's more blacks and Hispanics that have to work, but there are still white kids and stuff that have to work to support themselves, their families and stuff. But a lot of people who work around here, it's because they want to have a car, you know, that type of thing, and they have to pay insurance. But I think people in the inner city, they're paying because they have to help support their family more than kids around here, [who are] doing it so they can drive and that type of thing. Different situations."

"What do you think of affirmative action?" I asked.

"I think, [regarding] jobs, I think it's good. I think it's real good. But I think schoolwise it hurts white people a lot more. I mean, I don't know. I don't know." Here Howie seemed to realize that he was contradicting what he had just said about how blacks and Hispanics, because they tended not to be well-off economically, were disadvantaged in school. After he fumbled awhile, trying to decide on his answer, I asked him if his uncertainty had anything to do with a sense that affirmative action made it harder for white kids to get into college or get scholarships. He replied, "Yeah, 'cause, like, if I had a 4.0 GPA and maybe somebody else has, like, a 3.4 but was a minority, then they might get in. I mean, I don't see how that's necessarily fair. But, if they are good students, then they deserve to get in. You know?"

Although Howie's views on affirmative action were a bit ambivalent, he was one of only two white students I spoke to who had any degree of support for it at all. Indeed, affirmative action was the primary measure by which white youth gauged their relative advantages or disadvantages from others, and their assessment tended to be "disadvantaged." In an earlier chapter, I featured the narratives of Jonathon and Matt in which they expressed beliefs that their nonminority status disadvantaged them when it came to scholarships and such. Other students had similar responses when I asked them if they felt they had any advantages or disadvantages for being white. Billy replied, "Uh. No."

"Does it appear to you that nonwhites have advantages or disadvantages in this society?" I asked.

"Well, I wouldn't say advantages. Like, affirmative action [is an advantage], if you want to go that far. But from my standpoint, no."

Carli answered the question by saying, "I think I have disadvantages. I think we all do. I mean, affirmative action kind of makes me feel very disadvantaged." Matt had negative things to say on the subject, as well. He had made a comment that there should be a "young white American scholarship foundation," and I asked him why he thought that. He said, "Actually, I think they should just drop all the racial scholarships and just have different company scholarships, scholastic, sports, and maybe some income-based scholarships. Because this is America, we're all Americans. That's what I like to think."

"You don't have a sense that there are still some disadvantages minorities have in getting into good schools, jobs?" I asked.

"I think there was in the past," he replied, "but as far as my life goes I haven't seen disadvantages. In fact, I think affirmative action was an advantage for them, but I don't know much about that."

"Do you see yourself having any advantages or disadvantages?"

"[Disadvantages] just as far as scholarships. And at work I'm one of two males, [I] think because of affirmative action." I wasn't sure if Matt's latter point marked an advantage or disadvantage for him, but I didn't stop to ask because I already had in mind to ask him how, if minorities no longer had particular problems getting into good schools and jobs, he might explain why a disproportionate number of African Americans live in poverty in the United States. He thought for a moment then replied, "I guess that would be a good reason for affirmative action. Because [the United States] started out with slavery, they [blacks] didn't get a good start in life in America. Now that I think of it, affirmative action is probably a good thing. The thing to give them a better start. I don't see it as being their fault."

The somewhat spartan answers youth gave to questions of their relative advantages and disadvantages as whites were common at Valley Groves, as was the way the subject brought up the issue of affirmative action. At least half of the youth I spoke to said they felt that being white gave them no advantages, although a few of those said that whites *once* had advantages, but no more. Other youth answered somewhat ambivalently. I found it interesting and significant that Matt changed his mind somewhat after thinking about ongoing economic disparities between blacks and whites. A few other students I spoke to made a similar turn after I asked about present-day racial inequalities or provided some statistical facts about racial discrimination. This suggested to me that the youth were parroting the discourses and ideas they picked up from current debates about affirmative action without critically thinking about them, or that they simply did not have all of the information with which to think through and form an independent opinion on the subject.

In sum, white students at Valley Groves had more to say about white identity as a social identity, a sense of group position, than they did about white as a cultural identity, but still not a lot. Overall, the youth I spoke to felt uncomfortable in the company of a lot of people of color and believed that, as a group, they were not viewed favorably by them, blacks especially. Commonly they believed African Americans viewed them as "racist." They seemed to try to distance themselves from the accusation by acting in a color-blind, race-neutral fashion, by explicitly asserting they were not racist, and by pointing the finger elsewhere, namely at hicks. Furthermore, most students, whether whole- or half-heartedly, felt disadvantaged by their whiteness, particularly because of affirmative action.

Clavey: "Oppressor," Privilege, Racist Feelings

I originally met Melissa at the end of her sophomore year at Clavey when she, Linda, Sera, and Ann agreed to a group interview. Through her junior and senior years, Melissa remained very friendly to me, and after the discussion in her government class about the Million Man March, in which she played a central role, I decided to interview her again.

She had matured and grown more self-confident since I first met her. Her style had shifted from "alternative" to something a bit more "hippie." At least, that's how she told me others tended to see her. Fitting the hippie style, she usually looked as if she did not particularly care about her appearance. "[I wear] whatever," she told me. "Like I don't even brush my hair, and I feel totally comfortable. I don't brush it or do anything to it." But on the day we had our interview, her short and straight brown hair was so clean it picked up more light and air than usual. It flew around her face as we talked on a bench outside the faculty dining room.

"It's wonderful!" Melissa said to me when, as we sat down to talk, I reiterated my interest in her experience at Clavey, a "multicultural school." She explained that she lived outside of the Clavey school district in a fairly middle- to upper-middle-class part of town, but that she wanted to come to Clavey because, on the one hand, there was a "mix of different kinds of people" and, on the other, enough white people that they were "on the chart." She knew that it would be important to her to have other whites around to relate to. "You definitely can identify with your own kind," she said.

We talked a bit about that. She said that she felt that "every person was a bit racist toward other types of people in some way" and, hence, felt more comfortable with their own kind. I asked her if her experiences at Clavey had made her feel less prejudiced toward different types of people. This question sparked a long and very interesting response from Melissa that touched on issues that I heard other whites at Clavey express concerning their social location as whites:

"No, not at all. In fact, sometimes the contrary. . . . The first thing you need to learn when you come to this school is how to stay out of trouble, what are the rules, and how to understand each culture at a general level. Because you're going to need to relate to each person very quickly on their level as best you can. Especially if you're in the minority at this school; probably if you're a minority anywhere. You have to do that. You're kind of playing a game to get through the day and not offend anybody. Everything is so, you know, tense, usually, in a way. . . . Like, walking down the hall, the people that will usually tease me or yell at me or call me a bitch or will stand in my way and not let me down the hallway, tend not to be white. In fact, I've never had a white person do that to me. You know? And I'm not saying that white people don't, but there's never been one, you know?"

I knew the hallway people Melissa was referring to. In front of the entrances to the 30 and 40 buildings, groups of three to five African American males regularly hung out to socialize among themselves and scope out passersby. No one was exempt from being addressed by these guys. Friends or friendly acquaintances would usually be greeted with affectionate insults where others, arbitrarily picked out, might find one of the boys blocking their path with his chest thrust forward like a rooster ready to fight. One time, Patti and I were passing through the entrance to the 40 building on the way to her locker when one of the guys turned around and slugged the first person to meet his fist, an Asian boy, it turned out. Patti turned to me and said, "Don't you just love this school?"

Melissa continued,

"Like, I've been socked twice—not here, when I was in junior high—and it was a racial issue. I hadn't done anything racial, so I didn't quite understand what was going on. Like you're always getting this push and it's not coming from your own race. And it's really hard to ignore that. You really have to know that a lot of these students, these children are being raised in a really different way than you've been raised. I've been raised to never use violence as a way to solve my problems. Other people have been raised that the only way to solve problems is through violence. That's like all they've ever known. That's the only comfort they've ever known truly. If you come up here, mothers will come pick up their sons and beat them in front of the school! And you kind of walk by and you're like, 'You are beating your child publicly!' and nobody is turning their heads, nobody is looking shocked. Then you look around and go, 'Oh, god, I'm the only white person here; maybe this is normal for all these kids.' I've seen this twice up here where a mother has beat their child publicly. So it's definitely happening at the home. You know what I mean? It's like you can't break past that. Different cultures deal with things differently. It's a fact, it's not even race. Factually, generally, different cultures deal with things differently. You know, you have to face it and not just go around being politically correct about it, 'Oh, it's just a few.' No, it's a huge sum of this school, you know, a *huge* sum that are like that. It's a *fact* [pounding on the table for emphasis]; it's not like a maybe. It's definitely happening—you can definitely see it. You know what I mean? All of the fires, who sets them? Why are three quarters of the student body failing? And who are those that are failing? Look at that. There are reasons for these. You have to go back to the home. There are differences. You know?"

"Uh huh," I said. I took a mental note of Melissa's language, specifically the way she referred to African American students as "these students" and "these children," and earlier had spoken of getting to know students at "their level." This way of speaking positioned Melissa as a member of an "us" (whites) that stood in hierarchical relationship to a "them" (blacks). In this context, the implication was that blacks were culturally inferior to whites. I then asked Melissa to what extent she thought larger issues, like poverty or discrimination, weighed on the behaviors of blacks at Clavey and their families.

"Definitely, I hear every single day excuses for why they are doing what they are doing. 'Well, we haven't had equal opportunity' [said in semimocking voice]. It's like, you know, you *haven't*, and you *still* don't, but you *have to take responsibility for your actions* to a certain point. At least you have to take *some* responsibility to a point. You know what I mean? You are an individual, a human being who is separate [pounds table] from the world in one way or another. Constantly excuses are being made. Even you see the faculty here, they feel sorry for the students so they don't fail them because they didn't have equal opportunity. You have to fail the student if they should fail. That means that they haven't [pound] passed [pound] the *course* [pound]! They haven't *learned* [pound] what they are *supposed* to learn so they are not supposed to make it to the next level of learning. You know, learning is a process. You can't skip around. But it's like, 'Oh, all the black students are failing and none of the white ones are. Let's just make the grading policy a little easier. Let's lower our standards for them.' That's not helping them! That's hurting them! You know what I mean? You see it all over the place. What are you doing?

I mean, poverty plays a role, I don't think it's a huge role, but it definitely plays one. I don't know the facts but what I observe is a lot of Latino kids are pretty poor, the Asian kids and white kids tend to have money. Actually, I think all of the Asian people I know have a good amount of money, a few white people I know don't, and I think there are a huge amount of black people who don't. I mean, you drive down 35th to [the poor district in town] and you see a lot of Clavey students hang out around there. It's not a great area at all. I mean it's the ghetto and that's their home. You know? The whole lifestyle is more one of survival when you are in this poverty, like, ghetto, like, hungry starving, like, place where violence is just like really *alive*.

There's also less of a desire to be educated, I think, if you're coming home and being abused every day or you don't have a family, or you have a child and have no money and are on welfare. The idea of doing your homework and like going off to school and working with your teachers—I don't think it becomes that important. It's like, 'I need to survive; I need to get money. How should I? Drugs. That's a great way to get money.' You know? Excellent way to get money. You can get rich. It's really a sad situation, a cycle that continues and continues.

I don't know how you deal with that. You know? I don't know how to help the situation. A huge revolution needs to occur in this capitalistic world that we live in. This monetary hungry world, otherwise it just seems like it's in a decline. I don't know what the answer is—socialism, communism—I don't know what the answer is. I don't think any system is going to be perfect, but this one—there's a loss of value and morals and people aren't helping each other and working together. There's a loss of integrity and unity. You're not working together as a community; you're working more for your own few little people in the communities. It's really everybody who must work to-gether. If you ignore everybody and just think that you have this happy little life, well, no. If he dies, part of you dies. If he goes down, part of you is going to go down. We are on the same boat, literally. This is one earth."

At this point, I told Melissa that I agreed with her that we needed major social change to address the inequalities in this country, but that we lacked a clear vision of how that change might occur. I then said, "But, something you said sounded contradictory to me. Earlier you seemed to feel that the black family culture was to blame for the violence and lack of interest in school of many of the black kids here, and you denied the relevance of the wider society. But just now you seemed to advocate greater social responsibility for the situation many people of color find themselves in. Does that seem, like, contradictory to you?"

All she could say was, "But I don't know how to deal with it. I don't know how to help!"

Then she added,

"I have, you know, so many more opportunities than these people. And I worked really hard to get them, *really* hard. But when I was born, just being born, I already *had* so many opportunities. How do you deal with that? Not that it's a clean slate and you all start out like equal. You know? I don't believe there is an 'equal' thing, one type of 'equal' thing. There are different qualities and traits to have, some people have them, some don't, and that's okay. But I mean, to have so many more doors open to me, there's something *wrong* about that."

"In what ways have you had more doors open to you?" I asked.

"My upbringing. I've had more money. I've had supportive parents. Having the whole family thing and living in a *house*, having dinner, having a meal three times a day—not really, but always having food around. Having quiet when I want quiet; having space when I need space. I desire space. Um, getting to travel and learn about the world in that way. Having a great education. Having a ride to school, you know? Some very basic things like that. Having clothes that are warm when I need warm clothes; clothes that are clean, that smell good [chuckles]. Having showers. Basic things that I forget about all the time. In this modern world this is how we live so, you know, I forget how much I have. It's like, people don't have that. What are they supposed to do?"

"And to what extent do you think being white is also an advantage?" I ask.

"Oh it's a *huge* advantage. My brother's best friend is black and we always go out with him. He'll go in stores, and it's very obvious. These people, they'll watch him more than they ever watch me. Like he's going to steal something? No! He's a great kid! I'm more likely to steal something than he is! [laughs] But they don't know that. You know, just the way people view you, the way they look at me as opposed to a black person, it's like, 'She must be smarter. She must be more trustworthy.' It's like, 'She'll probably work harder at the job. She probably comes from a better family.' Me, who's done nothing except, 'God, she doesn't have much melanin, so she looks tasty.' You know? It's not fair.

And you know? I judge people that way all the time. If I'm walking down the street and there's a black person on one side and a white person on the other, I'm going to walk towards the white person. *Why*? Not that he's necessarily more to be trusted, but because I feel less likely that that [white] person will hurt me. I'm making these decisions all the time without really noticing, so it's like, it's *in* me, you know? This devil is in *me* also. I don't even know if it is a devil. I have no idea. It sounds so awful. It sounds so racist, it sounds so cruel, but it's almost *in* me."

This ten-minute section of my conversation with Melissa provides an excellent entree into discussing the complexity of white youth's experience of race at Clavey High, and students' struggles to come to terms with the ways "white" marked an identity of often disturbing social-political implications. Although, as I will show, white girls like Melissa had different experiences and interpretations of their experiences of white identity as a social category than did boys, and class differences fused with racialized differences to influence students' identities as whites, Melissa's comments touched on several issues that resonated in one way or another with all of the white youth I spoke to at Clavey. At the core of those issues were (1) an appreciation for racial-ethnic diversity, (2) stereotypes of whites as oppressors, (3) white privilege, and (4) beliefs among whites that their experience at Clavey made them more "racist."

First, unlike Valley Groves students, who expressed discomfort when outnumbered socially by nonwhites, Melissa chose to attend Clavey *because* she wanted to be in association with a range of different kinds of youth, even if it made her a racial minority in that context. She appreciated that *some* whites were around, because she felt she could relate best with them, but the idea of being surrounded by students who were not white was not, in itself, a significant issue for Melissa. Most students I spoke to expressed this same thing. They enjoyed the racial-ethnic diversity of their school and city and imagined always living in such a social environment. Several students explicitly told me that they felt uncomfortable when they went into the suburbs or other places that were predominantly white.

However, many white students at Clavey *were* "uncomfortable" with certain stigmas and stereotypes that pervaded the social atmosphere at school.

The word that perhaps best sums up the tone and flavor of those stigmas is "oppressor." While this was related to the stereotype that all whites are "racist," the latter term carried a different meaning and weight for white students at Clavey than it did for white students at Valley Groves. At Valley Groves, one might be called "racist" for merely acknowledging or organizing under racial distinctions. At Clavey, however, students made racial distinctions constantly, at times joked about racial differences in diverse company, and spoke candidly about race with very little pause, even when they said something that sounded prejudicial or stereotypical. To Clavey students, "racism" referred to a history and consequence of white racial oppression and inequality that white students well understood, both from their formal curricula at school and the informal education they received from their peers of color.

For example, most students, regardless of achievement level and racial-ethnic ascription, received a significant amount of history during the course of their time at Clavey that focused on the experiences and perspectives of oppressed groups in the United States. All students were required to take a world cultures course in their sophomore year that explored the histories and cultures of the range of different American racial-ethnic groups. Upper-level U.S. history courses might also revisit this broad perspective, particularly if the teacher was African American or white and very liberal. Also, some black teachers taught decidedly Afrocentric classes in history, social science, English, and chemistry.

I heard some white students complain about this education, saying that they had learned more about the histories of everybody except white people. One time, for example, Eric came into drama class from history, and the first thing that came out of his mouth as we approached each other was, "I am *sick* and *tired* of hearing about slavery and how the white man abused the black man. OK! I got it! Can we talk about something else now?" Despite complaints, however, most white students had taken in the lessons and were not mystified about why "white" carried the stigma of "oppressor." When I had first asked Eric what it meant to him to be white, he replied, "Well, white people have done some really bad things, [like] social Darwinists and a lot of perversion of Christianity. I suppose it's okay," his voice taking on a facetious tone, "except they go around and try to conquer everybody." Later he added, "[Nobody] thinks about the economic prison that our founding fathers and the people after that set up in a lot of ways [for blacks.]

You [referring to blacks] can't get hired in a lot of places, and along the way whites totally sucked the self-esteem out of [black] people."

Whether or not students got a formal education about white domination, whites at Clavey could barely pass a day at school without being reminded either of that history or of the anger toward whites that it had engendered among some African American students. In predominantly black classrooms, especially, any topic that as much as touched on issues of social injustice or race would engage black students and frequently lead to heated discussions about past and present experiences of African American oppression by whites. For example, one day, in Patti's history class, Mr. Edwards brought in a poem that was a moving ode to Native American resistance to cultural and economic annihilation. After reading it to the class, Mr. Edwards asked students to say the first words that came to their minds. African American students called out "oppression," "slavery," "anger." Mr. Edwards asked to whom they thought the poem was directed. "The white man," someone called out.

"What are some other feelings or thoughts the poem brings up for you?" Mr. Edwards asked. Then an African American girl called out, "Jeanie is my friend, but her ancestors enslaved mine, and I'm angry about that!"

Jeanie shot back, "What you talkin' about? My ancestors never enslaved nobody!"

"You know what I mean," the first girl replied. "I like you, you're all right, but the white man oppressed my people and I'm angry about that."

White Privilege

In addition to being singled out and negatively stigmatized as members of an oppressor race, white students' informal associations with African American friends and peers gave them experiences in a related but different aspect of whiteness—white privilege. Melissa was very cognizant of several ways in which she was privileged for no reason other than the amount of melanin in her skin. She recognized that economic benefits tended to come along with being white and that she was treated with greater trust by strangers and had greater opportunities because of that.

Many other white students shared Melissa's awareness of white privilege. In my interview with Murray, he said this about the advantages he had as a white student at Clavey:

"From my teachers I'm expected of a lot more than other students because I'm white. They respect me a lot more because I'm white. I'm given the benefit of the doubt a lot more. If I don't turn in a paper, I'd be given more slack than a black friend of mine. That' s a big stereotype. Like walking in halls. I've never needed a pass up at school, have never been asked to go to detention. But if I'm with a black person, I'll be stopped like that. I can leave school no problem unless I have anyone else [black] in my car."

Barry (the self-defined conservative Republican) had a different opinion than Murray about advantages or disadvantages of being white at Clavey. He felt blacks had the best advantage at school because they were the majority and all of the best members of the administration were African American. Outside of school, however, he observed a different story. He said, "I've noticed that affirmative action is sort of a roadblock going into college, but bottom line, in the workplace, most professional offices, white-collar jobs are still occupied by whites, specifically white males. Even with affirmative action, old executives are white men and they tend to relate better to white men and that sort of moves up. Whenever I talk to my dad, in his office, all people who make a lot of money are white men. So I see that [being white] is an advantage." Then Barry added, "Which is unfortunate, but, then again, it's not," to acknowledge both the unfairness of white privilege and his gratitude for it at the same time.

Daniel observed distinct advantages to being white, as well. "In this country white people get priority over others," he said. "Like with jobs, it would probably be easier for me to get a job in the suburbs, maybe in the city too. Also, since the majority of America is white, people don't look down on you." Both Daniel and Barry observed that, even with affirmative action, whites have better chances of getting jobs than other racial-ethnic groups. Daniel also believed that whites were advantaged because they were not looked down upon—the opposite perspective from the whites at Valley Groves who believed that they *were* looked down upon.

Finally, as one last example, Kirsten and Cindi also recognized certain privileges and advantages whites have in U.S. society. Recall that Kirsten was white and Cindi was part Chinese and white, though, as her discourse attests, she tended to place herself within a "we whites" narrative frame. I asked them, "Have you ever experienced at Clavey or elsewhere a time when you can say you felt ashamed or guilty to be white or could say you were happy to be white?"

"No, I don't think so," Kirsten responded. "I don't think I've ever felt like 'God, I wish I wasn't white.' But proudness—"

As if to finish Kirsten's sentence, Cindi chimed in, "You wouldn't necessarily be 'Yeah, I'm white and I'm proud!'"

"I think everyone should be proud of their race but it's never like 'Ho ho! It's mostly white people in our United States government, ha ha. I'm white!'"

Again finishing Kirsten's sentence but speaking over her last words, Cindi said, "Bragging about it," and in singsong fashion added, "I'm white! You aren't! Na na!" Then she broke into laugher.

"It's nothing like that." Kirsten went on, with Cindi still laughing. "Not that kind of proudness. Egotistical."

"Why not, I should ask. I assume I know what you mean, but why not?"

Kirsten replied to me, "Well 'cause, if it were the other way around and the African Americans dominated the government or whatever, and I was a major minority in the United States, I wouldn't want someone going around 'Ha ha, I dominate the United States government you little—.'" She purposely left the end of the sentence open to the imagination.

"There's more of us then there are you, so—," added Cindi, also leaving the rest of the sentence open to the imagination.

"Yeah, you just feel like, 'oh, thanks.' You know? And I just wouldn't want to do that because I wouldn't want to do something like that. It's like, *ew* . . ." said Kirsten with a tone as though she had just scooped a dead fly from her soup.

In short, white students I spoke to at Clavey High tended to have a dual awareness of the history of white oppression and contemporary white privilege.[2] While they sought to dissociate themselves from the history of white oppression, the legacy of that history, white privilege, was too obvious to deny. Dual awareness affected different students differently and elicited different types of responses in different discursive contexts. I have codified those responses as (1) social-political change, (2) exasperation, (3) guilt, (4) fear of retribution, (5) denial of certain privileges, and (6) shifting of blame.

In our discussion Melissa suggested that a "revolution needs to occur in this capitalistic world we live in." This was the "social-political change" response that many white youth had for addressing the unfairness they observed of race in the United States. Though not everyone thought revolution was the answer, exactly, most felt that social reforms were necessary to bring about social-economic justice for disadvantaged minorities in the United States. All but one of the white students I spoke to supported, at least, affirmative action. This was even true of Barry, the Republican. Although he believed that an affirmative action program based on class, not race, would be more effective, his basic concern was to improve opportunities for disadvantaged racial minorities through some kind of social policy.

However, often lurking behind fairly liberal-progressive political views were less hopeful, potentially immobilizing feelings. One of these was exasperation. Melissa touched on this when she exclaimed, "to have so many doors open to me, there's something wrong with that. . . . I don't know how you deal with that! I don't know how to help the situation. . . . I don't know what the answer is. . . . It's not fair!"

Melissa's exasperation came from feeling helpless to change the things she saw as unfair. In my conversation with Jessie, she spoke to another type of exasperation, more based on the personal toll stereotypes and heckling had taken on her tolerance and self-esteem. She told me,

> "When I was fifteen, I had very low self-esteem, incredibly low and . . . being a person with such low self-esteem I took everything to mean the worst it could mean and really believed that what people were telling me was that white people were the cause of everything bad that's ever happened. In World Cultures we learned about white, you know, white people suck, dah-dah-dah and just went on about how horrible it was to be white. I feel like I would have a lot more respect for just who I am in general if I was not white, I mean, if I was black or if I was a culture that was more prominent at this school just because you hear so much of this sort of [antiwhite] backlash, people being ignorant, and it really hurts you in a way. You can't separate that from yourself entirely."

"What are some stereotypes that you hear?" I asked.

> "White people have hell-a-lot of money. White people have, you know, two-parent households; all white people have never been abused. They have no reason to do drugs. It's always those white bitches who are anorexic and complainers, and why would you want to kill yourself if you were white; you've got everything, you know, everything. Oh my god, I've heard some of the most ignorant bullshit in gym. White women are bitches. They don't put out as much. I mean, aah, just all over the place."

Guilt was a third type of response that students had to the ascriptions and privileges of being white. Although I did not hear any Clavey students tell me that *they* felt guilty, several got defensive and said things like, "I *refuse* to feel guilty for something I had no part of." And many whites I spoke to believed that white guilt lay at the foundation of white identity, or lack thereof. They explicitly or implicitly named white guilt as the reason for which whites shied away from claiming a white identity. In Pickles' words,

> "[White people] feel guilty. They feel really guilty for what their ancestors did and a lot of them—I don't know if this is everywhere, but definitely here in [this] area—want to show them [blacks] that they are not like their ancestors. We [whites] don't really cling to each other. It's been taught that white identity is wrong, so we don't know what it is because we've blocked it out mentally. We should realize what white people do and other people generally don't do 'cause it's part of our culture. We don't recognize that because we're not allowed to have pride."

Eric, distancing himself from guilty whites, told me, "I went to Clavey public schools for most of my life and it's like, you see how a lot of white people deal with white guilt. They totally fold. They're just really afraid of black people. That's why there's Lakeview [private school]. It's a joke of a school [academically]. Lamer than Clavey, not challenging. But look at the ethnic make-up of Lakeview [predominantly white]. You don't think race is a factor? Absolutely! They don't want to think about that. It's an uncomfortable place for them."

"Uncomfortable because they feel afraid of blacks especially?" I asked.

"Definitely they feel afraid," Eric responded.

Eric's reply touched on the fourth type of response white students had to the mantle of "oppressor": the fear of black retribution through violence against whites. Melissa had been socked twice for reasons she believed to be racial. Many of the students I spoke to, male and female, working- and middle-class, had either been physically attacked for being white or knew someone who had been. That seemed to occur mostly in junior high school, although after the Rodney King verdict, a Clavey student was hospitalized after being beaten up by a group of black males.

Also, just about every time a fight broke out at school, which was at least once a week, of priority in the rumor mill was whether or not the fight was intra- or interracial, and if it was the latter, was it racially motivated. One day, I saw a large stampede of youth running toward the Junior Circle. This was the sign that a fight had broken out, so I joined in to see what was going on. As I did, a student I knew, a working-class male of mixed white and Arab descent, yelled to me, "It's a race riot! Be careful! Here, stick by me. I'll protect you." The student was joking, but his humor drew on the tension that he could well have been telling the truth.

In my interview with Patti, who enjoyed having diverse friends and at the time was going out with an African American boy, she told me that she got upset when classroom discussions got "racial." "I've always believed in unity, not everybody for themselves," she said. I asked her if she thought that African Americans still had to confront social injustices today in the United States. She replied,

> "You know how it seems—if you look at it nowadays, it's more like the black people and the gangs, they're taking over in a way. They're shutting us out. It's more, like, because of the anger that happened to them a long time ago that they're so angry that they're going to do things to us. Like, who has more rule over—take downtown Clavey—who has more rule over it? White people are afraid of blacks now or any other kind of group now because they feel like taking over. It's them who have the guns, not us. So we're just like shoveled away, and I don't see why. I think it's the anger. That's what bothers me."

Patti's concerns were expressed more dramatically than those of other students I talked to, but the dramatics serve well for making this point. Many white youth at Clavey feared black anger, and school fights and occasional racially motivated verbal or physical attacks by blacks kept white students in states of alert. As Melissa said, they learned the rules of survival and stuck close to them to preserve the peace.

The fifth type of response to the social position and ascriptions of whiteness was denial. While several youth took the position of denying any responsibility for the "sins of the ancestors," more common was denial of the stereotype that "all whites are rich." When I spoke to African Americans and other students of color at Clavey, this was more or less the first thing they implied about whites at Clavey. "They seem to be well off"; "A lot of them live in the hills"; "They're all rich—that's the stereotype anyway" were some of the things they said. Working-class students I spoke to were most intolerant of this stereotype, for obvious reasons. Many of them had grown up and still lived in the same low-income projects as black kids in the school.

During my interview with Tina, whose family had lived for some time in the urban projects, we discussed demographic shifts and the "minoritization" of whites in California and the United States. I made a comment about how whites have had the "privilege" until recently of being unintimidated by claims for power by minority groups.

Tina immediately shot back, "Only *some* whites. *Some* whites have had that. That's what everybody thinks. 'You're white, you've had it good. You must be rich and live in a big house.' *No!* I live in an apartment. My back yard is about as big as this table. I grew up around drugs, not in a good neighborhood. I wasn't born in the hills, don't have my own car. But that's the way it's perceived. On the other hand, a lot of blacks aren't just from the ghetto and stuff like that."

Several middle-class white students who lived in the wealthy "hills" or other nice neighborhoods also took issue with the assertions that they were rich. Jessie touches on this above when she talks about the "ignorant" claims that all whites are rich. In my conversation with Cindi and Kirsten, they brought up the issue of the presumed richness of whites when I asked them what they saw as *disadvantages* to being white. Kirsten said, "Well, I think a lot of people—[cutting herself off] if you go to Clavey and you're white, then everyone thinks you're rich for some reason. Cindi and I are way not rich. Like, some of our parents don't work."

"Our fathers are jobless," Cindi elaborated.

"And so, like, my father started our addition like five years ago, when I was eleven, and because we don't have the money to add on, we've been trying to save so we can put on garage doors. So I don't think I'm in any way rich."

Kirsten and Cindi's fathers were jobless and they were short on cash, but Kirsten's family apparently owned a home. Possibly Kirsten did not recognize her home as an economic asset that most black families do not have and, thus, how she could appear to be "rich" in that respect. My point, however, is not to argue who was or was not *actually* rich, but how the stereotype raised white students' defenses. Eric told me one day, "It's not cool to be rich around here, so you play it down." My sense was that it was not cool because of all the ways it articulated with other sentiments and experiences of white identity—white privilege, white guilt, white stereotypes, and exasperation over helplessness. As Melissa said, she was "born" into having a house, food, and living in a nice neighborhood, and the unfairness of that plagued her.

More often than verbally denying class status, white youth at Clavey played it down in their clothing. "They dress like they aren't rich," Anthony, a black male, told me. Most white students generally wore casual, understated clothing, not the glossy, Gap look of Valley Groves students. Punk, alternative, and hippie students looked particularly grungy, and although wearing old, torn, and worn-out clothes was true of those students at both Clavey and Valley Groves, they looked significantly *more* torn up and grungy at Clavey than at Valley Groves. The "alternative" look at each school, especially, was hardly recognizable as the same subculture because of the different ways youth interpreted the "grunge" aesthetic. The most vivid difference was in what girls did with their hair. At Valley Groves, alternative girls' hair was always short, clean, shiny, and often pulled back with colorful little plastic clips. At Clavey, girls' hair could be short or long, and in either case would look like it hadn't received a brush or washing in days. In contrast, African American students at Clavey tended to dress with obvious concern for cleanliness, beauty, fashion, and expensive looks. Scholars have argued that black students will put great effort into their attire to compensate for lower-status background and/or to mock the limited access of African Americans to wealth.[3] I suggest that white students at Clavey operated under the same impulse, only in the opposite way. They waged a type of "sartorial warfare"[4] against the stereotype that all whites are rich.

The last type of response to white social location was to shift blame for social inequalities off of whites and onto the "victims," particularly African Americans and their families. Melissa blamed the black family for instilling violent behaviors in their children and not pushing them to work hard in school. She also asserted that African Americans were not taking enough personal responsibility for improving their lot. These types of response seemed to come up precisely when the issue of academic achievement was on the mind of the speaker. Often, when I asked youth to explain why there were disproportionate numbers of whites and Asians in the accelerated classes and African Americans in the standard curriculum classes, they invariably raised meritocratic and/or cultural arguments. They claimed that African American youth didn't work hard enough or take school seriously, and thus could not get the grades to be in the accelerated classes. Linda commented, "It's so sad because these kids could be pushed so far beyond what they are [doing]. Like, it's unbelievable. When I see a twelfth-grader holding a geometry book, I cringe inside me. Because, *you can learn*, you can do it! People are so lazy, they don't care. They have no goals, no ambitions. It's frustrating. I don't get it!"

"I Feel More Racist"

Related to the occasional tendency of some white students at Clavey to place the blame for the underachievement of students of color solely on those students themselves, but in a category all of its own, was the claim by several whites I spoke with that their experience at Clavey had made them "more racist." Unlike white students at Valley Groves, who believed they were stereotyped by blacks as "racist" and who explicitly denied the charge, some whites at Clavey wrung their hands over feelings that they *were*, in fact, racist, despite conscious desires not to be. By "racist" these students tended to mean either that they held negative stereotypes of people of color, African Americans especially, that had been confirmed by their experience rather than debunked, or that they had failed to learn how to make racialized boundaries insignificant when it came to, for example, choosing who their friends were. When I asked Melissa if the multiracial, multicultural experience that she thought was "wonderful" had made her feel less prejudiced toward different kinds of people, she said, "No, not at all. In fact, sometimes the contrary." She felt that her experiences of being harassed in the halls and observing who in the school was creating trouble and failing in classes had confirmed certain stereotypes and reinforced prejudices. She came to believe that "it's almost innate" for groups to be a "bit racist" and want to stick to their own kind; that some people naturally had qualities that others did not; that "factually, generally, different cultures deal with things differently" and that African Americans were particularly different. And, finally, she expressed her racism as a "devil" in her, a despicable and evil thing that she had little power to rid herself of.

Several other students, including students of color, expressed to me that their experiences at Clavey reinforced stereotypes. Often this was done offhandedly, as this comment by an Asian American girl I interviewed: "There are stereotypes that the African American students are all gangsters and violent, that whites are snobby, stuck-up and rich, and, you know? They're *true* for the most part!" Other times, however, youth were more disturbed by the implications of having their stereotypes confirmed. For example, Barry told me, "You know, the tragic thing about being here is that, I think, coming to school here almost makes you racist. Because you see all the stereotypes you ever heard of and you start to realize that they're all true for the most part." Jessie said, when I asked her why she chose to come to Clavey High,

> "My parents wanted me to, and I did too, but they had in mind that it would help me not be like other whites, racist and scared of black people. But in some ways, I feel more racist now than before [I came here.] You know, like last week I got mugged by a group of black kids outside the library, right over there [pointing toward the main entrance]. And this was during school! That shit happens all the time and it has its effects. Like, I'm scared of groups of black guys now, you know? And I know not *all* blacks are like that, but still, the reflex is there."

In a less explicit way than the students above, several other white students expressed a similar type of sentiment about feeling more racist. They expressed unhappiness with or frustration over the kinds of racialization that went on at school. Recall, for example, the conversation with Melissa, Ann, Sera, and Linda back in chapter 3. At one point the girls were talking about multicultural week at school and how students were asked to wear tags that said, "I'm proud to be   ." Sera and Ann pointed out that students were supposed to fill in the blank with their racial-ethnic culture, and they seemed in agreement: "That puts up a blockade!" In my interview with Eric, he made a similar comment. He said, "You've seen these t-shirts? They're so helpful. They're really able to dole out the color lines. They say, 'Love sees no colors.' Why don't you get a sign that says, 'Don't beat me up?!'"

These types of responses may have stemmed from the notion, common to popular interpretations of the "color-blind" ideology, that to see racial difference is itself racist. However, Clavey students tended not to believe in a color-blind ideology per se, especially not as a legal or political ideology. They did, however, seek a form of "color-blindness" at the personal level, meaning that they would get past *judging* and stereotyping people by the color of their skin. The idea of getting to know kids of color as individuals and making friends with them was what drew most of the students I spoke with to Clavey High. However, the emphasis many students of color placed on racial-ethnic difference made that effort difficult if not impossible for some white students. This was so, I believe, because some white students were not able to think of racial-ethnic difference without assuming that difference meant "unequal." "Different but equal" was not a concept they could wrap their minds around, so the emphasis on racial-ethnic difference that was so prevalent at Clavey reinforced notions held by whites that racial-ethnic lines, at best, were impenetrable and, at worst, marked unequal status and exasperated tensions between groups. Hence, to emphasize your race-ethnicity was tantamount to throwing up barriers or asking to be beaten up.

Shades of White

The social identities of white youth at Valley Groves and Clavey high schools differed widely between the two schools and, at Clavey especially, within them, revealing a multiply layered spectrum of diverse shades of white. The existence of that spectrum and the dynamics by which different shades emerged, stood out, or receded can be explained by the different ways interracial association, institutional structures, the local interpretive community, and other personal identities—like gender—interacted with and affected one another in certain contexts.

At Valley Groves, white students believed that people of color looked down on them and saw them as racists, but no one told me that someone of color approached them directly and said, "You are a racist, and I will tell you why I think that," or otherwise said anything explicitly negative to their face. I presume they picked up those ideas from indirect sources like the media, popular culture, and, possibly, other whites. And because the "racist" ascription had an ethereal source, Valley Groves students were able to distance themselves from it. They didn't *feel* racist, and unexamined racist things they did were not pointed out to them, so they could more or less confidently deny the charge and/or project "racist" onto others, in this case, the hicks.[5]

The belief that white people were a disadvantaged group was similarly developed largely among whites themselves in and around Valley Groves and not from direct association with people of color. The late sociologist of race Herbert Blumer argued that white racial identity is defined collectively through: (1) *remote* (not face-to-face) interracial association; (2) in the "public arena," such as legislative assemblies, public meetings, the press; (3) around "big events" that raise fundamental questions about race relations; (4) with renowned individuals or intellectuals; and (5) under the direction of strong interest groups.[6] At the time of this research, Proposition 209, California's anti–affirmative action proposition, fit the bill vis-a-vis Blumer's model. It was a ballot initiative with financial backing from right-wing interest groups and the support of such renowned individuals as the Republican California governor at the time, Pete Wilson, and University of California regent and intellectual, Ward Connerly, who is African American. Anti–affirmative action proponents, who in the end won the battle, waged their fight on "reverse racism" and similar arguments that located whites as blatantly and unfairly disadvantaged by affirmative action and other redistributive racial politics.

I propose that white students at Valley Groves bought into the construction of white as a "disadvantaged" identity that was forged out of the debates on behalf of Proposition 209. They did so largely because the argument jibed with their race-neutral common sense, itself a product of remote association with people of color. Racialized differences and inequalities were not a part of the white students' lived experience, so they firmly believed that inequalities were not an issue elsewhere as well; hence, there was no need for affirmative action. Meanwhile, practically the only occasion in which white students were forced to think of themselves racially was when they pondered their futures in college and the odds on their behalf for admittance or scholarships. In light of the propaganda against affirmative action legislation, they interpreted those odds to be slim and affirmative action to be discriminatory against them as whites. In short, the resonance of anti–affirmative action discourses with the students' race-neutral common sense allowed those discourses to become "hegemonic," to ring as "truth" to the youth. This explains why both conservative *and* liberal students opposed affirmative action on the same grounds—unfair disadvantage to whites.

At Clavey, white students' close association with students of color constantly pulled the rug out from under hegemonic discourses and constructions of white identity. Students of color were (at times, literally) in white students' faces, accusing them of complicity in the reproduction of racial inequalities in the United States. Formal classroom curricula and informal dialogue with peers of color left no escape for white students from the realities, past and present, of race and white racial oppression. At the same time, first-hand experiences of being treated better and with more trust than peers and friends of color made it clear to Clavey whites that they were not disadvantaged but, in fact, privileged. Many translated that into the need for sweeping social reforms to redress social inequalities, including support for affirmative action.

However, as I have pointed out, white students' experiences of their whiteness did not always lead to progressive political thought or action; instead it took disturbing turns into exasperation, guilt, and sometimes victim-blaming discourses and "racist" self-images. These different responses were shaped by the ways interracial association was structured and made meaningful in different contexts. Broadly speaking, two types of contexts influenced white racial identities most differently: contexts in which intergroup association was structurally polarized and/or stratified and those in which intergroup association was not. In the moments or situations when intergroup association was dichotomized or stratified, white youth tended to reach for and find resonance with abstract constructions of whiteness as norm and superior, and blackness (which at Clavey could include Latinos) as defective and inferior. In these moments, white youth tended to say the most prejudicial-sounding, stereotypical things about other students, African Americans especially.

One of these moments was when white youth, usually high-tracked white girls, sought to make sense of or explain their academic advantage at school. As I have already argued, the tracking structure stratified youth by race and defined track distinction along terms that reinforced racial stereotypes. Black and Latino youth were marked as lazy, rowdy, and out of control, whereas white students and some Asians were marked as the good students, industrious, and well mannered. I also argued that, to an extent, all youth embodied and played out these racial meanings in their informal interactions at school. Those embodied stereotypes provided the grain of "truth" that white youth observed in their experiences at Clavey, the grain of truth that youth reported made them feel "more racist" because they found that their experience of racial difference reinforced the negative stereotypes they had wished to be rid of. In short, a feedback loop was in place at Clavey whereby social structures and stereotypes of different youth influenced behaviors that, in turn, reinforced or "proved" the need for racialized social structures and the veracity of the racial stereotypes.

High-tracked, usually middle-class girls like Melissa, Linda, and Jessie spoke more stereotypically about black students than any others. White boys spoke the least stereotypically of all. This could be explained by the fact that, since the girls were talking to me, a (white) woman, they may have felt more comfortable disclosing their feelings than the boys did. Secondly, *as girls*, they may have had more access to their feelings and ability to communicate them than did the boys.[7] However, derogatory stereotypes did not come up all of the time, only when the issue of academic achievement was on the table. I propose that what I have described as the interdependent, multiracial self was at play here. White girls could least accept that their academic status was not the result of their own hard work. Their self-esteem depended on it. Women and girls have relatively recently won the right to achieve to their own full potential, and they still face discrimination and fears of inadequacy.[8] Blacks have historically played the role of the gauge by which whites can measure their own status. The lower the status of African Americans, the higher the status of whites and the more whites can assume greater competency for and entitlement to that status. I suggest that African American youth played that role for white girls. Explaining black underachievement in terms of competency, not discriminatory practices, allowed white girls to feel confident in their own academic abilities.

Another moment when racial identities were polarized was when white and black youth were in a position to debate history, black-white history in particular. As I have shown, in those moments, race talk could become very polarized and sometimes hurtful. Friends could suddenly split into "oppressed" and "oppressor." When white youth felt the "oppressor" stigma on them, feelings of guilt, exasperation, anger, and denial emerged. And to the extent that many whites at Clavey carried the same mantle and experienced the same feelings about it, a collective identity emerged among them. As Jessie told me, "I do find myself relating to people in this setting at school because they're white as opposed to because they're a classmate or something. We'll see each other and relate instantly. With people of other cultures, often times I feel like there is a chance they'll assault me. I don't mean physically, but like they will, 'I don't want to talk to you because you're white.'" Jessie did not expect to be assaulted by whites; she expected a kind of solidarity based on shared experience.

The "oppressor" stigma and the negative feelings that went along with it, I believe, was another cause behind the types of stereotyping I observed at

Clavey. A baseline premise of social-psychological theory of collective identity formation is that individuals need a positive group identity, and positive identity is derived largely from intergroup comparison.[9] That means that satisfactory group identity is often manufactured through negative evaluation of an out-group. In the United States, in those places where white identity is fully conflated with the norm and/or American identity, whites might tease some pride out of that, but in general there is little out there in common discourse that defines "white" identity, period, let alone a positive white identity.[10] For white youth at Clavey, add to that the fact that they were frequently face-to-face with negative stereotypes and the most unseemly aspects of whiteness. Jessie, who said, "you can't love yourself and hate your culture," sought out aspects of white culture that she could feel positive about, but she was unusual in that respect. Given that white youth at Clavey had no help from teachers or the wider society in how to carry or constructively counter the negative stigmas of white identity, I believe they spoke negatively about other racial-ethnic groups out of a pressing need to grasp a positive sense of self. And the fact that white *girls* tended to speak most negatively of all points to the particular difficulties girls face with self-esteem because of their gender status. For white girls at Clavey, the negative stigma of being both white and female, codified for Jessie in the term "white bitches," may have made them particularly susceptible to using negative stereotypes as a means of not becoming absorbed in negative views of themselves.

However, those were *those* moments, the moments when race was most polarized and charged between students. Then there were the moments when youth would be doing things together, the exact same things, such as walking down the hall, browsing in a store, or riding in a car. At those times, the lines of sameness—as students, as youth, as friends—made "race" a less salient concern, if a concern at all. Or moments when white students, for whatever reason, were able to stand back and see the way white privilege was structured into the social fabric, in "good old boys" networks, in government rule, and in the distribution of wealth, opportunity, and life chances. At these times, white youth at Clavey recognized that they were unfairly privileged and felt that something large-scale had to be done to rectify that. This was why, I believe, so many white students at Clavey supported affirmative action and other redistributive political efforts (even, in some cases, revolution!). So, while on occasion youth espoused negative, stereotypical attitudes about African American and other disadvantaged groups, attitudes that could justifiably be called prejudicial or "racist," on other occasions they felt and expressed attitudes with radically different implications that might as easily be called "antiracist." Both were genuine.

What are we to make of this? Were Clavey whites racists? Were Valley Groves students? Advocates of "modern racism"[11] argue that contemporary forms of racism are more covert, subtle, and indirect than traditional, more blatant forms of racism. Hence, whites will appear to be nonracist and egalitarian while holding deep-seated antiblack sentiments. They stress that contradictory statements by whites reveal this hidden racism, the true "racist" self. My work suggests that this interpretation is oversimplified largely because it derives from either/or ways of thinking. The white youth in this study understood the meanings of race and racial inequalities through a lived experience that fostered *both* racist *and* non- or antiracist sentiments and politics. What must matter in the end is not whether or not white Americans hold negative views of blacks and other disadvantaged people— it must be that the majority of white people born in the United States are inculcated with such views—but how well they succeed in putting aside those views to uphold and practice more egalitarian beliefs, feelings, and political behaviors. The question of what pedagogical and institutional changes in schools are needed to help youth foster such practices is a central concern of the next, concluding chapter.

Conclusion

Beyond Whiteness

[W]e are all androgynous, not only because we are all born of a woman impregnated by the seed of a man but because each of us, helplessly and forever, contains the other—male in female, female in male, white in black and black in white. We are all part of each other. Many of my countrymen appear to find this fact exceedingly inconvenient and even unfair, and so, very often, do I. But none of us can do anything about it.—James Baldwin, "Here Be Dragons"

When all the voices of the self are fully owned, they are less likely to be projected onto others. In this way, self-acceptance translates into acceptance of the other. —Anne Caroline Klein, *Meeting the Great Bliss Queen*

The Everyday Processes—"Currents"—of Racial Identity Formation

In the introduction to this book, I likened identity to a river. At particular times and places, rivers will appear smooth and steady, then suddenly break up into something chaotic, with some waters flowing downstream, some flowing upstream, and others even defying gravity. By way of a recapitulation of the theoretical argument, I will elaborate in detail on the various processes that shape the flow and character of that river. I call these processes "currents" to metaphorically evoke their fluid, constantly moving character, as well as the easy facility with which they can both blend together and disarticulate. They are: (1) association with people of color; (2) "us-them" boundary-making processes; (3) the ways class, gender, and other identities interplay and influence one another; (4) the multiracial self; and (5) the meanings derived from the structural-institutional context.

Association with Racialized Difference

A main assumption underlying this research from its inception has been that the *experience* of racial groups in *association* is the "elementary ingredient of race relations."[1] People must experience a racially defined "other" for there to be a "racial" self.[2] (I say "racially defined" because it is not difference per se that constructs identities, but how semiarbitrary differences are social-politically marked and defined.) Collective identities take shape through processes by which in-group members define, adopt, and police criteria for group membership with respect to an out-group.[3]

White people are the only members of the U.S. population who have the option to live in entirely racially homogeneous environments, where they have little or no direct contact with people of marked racial-ethnic difference, and where their cultural-political milieu is homologous to their sense of what is natural or common sense. At Valley Groves High, such white racial homogeneity explained, in large part, why white students' racial identities were constructed as "normal": without close association with marked "nonwhite" racial-ethnic difference, there was no defined "white" identity.

However, in the age of global communication and mass media systems, individuals—particularly in industrial societies—would be hard pressed to have no association whatsoever with people of different racial ascriptions. If individuals do not encounter racial-ethnic difference in their workplace or neighborhoods, they will at the movies or on their television sets. Therefore, I have found it useful to speak of *proximities* of association and the types of identities different proximities of association with racial-ethnic difference help construct. White youth at Valley Groves and Clavey high schools lived not far from one another and watched the same television, read the same newspapers, and went to schools structured in relatively similar ways. Many even lived in very similar "suburbany" neighborhoods. Yet, white youth at Valley Groves, who had little association with racial-ethnic difference outside of the media and popular culture, had very different interpretations of racial discourses, perceptions of racial-ethnic others, and "white" racial identities than their counterparts at Clavey High, who had daily, face-to-face association with students of color.

My argument has been that varying proximities of association make for varying "white" identities because of the bearing proximity has on the other processes or "currents" of identity formation that I discuss below.

Further understanding of the effects of proximity of interracial association may become increasingly important as demographic shifts in the United States place more and more whites in close, direct association with people of "nonwhite" racial-ethnic ascriptions.

Defining and Negotiating "Us-Them" Boundaries

These are the processes by which in-group and out-group terms and membership criteria are worked out in practice and maintained. This current is itself composed of multiple, intertwined, and complex processes. One is what Blumer and Duster describe as the "give-and-take, the clash and testing of divergent interpretations."[4] In-group members negotiate their identities and who they think out-group members are with respect to how out-group members define the in-group and themselves.[5] These processes of give and take never settle entirely within fixed boundaries. To maintain distinction, racial boundaries are in continual negotiation. Among the youth in this study, whose racial identities tended to be most vividly expressed through styles of clothing, musical tastes, and other consumer interests, the boundaries of otherness and whiteness were in daily, perceptible processes of negotiation and change. As Imani said to me about African Americans, "When people . . . copy us, we change it as fast as we possibly can." At Clavey, in particular, students, including white students, were quite aware that if they were going to have a racial-ethnic identity, they would need to construct it and be constantly vigilant of its borders.

Very closely related to this (indeed, these processes are only analyzably distinct, but in practice integrated) is a second process that Stuart Hall refers to as the "play of history and the play of difference." White students at Valley Groves and Clavey defined white identity not as the result of a black-white identity paradigm, but in terms of being not-black, not-Asian, not-Latino, not-"minority," and not-"ethnic," as well as not-rich-white, not-racist-white, and so forth. All of these constructed what it meant to be "white," and each put a different social-historical-cultural light on what distinguished whiteness and white identity.

Another us-them boundary-making process engages power relations in a given context. This is more tricky than it might seem, given that, in the wider society, white people wield considerable political, economic, and cultural power. However, in everyday interactions, power relations between groups can be diffuse and negotiable.[6] This was particularly true at Clavey between youth in face-to-face negotiations over cultural definitions of racial identity. Often, those negotiations were power-*inverted* in that black and other youth of color were the ones defining the terms of the negotiations and wielding considerable cultural weight over whites. Furthermore, in schools, youth are put into different power relations with one another at different times. They might work together under conditions of competition on unequal terms (such as the academic market), competition on relatively equal terms (such as sports), noncompetitive relations on unequal terms (such as so-called equal-status work on joint projects in which one group—usually whites—actually has an advantage), and noncompetitive relations on equal terms (such as equal status work on joint projects in which different strengths and advantages of different individuals are accounted for).

What is important about this is that, in situations where the white students at Valley Groves and Clavey felt their power or privileges threatened by another group, their perspectives on race matters and racialized groups became conflictive, stereotypical, and defensive,[7] but under more equal-status, nonthreatening association, their identities and perspectives were relatively porous, generous, and egalitarian.

A final us-them process involves personally experienced feelings and fantasies associated with different relationships with racialized people. Nancy Chodorow[8] makes this argument with respect to gender multiplicity. She asserts that the meanings of gender at any given moment for an individual are both a function of discursive constructions of gender and intrapsychic and emotional events. Images of specific relations, like daughter-father, daughter-mother, sister-brother and so forth, and the fantasies, moods, and emotions tied to those relations will animate different meanings of gender and the self. She asserts, "The clinical encounter demonstrates the moment-to-moment shifting and developing of gender and its varying salience, complexity, and multiplicity as different elements in the gendered sense of self become important (and as gender itself is more or less salient in a current moment or period of transference). Now the controlling intrusive mother is central in the creation of gender, now the dominant father, now the excited little girl, now the one humiliated by her excitement."[9]

What was true of gender in Chodorow's study was true of race in mine. Feelings and fantasies about white-black relations raised a very different sense of self and whiteness than the feelings and fantasies associated with a white-Asian relation, or a majority-minority relation. As white youth moved from one thought about a relation to the next, or one face in the hall to the next, their identities as whites shifted accordingly.

Interlinking and Blending Identities

This current, introduced first by women scholars of color,[10] is possibly the most recognized as that which diversifies racial identity and makes it multiple. It comprises the multiply merging, articulating, and disarticulating social locations individuals are categorized into and may identify with, such as race, ethnicity, nation, class, gender, age, religion, and sexuality. The experiences individuals have of these different social locations are often integrally tied to one another: sometimes they intersect or cross-cut one another, other times they are so fused as to be inseparable. In earlier chapters I discussed how race, gender, and achievement status at school intersected in ways that sometimes put white, high-achieving girls on the defensive when talking about racial inequalities in educational outcomes. When achievement status was not salient in the discussion, the girls' postures softened and their views of racial inequalities turned considerably more concerned with the unfair distribution of privilege along racial lines. White, middle-class girls also tended to have more multiple and complex feelings and thoughts about race than white, middle-class boys; I attributed that to the ways white girls' experiences of being both sexually and racially objectified complicated the girls' views on race and did not allow them to maintain a safe distance from it.

The above are all examples of how identities can intersect and inflect one another. But often race, class, and gender do more than intersect, they coproduce and implicate one another, blend and fuse together. In students' discourses, class "spoke through"[11] the language of race such that white meant one was "rich," "suburbany," and "lived in the hills" (read middle-class), and black or Latino meant that one "lived in the flats," "acted ghetto," came from "single-parent" families, and lived among violence (read poor). Working-class kids who had adopted the styles and mannerisms of the poor and working-class black friends they grew up with would be categorized "black." And, finally, gender, too, spoke through the languages of race and class, such as in stereotypes that all blacks were "tough," "criminal," and "street-smart" (read male) or Asians were "smart," "geeky," "studious," and "reserved" (read feminine).

The Multiracial Self

This current may be the most difficult to grasp intuitively because it most challenges the notion of the self as unified and autonomous. That idea of the self grew out of the Protestant Reformation, the Enlightenment, and the rise of mercantile capitalism—all of which tended to isolate the individual, whether in relationship to God or to other humans—and it continues to be the dominant paradigm for the self in Western industrialized societies.[12]

In chapter 4 I discussed and illustrated several facets of the multiracial self. I argued that the self is multiracial by virtue of the interdependent nature of racial-ethnic identities and the multicultural competencies people have. One type of interdependency involves the processes by which individuals construct selves. George Mead[13] argues that to achieve a sense of self, the individual must become an object to him- or herself. This involves internalizing how other individuals see the self and looking back at the self through the other's eyes. For over a century, black scholars, such as W. E. B. Du Bois, James Baldwin, Zora Neale Hurston, and Frantz Fanon have given testimony to the experience black people have of seeing themselves through the eyes of whites.[14] I argue that white youth in this study became "white" only when they saw themselves through the eyes and minds of African Americans, as well as Asians, Latinos, and other racial-ethnic groups. The youth were populated by racial others and, in that way, carried multiple racial identities and experienced being multiply racialized.

A related interdependency is expressed in the ways individuals see, define, and evaluate themselves and/or their group vis-a-vis others. For example, the self is often defined through negation of others—I am white because I am not black. It can also be defined with respect to difference from others, from being like or unlike, or having more or less than others. White youth at Clavey and Valley Groves needed racial-ethnic difference to define themselves. They measured their relative cultural and social merits and demerits, advantages and disadvantages, entitlements and bankruptcies by comparing themselves to racial-ethnic others. Baldwin pointedly summarizes this type of interdependency in these words: "In a way, the Negro tells us where the bottom is: because *he is there*, and *where* he is, beneath us, we know where the limits are and how far we must not fall."[15]

Psychoanalytic theories of race suggest yet another type of interdependent, multiracial self. They argue that individuals resolve primordial ambivalence about "good" and "bad" aspects of the self by expelling all that is "bad" and projecting it onto others.[16] The "other," then, *is* the self—the feared, anxiety-producing, and rejected aspects of the self that the individual cannot tolerate. In this research, it seemed that splitting and projection, whether it was expressed in terms of projecting "angry" and "violent" characteristics to other people's music, or projecting insecurities about one's achievement status, more radically polarized students and constructed white identities that were less porous and more symbolically violent than white identities constituted from other dependencies.

Finally, the multiracial self might also be called the multicultural self. Today, "race" is defined as much, if not more, by cultural differences as by biological or phenotypical differences. Among young people, this is particularly true. Clothing styles, musical tastes, speaking styles, body language, and leisure interests define who is "authentically" black, white, Asian, and Latino. Youth, like those at Clavey High, who live around and go to school with a culturally diverse range of youth, will learn or acculturate to a wide repertoire of cultural forms and practices. They will not practice all of them, however, because of sanctions applied by in- and out-group members for crossing racial-cultural boundaries. So, for example, when white youth at Clavey had competencies that were marked "black"—like enjoying rap music or speaking Black English—they suppressed them, unless and until a situation arrived where it was either safe or beneficial to bring forth their "blackness." The same was true for African American, Latino, and other youth of color and their "white" competencies.

In sum, the multiracial self means that *race* is premised on an interdependent relationship between the self and other that is not only an external relation, but also—and possibly most significantly—an internal relationship. The self and other are one and the same. And this internal self-other relationship is itself multiple. The experience and definition of the racial self shifts, if sometimes minutely, depending on the social-discursive context and how the internal other is defined and dealt with.

Hand in hand with the above interrelational processes by which white people construct a sense of their racialness is the ways racial-ethnic difference is structured by and interpreted from the wider structural milieu. From the way a speaker's podium is elevated above rows of indistinguishable chairs; to the ways individuals and groups are politically, economically, and residentially situated; to the common values, beliefs, ideologies, conceptual terms, and discourses of the society, we live in a wide and complexly interwoven network of implicit and explicit meanings. Spatial, material, social, and discursive structures shape people's experiences and condition how they understand or make sense of them. To the extent that individuals internalize these structures—identify with them and take them for granted as "truth" or "common sense"—their everyday practices and beliefs tend to reproduce dominant structures and the conditions of existence.[17] A dominant feature of the social structure in the United States today is the hierarchical relations of class, gender, race, ethnicity, and age. Implicit racial meanings reside in such phenomena as racially stratified labor markets, neighborhood segregation, the ghettoization of African Americans, and the achievement gap between white and nonwhite youth in schools. As individuals live, work, and interact socially within these webs of racial meanings, their racial identities and attitudes take shape.

Schools are noted for being primary sites for the inculcation of dominant norms and expectations that will help reproduce the dominant social-economic relations of the wider society. From the ways youth are sorted into divergent types of classes and distributed different types of knowledge and skills,[18] to the ways linguistic, curricular, and pedagogical biases reward some (usually middle- and upper-class white) students and disadvantage others,[19] schools reinforce if not constitute race, class, and gender differences and make them seem natural and self-evident. I have argued that, at Valley Groves and Clavey, racialized tracking structures, "multicultural" curricula and practices, Eurocentric curricula and pedagogies, and the racial constitution of authority figures, among other things, all contributed to reinforcing and constituting "race," racial distinctions, and racial identities.

But the meanings derived from social structures, in the wider society as in our schools, are not entirely fixed or unambiguous, and this may be particularly true of racial social structures. The social-structural milieu is an indissoluble mix of political, economic, cultural, and social structures and ideologies, and, as such, is internally incoherent and contradictory. The implicit and explicit meanings individuals draw from social structures depend on the social relations they are engaged in.[20] People's communities form the interpretive bases from which meanings are made, which means that social-discursive events and structures can be read differently in different social contexts. White youth at Clavey, because of their direct association with students of color, had very different interpretations of the discourse of "color-blindness," the politics of affirmative action, and the meanings and racial significance of the Million Man March than their counterparts at Valley Groves.

Moreover, research examining the interface between broad social structures and the meanings individuals ascribe to race tend to assume that social structures speak in one voice, even if they are variably interpreted at the local context.[21] My research has suggested otherwise, that social-discursive structures are multivocal and contradictory, and likewise influence individuals' subjectivities. More than a half-century ago, Gunnar Myrdal[22] argued that American ideals of justice, democracy, and equality were in conflict with practices of racial segregation, inequality, and prejudice. He asserted that the "American creed" needed to be extended to blacks in order to resolve that contradiction and bring about racial equality and harmony. However, although the Civil Rights movements in the 1950s and 1960s abolished legal segregation and enacted legislation geared toward increasing social and economic equality for blacks and other disadvantaged peoples, we have not entirely rid ourselves of the old regime. Racist and antiracist structures exist side by side.

Youth in schools spend their days among such contradictory racial structures. Eurocentric core curricula are practiced alongside rigorous challenges by teachers, administrators, and students to Eurocentricism; hierarchical and stratified structures, which at Clavey were clearly racially organized, exist alongside egalitarian and pluralist ideologies and "multicultural" efforts to lift up minority youth academically.[23] Multicultural programs themselves contain contradictory messages. At Clavey, multicultural practices included monthly "cultural" assemblies, a special week of activities that celebrated different traditions, and a class or two in African American literature. These activities were designed to give voice to marginalized youth and bring their experiences closer to the center, but by virtue of the fact that they took place outside of the core of school practices and curriculum, they reproduced the marginality of those same youth.

Contradictory school structures are only one part of the confusing social-discursive milieu in which young people find themselves. Since the 1960s, new conceptual terms for defining race and making sense of the conflicting institutional and social arrangements of race have proliferated from the political right to the political left.[24] Howard Winant and Michael Omi[25] argue that the Civil Rights movement resulted in the replacement of explicit racial domination with racial hegemony. Hegemony is rule by "consent,"[26] which in practice has meant open contestation between dominant and subordinate interests and, ultimately, the successful incorporation of oppositional demands and discourses into the ruling order. Winant argues that racial hegemony has engendered a number of conflicting "racial projects," that is, ideological and discursive efforts to shape the meanings of race.[27] Some of these conflicting racial projects include "color-blindness," a highly individualistic and meritocractic approach to social injustice that denies the significance of race, and cultural pluralist discourses that celebrate (and reify) racial-cultural differences and seek "different but equal" rearticulations of race relations. Other contradictions, which the young people in this project particularly struggled with, include competing values of personal responsibility and humanitarian social responsibility; normative whiteness and the pressure to define oneself culturally; universalism ("We are all human") and racialism ("There are differences . . ."); and competing claims that to see and talk about race is "racist" and to deny or dismiss it is "racist."

The white youth in this study internalized these multiple and contradictory meanings of race through their everyday experience, through their daily encounters with racist and non- or even antiracist practices, structures, discourses, and social interactions. They might choose which meanings to hang their hat on, but were hard pressed to completely free themselves of both the negative and the positive conceptions of race their daily practices instilled in them.

The Cultural

I hesitate to place this discussion of the "cultural" under the rubric of the "structural" because I do not want to suggest that the former can be reduced to the latter. However, the two are integrally interlinked, and culture does have a "structuring" influence on people's lives. "Culture" is the name we tend to give to the entire set of beliefs, habits, "expressive symbols and values in terms of which individuals define their world, express their feelings, and make their judgements."[28] Social, discursive, and ideological structures contribute to some of those beliefs and values, but not the entirety. The rest are derived from the experiences of people in their day-to-day lives, experiences that can contradict and "penetrate" the dominant logics.[29] In practice, culture mediates the relationship between individuals and society as the arena for *both* the active production and reproduction of social relations of everyday life *and* resistance to and change of the same.[30]

My research focused to a considerable degree on the cultural, the meanings youth gave to their identities, relationships, everyday rituals and behaviors and the expressive forms they adopted and practiced as a means of self-production. It was my main means for exploring "internalized" social structures and internalizing processes, as well as counter, alternative, resistant, and/or emergent meanings. Through the cultural, particularly popular consumer culture, the young people in this study articulated a sense of self in accordance with ascribed criteria for racial membership, but not always in seamless fashion. The cultural, like the structural, offered a cockeyed and confusing map with which to navigate one's racialness and make sense of race relations.

Into the Twenty-First Century

I have found that the continuous interplay, blending, and fragmenting of these identity-making currents—association, defining us-them boundaries, interlinking identities, the multiracial self, and the structural-institutional context—are what render racial identity formation, including white identity formation, a complex, ever-evolving process and racial identities multiple and contradictory. Racial identities and consciousnesses cannot be disarticulated from the variable dynamics of the social relations and structural-political-cultural milieu individuals and communities are embedded in. This means that in order to effectively examine race, racial identities, and racism, we need to pay attention to the different relational and structural currents at play in the construction of those phenomena, and be vigilant of particular relational-structural confluences at different times and places. As I have tried to show in this book, at Valley Groves, the particular configuration of these identity currents and structures was tantamount to a river when the stream bed is wide, with very little gradient, and no obstacles in its path. White students' identities sustained measurable degrees of coherency, stability, and unity among whites and within their own minds. And just as fish in the sea might have a hard time defining water, white students at Valley Groves had a difficult time defining whiteness and disarticulating it from everything else that seemed natural and normal to them.

At Clavey High, on the other hand, white students' identities were like a whitewater rapid with differently configured waves and counterintuitive dynamics. There, white youth were more conscious of the turbulent racial waters they were embedded in, and their reflections on race and their own identities took multiple forms and frequently shifted, sometimes in contradictory ways, depending on the social-relational context.

The difference between Valley Groves and Clavey in how white students reflected on and expressed their identities as whites has particular implications for scholars, educators, and activists concerned with constructively addressing white privilege and unintentional racism among white youth. First, we need to know the specific youth we are concerned about, the types of association they have with racially ascribed differences, and the interpretive framework with which they organize and make sense of those differences, and then tailor antiracist pedagogies, curricula, and intervention programs to suit them, ideally with their help.[31] Second, antiracist efforts need to contextualize the different meanings youth ascribe to their racial identities and relationships since those meanings are at the root of race-based misunderstandings, tensions, and conflicts and not racial differences in themselves.[32] Finally, the role of local popular and youth cultures as sources for defining racial differences and identities *and* for cross-racial integration and bonding should be of particular concern.[33]

Moreover, in this study, white racial identities were not only multiple across contexts but within contexts and even individual minds. They were made multiple by the ways race, gender, class, age, and other identities influence one another, and also by the quantity and quality of association with people of different racial ascriptions. Individual multiplicity was further enhanced through the inculcation and/or adoption of multiple and contradictory racial social structures, discourses, and relations. White students at Clavey appeared to be more racially multiple than those at Valley

Groves, I argued, because of their close association with a range of young people of color. Many were both "cultureless" and culturally defined (and everything in-between), and both "racist" and antiracist (and everything in-between).

Thinking in terms of racial multiplicities and both/and continua instead of either/or dualisms necessarily changes the way we think about influencing white people's political behavior. Encouraging multiplicity and bringing it to light might be a way to undermine essentialist notions of race and reveal the arbitrariness of the structures and institutions that uphold white privilege. Moreover, this perspective shifts how we define "the problem" and what our analytical focus is. Recall Melissa, who said, "There's this devil in me," upon reflecting on the negative stereotypes and prejudices she held despite personal experiences that belied those stereotypes and conscious awareness of her privileges as a white person. I believe that when Melissa revealed to me the "devil" in her, she was not hiding anything or looking to be absolved so that she could continue benefiting from white privilege guilt-free. She was asking for help in somehow controlling if not eradicating that part of her that she abhorred, a part she obtained by virtue of living in a structurally white-dominant society but that was by no means dominating her consciousness. If we reduce the whole of Melissa to that "devil" in her, then we lose the opportunity to nurture and bring to the foreground her antiracism. Our analytical foci may need to be less on what makes white people "racist" and more on what makes them actively non- or antiracist.

On a less optimistic note, while the main emphasis of this text is on the different racial consciousnesses and identities across different demographic contexts and within them, my research also revealed certain commonalities between the two sets of students, most significantly, the construction of white as norm. While normative whiteness was less ubiquitous and salient at Clavey than at Valley Groves, it was there all the same, covertly reproducing notions of white superiority. This suggests that, because of the ways white dominance is institutionally structured into the society, interracial experience alone is not sufficient to fully counter its effects. Deep and wide structural change is also required.

However, I suggest that, rather than privilege the commonalities among whites *or* the diversities among them, it behooves us to keep them in "productive tension."[34] A focus on this productive tension will, on the one hand, keep us away from tendencies toward structural determinism, such as what lies beneath claims that white dominance, by virtue of the ways it infuses many aspects of U.S. society, affects all whites equally and consistently. On the other hand, it would keep us from attributing too much volunteerism behind the contradictory feelings and beliefs whites often hold about race and their own racial identities. Such a productive tension would keep the constructed nature of race in the foreground and move us away from reproducing hard and fast, intractable racial distinctions that effectively mute cross-racial dialogue and immobilize antiracist political agency. Examples of this immobilization abounded at Clavey; Melissa was one case in point. She felt powerless to do anything that could help span a bridge across what seemed like a deep cavern of inherent differences between differently racialized peoples. Overall, a focus on the productive tension between the commonalities and differences among whites may reveal new and more effective strategies for abolishing white domination with the active participation of white people themselves.

This research begs the question of what becomes of the racial consciousness and identities of the young people at Valley Groves and Clavey as they settle into adulthood. Do they maintain similar racial politics? Do white Clavey alumni sustain complex, multiple, and contradictory racial consciousnesses and identities or do their identities unify and calcify? If my argument that the types and structure of interracial association shape white racial consciousness and identities is sound, then that should apply to adults as well as youth. That would mean that the racial consciousness and identities of Clavey alumni could become unified and rigid if they end up working and living largely among other whites, and the opposite could occur to former students of Valley Groves if they find themselves working and living among people of color. As this book was going to press, census reports for the year 2000 announced that non-Hispanic whites in California had dropped to 48.7 percent of the state population. The article accompanying this news asserted that the dip in the white population to a numerical minority had occurred sooner than expected and portended the same for the nation as a whole. This news leaves little doubt that the youth of today will be living in a nation of significant racial-ethnic diversity and in which they may not be the numerical majority. We might, then, expect tomorrow's white adults to experience forms of racial multiplicity like Clavey whites did.

Having said that, the bad news is that, as California and the country have grown increasingly diverse, racial-ethnic neighborhood and school segregation has also been increasing.[35] Meanwhile, the reign of a conservative agenda in our public schools threatens to make standardized testing and "school choice" options long-lived trends. Both reforms have the potential to further segregate youth by race and class as well-to-do white parents exercise their power to track their children into separate classes for the "gifted" or remove them from low-performing schools, which tend to have poor and working-class white students and students of color, to high-performing schools, which tend to be predominantly composed of middle-class and white students.

Moreover, an important difference between adults and young people is that the identities and world views of the former tend to become more "fixed." Fixity is a function of positioning oneself sociopolitically, and adults—as workers, parents, and full citizens—are called on more than youth to speak from a clear and uniform sociopolitical location. Still, we tend to assume that adolescence is a formative time for adult identities and world views; otherwise, it would make no difference to us what kind of schooling our children got.

With respect to what can be done to counter some of these troubling social-political trends and nurture the next generation of young people to live and work together with dignity and respect, this research is suggestive of a few endeavors. First, we must work to reverse the movement toward neighborhood and school segregation. Racial and ethnic integration remains a paramount necessity for preparing all youth for effective democratic participation in the twenty-first century. By integration, I mean more than desegregation, although the latter is a necessary condition for the former. Integration is, in the words of Dr. Martin Luther King Jr., "the positive acceptance of desegregation and the welcomed participation of Negroes into the total range of human activity. Integration is genuine intergroup, interpersonal doing. . . . Integration is the ultimate goal of our national community."[36] The focus on integration in schools goes beyond the current, almost pathological, obsession with schools as training grounds for the workforce and reintroduces the value of schooling for teaching youth personal and interpersonal respect, cooperation, tolerance, and reflection, skills that are necessary for effective, democratic participation.

The focus of desegregation has always predominantly been on black and, more recently, Latino youth, and for good reason. Initially, court-mandated desegregation was an effort to advance equal opportunity for African American youth and improve their life chances over those of their parent generation. Where desegregated schools emerged, they raised considerable debate over whether or not desegregation has helped or further harmed students of color. On one side of the debate are concerns, for example, that students of color gain greater self-confidence and self-efficacy in schools populated primarily by them; on the other side are concerns about the correlation between racial isolation and concentrated poverty.[37]

My research suggests that deeper examination of the effects on *white* students of racial isolation versus racial diversity may tip the scales toward more support for desegregation and integration. At Valley Groves, white youth were naive to the realities of black and other disadvantaged racial-ethnic groups and uncomfortable in close association with people who had different life experiences than they. As the United States moves increasingly toward greater racial and ethnic diversity, its social and economic well-being will depend on the ability of people to work together with mutual understanding and respect. White youth at Valley Groves were ill prepared for that. In contrast, white students at Clavey were very aware of the ways race mattered in the United States, even to the point of acknowledging white privilege. And Clavey whites were experienced and comfortable with working with youth from a range of different backgrounds and identities. Studies have shown that these types of knowledge that youth acquire through early experiences of diversity are perpetuated throughout their lives.[38]

Not that Clavey was perfect. In fact, while it shows the potential of desegregation, it also illustrates the dangers of desegregation without *integration*. The school population at Clavey High was resegregated within, and white students at Clavey expressed racial prejudices and intolerances that exceeded those of whites at Valley Groves. But I have argued that these sentiments were fickle, and not a product of the experience of diversity but rather how that experience was structurally and discursively *framed* for youth. That framing was, itself, contradictory—racist and antiracist school practices and discourses existed side by side at Clavey. Placing different youth together cannot, in itself, bridge racial divides when there are no provisions for making sense of the integration experience and when school life is not structured to allow all youth to meet and mutually share their cultures, experiences, and perspectives in common goals of personal and social betterment.

This leads to my second point. To achieve integration, we need to eradicate the racist structures in our schools and develop new structures and practices that neither cast difference as "other" to the white norm nor root difference in notions of cultural primordialism and essentialism. In this book I discussed two school practices in particular that were racist to the extent that they reproduced racial hierarchy and white domination: tracking and "add-on" multiculturalism. Tracking has been a controversial subject for some time, and the issues of sustaining ability grouping versus employing some form of detracking are complex and not easy to resolve.[39] Still, I am not satisfied that enough weight has been given to the effects of tracking on constituting and reinforcing racial distinctions, meanings, and stereotypes (including white supremacy), and making those things seem self-evident and merited.[40] The reproduction of racial meanings and white dominance needs to be acknowledged as something that works hand in hand with poor academic resources to create wide achievement disparities between white and nonwhite students. We need to continue to seek out viable solutions to all educational practices that segment and hierarchize students by racial, ethnic, and class location.

It is also time to redesign "multiculturalism" from the ways it tends to be most often practiced in schools into an institutional and pedagogical practice with transformative potential. In this research, two types of multiculturalism were simultaneously at play in the schools: "conservative multiculturalism" and "left-liberal multiculturalism."[41] Peter McLaren argues that conservative multiculturalism is an assimilationist model of multiculturalism, in which white is posited as an "invisible norm by which other ethnicities are judged."[42] This type of multiculturalism was at the institutional core of both Clavey and Valley Groves high schools. Left-liberal multiculturalism "tends to exoticize 'otherness' in a nativistic retreat that locates difference in a primeval past of cultural authenticity."[43] This was the concept of culture, identity, and multiculturalism that students, particularly Clavey students and teachers, tended to adopt and promote. Conservative multiculturalism marginalizes and dismisses the different experiences and cultures of students while left-liberal multiculturalism reifies them into tightly bound fictive identities that reproduce notions of inherent, durable, and unbridgeable differences between people.

A recoded and transformative multiculturalism would take as its premise that, as Stuart Hall puts it, "we all speak from a particular place, out of a particular history, out of a particular experience, a particular culture, without being contained by that position. . . ."[44] Speaking less out of essential differences and more out of all of our different histories, life experiences, languages, epistemologies, family or peer cultures and ideologies will illuminate the ways differences are socially and politically constructed (hence fluid and mutable), as well as the multiple axes of "sameness" that cross-cut axes of difference.

This new multiculturalism, which might be called "critical multiculturalism,"[45] would be inclusive of white students and possibly have the most profound impact on them. White youth would be challenged to critically examine and deconstruct what being "white" means to them. This would *not* happen through introducing European American "ethnic clubs" or cultural assemblies, but by helping white students explore the historically constituted experiences, identities, and epistemologies of whiteness and the bearings they have on the construction of white as normal, postcultural, or however else students make sense of being "white." As Henry Giroux argues, pedagogical practice such as that would give white youth "the opportunity to rethink the political nature and moral content of one's own racial identity, and the roles it plays in shaping one's relationship to those who are constituted as racially 'other'."[46] This type of critical self-reflection might help white and students of color move productively through times when different interpretive frameworks are hindering cross-understanding, such as when African American youth need to express pain and anger about slavery but white youth won't listen because they cannot see how the "past" matters. It would also offer white students a means of moving past immobilizing feelings of guilt or denial and toward reformulating their identities in ways that challenge dominant interests, cross boundaries, and help develop a range of personal connections and political coalitions.

In their article "Communities of Difference: A Critical Look at Desegregated Spaces Created for and by Youth,"[47] Michelle Fine, Lois Weis, and Linda C. Powell propose a framework for constructing "true" integration in schools that addresses the concerns I've raised here. They start with equal status contact theory, which posits that (1) "contact should occur in circumstances that place . . . groups in equal status," (2) "contact should involve one-on-one interactions among individual members of the . . . groups," (3) "members of the . . . groups should join together in an effort to achieve superordinate goals," and (4) "social norms, defined in part by relevant authorities, should favor intergroup contact."[48] Fine, Weis, and Powell assert, however, that, in practice, equal status contact theory tends to bracket differences between youth under "we are all the same," and that this threatens to reproduce white privilege and racial opposition in "the guise of neutrality or 'color-blindness'."[49] They propose that equal status contact be accompanied by three political and social conditions: (1) "a sense of community"—namely, of shared ideology, identity, and vision; (2) "a commitment to creative analysis of difference, power, and privilege"—what I have described as "critical" multiculturalism; and (3) "an enduring investment in democratic practice with youth."[50] By the latter condition, Fine, Weis, and Powell mean letting youth take active leadership roles in constructing multiracial communities, which in my mind means youth's participation in designing integrationist practices and structures in the school, creating safe spaces for intergroup dialogue, rearticulating the lines of sameness and difference, and all around improving the quality of their experiences of race in school. Institutional and pedagogical practices that employed the four values of equal status contact, community, difference, and democracy would go a long way in bringing about true integration and, possibly, a radical rearticulation of "difference" and distribution of power that could take us beyond "race" and "whiteness" altogether.

Appendix

Methods and Reflections

Consciousness and identities are not matters that lend themselves to precise measurement. I assumed from the beginning that analyzing white racial consciousness and identities would be particularly difficult, given that white identity and culture tend to be undefined and taken for granted for white people, and race is a topic that is subject to different interpretations and, often, uncomfortable sentiments. For these reasons, I chose to use predominantly qualitative methods to conduct this research. Participant observation, ethnology, and in-depth interviewing combined enables a researcher to cross-reference what people say with what they do; triangulate between what participants say, what they do or what *other* participants say the first ones do, and what existing literature suggests; dialogue with participants about beliefs, feelings, and attitudes in order to come to agreed-upon understandings; and, most importantly, gain an "insider" perspective—all of which can open understanding to the most opaque thoughts and cultural practices of a people.

Qualitative methods, like quantitative methods, are not without their pitfalls and problems. Those that most concerned me when designing and carrying out this research were (1) controlling for factors such as region or socioeconomic class that might undermine my ability to assert the role of intergroup association in shaping white identities at my research sites; (2) getting access to the preferred sites; (3) achieving an adequate "sample" of different types of students in each school; (4) approximating as closely as possible the "native point of view," which meant paying close attention to how my own racial ascription, class background, gender, and age affected how students responded to me and how I interpreted their responses; and (5) achieving resonance, that is, making findings and drawing conclusions of wide relevance.

Choosing Comparable Sites

White people's experiences, histories, and identities are very different by region, class, gender, and age. Since I was interested in examining the influence of interracial association on white identity, I sought to control for those other influences without losing sight of the fact that they are all symbiotically related. I looked for two high schools in the same region, of similar size and socioeconomic demographics, but widely different in racial-ethnic demographics, with one school being predominantly white and the other minority white. I first studied the government documents and census data of various regions to find cities and towns with the desirable demographics. When I narrowed the possibilities down, I then consumed school board statistics and information about the public schools in each area, including race-ethnic make-up of the students and staff, AFDC and free lunch recipients at the schools, test score averages, total number of students, and sizes of the campuses. Through this process, I chose the cities of "Clavey" and "Valley Groves" and determined two good candidates for the multiracial site and two for the predominantly white site in each, respectively. At that point, I started visiting the schools themselves. I contacted either the principal or the student activities director and asked permission to visit the school for a day. These visits allowed me to scan the school demographics and observe some of the students' social geographies and interracial interactions. I also spoke with the principal or other administrators about the possibility of conducting the research at their school.

In that way, I decided upon "Valley Groves" and "Clavey" high schools. Given that urban cultures and politics tend to differ from suburban cultures and politics, originally I wanted the two schools to be either both urban or both suburban, but I could not find two sites that met my other demands and were also in the same suburb or city. In the end, I came to realize that the questions of white identity in a racially isolated compared to a racially diverse context are integrally tied to the core of what defines suburbs and cities and that it was erroneous of me to imagine otherwise. Nonetheless, in the field, I took measures to counterpose potential skewing of my data to the political left (at the urban school) or the right (at the suburban school) by interviewing both liberal and conservative students at both schools and taking suburban and urban cultural differences into account in my analysis.

I was also concerned about socioeconomic differences that tend to exist between suburbs and big cities. As I argue in this book, class-based habitus and experience can intersect and/or fuse with race-based habitus and experience in ways that significantly shape racial identities. Hence, youth from working-class backgrounds will likely have different racialized identities than youth from middle-class backgrounds. Clavey was an excellent site for the research because it had a wide class range and the most significant number of middle- and upper-middle-class white students of all the schools I considered. It also had high academic achievement and the lowest number of students on AFDC or free lunch assistance compared with other high schools in the district.[1] Socioeconomically, it seemed to be the closest I could get to a "suburban" type of school within a multiracial urban area. Valley Groves appealed to me because it was one of the most "white" schools in the region and, although fairly solidly middle-class, the students came from upper-middle-class as well as working-class families. Although it did not perfectly match the class range at Clavey, it at least *had* a class range. Finally, in an effort to control for class differences on the ways youth thought about themselves as whites, I chose to focus on youth from middle-class backgrounds in both schools.

Getting Access

In order to gain access to the schools, I was required to submit a detailed research proposal to the local departments of education for their approval. I had no difficulty getting that approval from both districts. I next needed the approval of the school principals. The principal of Valley Groves welcomed my research enthusiastically, but the principal of Clavey had initial reservations. He told me that my research "scared" him because he was afraid that talking to white students about race would raise the objections of other students, especially the black students. I explained that I would not be talking only to white students, but to African American, Asian, and other students of color as well. This did not appease him, so I asked for a "probationary" period of two weeks, after which, if he still had concerns about my presence on campus, I would respect his wishes to go elsewhere. In that two-week period I became productively involved in some student committees while also sitting in on classrooms and hanging around the campus with students. When I next checked in with the principal, he was sufficiently convinced that I would not cause any trouble, and he granted me long-term access to the school.

Sampling

I did not randomly sample for interview participants because I had very specific desires regarding to whom I wanted to speak: liberals and conservatives; whites, blacks, Asians, and Latinos; punks, hippies, homies, alternatives, rappers and such; high achievers and low achievers; girls and boys; middle class and working class. So I sought out interviewees largely through a directed "snowball" method. I started out by going to classrooms and club meetings and asking for volunteers. After speaking with some students from the lists I generated, I asked for recommendations of whom else to talk to. In order not to find myself circulating within one or two crowds or speaking only with the most willing students, I directly approached students I observed in classrooms, in school workshops, or in their cliques on campus and asked them if they would be willing to be interviewed. For the most hard-to-find, marginalized, or "counterculture" students, this was my most successful method. At the same time, it had its weaknesses. I am a relatively shy person and that, combined with, in some cases, oversensitivity to racial and age difference (which I will elaborate on shortly), caused me at times to be too self-conscious to approach individuals in groups that kept closely to themselves. At Valley Groves, those groups were the hicks, homies, and druggies (although I did manage to speak informally with several of the latter), and the nonmainstream Latino and Filipino students. At Clavey, they were the Latino groups generally and the "newly arrived" Asians. Although I do not feel that the absence in this book of students from these groups greatly compromises the analyses I have made, I do believe that their participation would have added nuances, enriched, and, likely, strengthened my overall argument. That is particularly true with respect to my analysis of the implicit ways socioeconomic class influenced the ways certain students—hicks, homies, and druggies especially—were categorized and stereotyped.

Overall, I formally interviewed over sixty students at Valley Groves and Clavey high schools. They included, at Valley Groves, fourteen white youth, one Filipino female, and a group interview with ten African American students, and, at Clavey, twenty-two white youth, ten African American youth, two Chinese American, one Filipino, and two Latino youth. A little over half of my interviewees were female. I also sought to interview youth with different political orientations and subcultural affiliations to be able to compare those with similar politics and consumption practices but in different schools.

Most of the white students I interviewed were middle class but a few were working class. I judged socioeconomic class by, on the one hand, considering parent occupation and quality of life, such as the neighborhood the student lived in, whether or not he or she lived with a single parent or both, and how many siblings the student had. On the other hand, I took into consideration the "class" the student seemed most to identify with. Julie Bettie[2] makes the useful distinction between "performativity," the unconscious habitus one might adopt from the family culture, and "performance," the conscious or semiconscious choices youth make to act in certain ways to enhance their mobility or gain acceptance from their closest peers. For example, one of the participants from Clavey lived in an apartment in a low-income part of town with her mother, who was a nurse, and older brother. Although her mother's salary and education might rank her "middle-class," as a single mother of two children, the lifestyle she was able to provide for her children was modest and in keeping with the styles of the working-class people in the neighborhood. Moreover, this student hung out primarily with working-class friends and had low ambitions for herself educationally and careerwise; her presentation of self was decidedly "working class."

Authenticity

A goal throughout my research was to capture, as best as possible, the "real thing" at Valley Groves and Clavey, to satisfactorily document students' everyday experiences and practices at school, and interpret the meanings they gave to those experiences and practices. My motivation for doing so was, deep-down, more guided by the desire to respect and do justice to the young people in this study than it was to win the approval of my peers for having conducted "good science," although I certainly recognize the necessity of the latter. And, while holding this objective dearly, I also knew (and continue to respect) that it is impossible to extricate oneself from one's findings and analysis. In short, I make no claim to have documented here the "authentic" native point of view.

That said, I did *try* to grasp that view, and to do so, stayed alert to three main concerns: (1) interpreting and representing the voices and practices of the students respectfully and with as much of their own input as possible; (2) being aware of when students might be saying something solely for my approval regardless of their gut feelings; (3) being mindful of the ways my race, class, gender, and age influenced the ways students responded to me and how I interpreted them.

To address the first two of those concerns, I spent extensive time in the field and took every opportunity to talk to youth informally as well as formally. I began the research in the spring semester of 1994, spending three to four days at Clavey while I considered a suitable comparable site. To get acquainted with the place and meet youth, I spent most of my time observing an advanced drama class and the leadership class. I also served on the Principal's Advisory Committee on Race and Ethnic Diversity as adult support for the efforts of the students on the committee. Initially I intended to spend the fall semester of 1994 at Clavey as well, then spend the spring semester of 1995 at Valley Groves and end the research there. However, quite quickly I realized that would not be enough time to capture the complexities of student life in the schools. I ended up focusing the full 1994–95 school year on Clavey, attending it three to four days a week and visiting Valley Groves at least once a week, and the next academic year, reversing the focus and spending most days at Valley Groves and visiting Clavey once a week or so.

In both schools, I began making relationships with students by asking them if I could shadow them through a week of their courses and after-school activities. I did this with four or five students, each of whom was in a different academic track or academy. After that, I would visit students in just one or two of their classes before interviewing them. Classroom observations allowed me to get a sense of the youth's formal social world, of intergroup dynamics in classrooms, of different teacher styles for different types and tracks of students, and the kinds of material and subject matters taught to different types and tracks of students.

When not in classrooms, I hung out with youth at various sites around campus during the break and lunch hours. I frequently stayed after school for sports events, theater rehearsals, and other extracurricular activities. I also chaperoned the Junior and Senior Balls for two years. These observations gave me a fuller sense of youth's informal activities and social worlds. I could observe the performances of identities as well as interactive processes of identity formation. And my awareness of youth's informal practices allowed me to explore the meanings of those practices and rituals in my formal and informal discussions with students.

To bring me closer into the students' social and cultural allegiances, on weekends I explored some of the cultural activities youth were interested in. I listened to the local rap, alternative, and heavy metal radio stations; bought the latest hits on commercial and independent labels; studied music students had given to me; watched MTV; read music magazines and "fanzines"; went to punk and alternative rock clubs; and attended a rave that had been organized by some students I knew.

Formal interviews took place on campus, in coffee shops, and in students' homes and generally lasted from two to four hours. They were all tape-recorded, transcribed, and coded. In the interviews, I explored youth's experiences at school, their experiences of racial difference, how they thought of themselves racially, how they thought of racial-ethnic others, their cultural interests and other significant identities, and what types of meanings they gave to their interests and identities. Interviews and informal discussions were also a time for me to check out my interpretations of school practices, youth cultures, and other events around campus.

Besides simply spending a lot of time in the field and interviewing a wide range of students, winning the *trust* of youth was what I knew I needed most in order to get inside their lives. To an extent, being on campus everyday was enough to make students trust me. In the fall of 1995, after my first year and a half in the field at Clavey High School, I ran into Melissa, Linda, and Ann. We stopped to talk, and after catching up with one another, the conversation turned to Clavey. They said that their experience at Clavey was so unique that they felt that no one, not their parents, nor their siblings, nor friends outside of the school, could ever understand. Ann said, "Only we understand—that's why we are so close—and *you*, because you've been there. And this book you are writing is going to be so great because no one, *no one* has spent the time you spent there and talked to the kids you talked to."

However, simply being on campus was not really sufficient for winning students' trust: how I presented myself was key. Although I looked somewhat younger than my age (thirty-eight when the research began), I made concerted efforts to minimize the effects of age difference on how students related to me. I did not associate with other adults on campus. I dressed in casual attire that I was comfortable in, which happened to be similar to the attires students were comfortable in: blue jeans, sandals or athletic shoes, t-shirt or sweatshirt, no jewelry except four tiny hoop earrings—one in one ear, three in the other. I had students call me by my first name, and I did not talk down to them, judge them, or otherwise present myself as an authority figure. To the contrary, I saw the *students* as the authorities, and they seemed to appreciate that regard. Those efforts, on top of having developed some popular-cultural frames of reference with the students, contributed to my developing some very close relationships with several of the students and fairly wide access to different peer groups and cliques on campus. Having stood in the middle of secret hide-outs, food fights, fist fights, profane tongue lashings, and over-the-top fits of goofiness, I can say that in most cases I seemed to have little impact on students' behaviors.

This was particularly true at Clavey, where students, of all racial-ethnic ascriptions, were particularly open to me and welcoming of my participation in their school lives. I made close friends with several of the youth and have retained a few of those to this day. Moreover, my presence on campus at Clavey seemed so inconsequential to students, whether it be when I was in classrooms or sitting among them in the yard, that at times I felt invisible. This had its merits in that I sensed that youth were not significantly altering their actions or censoring their speech because of me. It also posed problems since, as I've noted, I am a rather shy person and could not always step easily out of my invisibility to engage with youth.

Winning the trust and ease of Valley Groves students was not as easy as at Clavey. Although I felt that students were being honest and candid with me in our interviews, I did not develop any close connections with particular students at Valley Groves, despite many efforts. I was also very visible. I seemed to mystify youth since I was clearly too old to be a student, but I did not carry myself like a teacher or administrator. My backpack seemed to bother them the most—I heard youth talking behind my back about how I was obviously trying to look like a student by wearing a backpack. Oddly, off campus, at the local coffee shop where many of the skaters and druggies hung out, students were more open to me and inviting.

Overall, these differences in the ways students perceived and trusted me resulted in an imbalance that I believe is evident in this book. I had more to say about Clavey because I got more "inside" students' lives there. I also enjoyed being at Clavey more, since I had friends there, so spent more time there. I do not feel, however, that I missed out on or misread racial meanings at Valley Groves. Similar studies of racial formation in suburban schools have given me that confidence.[3] My explanation for the differences in the ways youth responded to me is, first, that suburban culture is more protectionist and isolationist. Youth may have felt more suspicious of "outsiders." Second, as a student in one of my undergraduate classes suggested to me, it may have been that the Clavey students, attending an impersonal and disciplinary urban school, were more starved for adult attention around school than the white students at Valley Groves, who as a matter of course received a lot of individual attention from teachers and administrators. Finally, I came to believe that Valley Groves students were less comfortable with diversity in all of its forms. Hence, relating to an older person felt alien and awkward to them, whereas Clavey youth had learned how to cross boundaries of age, race, class, and such to meet the individuals behind the categories.

Of course, winning students' trust or not did not ensure that they would tell the "truth" or not say things they thought I would like to hear. One problem with getting to know students so well is they came to know me well, too, and may have sought my approval by saying things they knew would please me. I cannot say without a doubt that this did not happen or that I was always aware of it when it did. I can only say that more often than not I found myself surprised by how candid and unguarded the young people were, and how unflinchingly they would say things that were, in fact, shocking or disturbing to me. They seemed far more interested in being seen and heard for who they were than in pleasing me. Usually, after an interview, students would thank me—thank *me*—for giving them an opportunity to speak their mind.

I also took certain measures to not influence students' responses based on their expectations of what I wanted to hear. I conducted most of my interviews when I first met students, before they knew me very well. I presented myself as a U.C. Berkeley graduate student doing a comparative research project on youth cultures, identities, and race relations in high schools. I usually did not reveal that I was specifically interested in *white* youth and identity until some point toward the end of the interview, if at all. If youth probed into my research interests, however, I would not lie, but I would tell them that I did not want to reveal anything before we had our interview for fear of influencing their responses. They understood this.

With respect to the ways my own race, class, gender, age or other aspects of my social location or personality influenced students' responses, it seemed that sometimes they worked on my behalf and sometimes not. I have already touched on the issue of my age difference and the impact that seemed to have on Clavey and Valley Groves students. My racial ascription may have also played into why Clavey whites were more comfortable with my age than Valley Groves whites. At Clavey, where racial distinctions were so significant, being white seemed to be an asset with white students. I got this sense because different students spoke about a kind of instant solidarity they felt with other whites, even strangers. It seemed also that racial solidarity was part of what made age differences between me and white students less significant to them. With students of color at Clavey I am less certain of the influence of my racial ascription. For the most part, they seemed very candid with me, including speaking critically about white racial dominance and saying unflattering things about white people. However, race *did* limit my ability to hang out informally with groups of students of color in the ways I did with groups of white kids, thus limiting my understanding of the former's internal dynamics.

At Valley Groves, my whiteness had its pluses and minuses. For white students, my racial appearance was familiar and safe but also made my differences stand out more. White students there drew sharper distinctions between different kinds of whites than at Clavey, hence, being an "adult" white drew greater suspicion, I believe. This limited my access to students' inner circles, as I discussed above. With respect to students of color at Valley Groves, the limitation of my racial ascription was more self-imposed than imposed by the young people. The students of color who were not integrated into the mainstream of the school seemed protected and withdrawn. (This may have been completely in my white imagination, I don't know.) I was hesitant to invade their safe spaces. Hence, I did not speak to as many students of color at Valley Groves as I would have liked and chose to do a group interview with the Black Student Union instead of try and approach African American youth individually.

Gender had the most obvious effect, to me, on my research processes and relationships with students. Here the effect was caused both by how girls responded to me and how I responded to them. Although it was unintentional on my part, I found myself more among girls, of all racial and ethnic ascriptions, than among boys. Girls, at Clavey especially, seemed quite comfortable with me. They did not mind my hanging out with them individually or in groups, whereas most boys, with a few significant exceptions, opted out of my sticking to them during their social time. I, too, felt more comfortable among girls. When we got together we would talk about things "girls" talk about—relationships, sex, hair, bodies—and the presumed comradery was like a safe haven for me when I felt overwhelmed by my experiences in the field. Whereas I assumed gender difference might tweak students' responses to me in the interview situation, I was not prepared for this "presumed comradery," which struck me most by the degree to which it transcended differences in age, class, and race. With respect to the research, the result was that I spoke with more girls than boys and on deeper levels—a fact that I believe is evident in the book. However, at Clavey especially, I did become close with a few boys, one of whom was a critical "informant" for me.

My experiences in this and other ethnographic research I have conducted have convinced me of the value of working with a team of ethnographic researchers that is diversified by race, class, gender, *and* age, especially when the research focus includes youth. Although I don't think that the race, class, gender, and age of the researcher limit research findings in such a way as to render them insignificant or false, I do believe that they can limit the depth and breadth of the findings and analysis.

A final comment on the subject of the "native point of view": While doing this research, I assumed that the young participants were the experts. I took their words at face value, and when I made analytical interpretations of their practices, I ran them by the participants to see what they thought. If some agreed and others disagreed, I either went with my original thoughts, usually modified, or expressed alternative interpretations. If everyone I spoke with disagreed, then I dropped whatever interpretation I had in mind. I believe that this kind of dialogical engagement with the "subjects" of research is one of the main strengths of qualitative research, when applied. I also believe it is of highest importance when working with young people. Too often social science ignores, discounts, or dismisses young people, assuming that they lack the wisdom or maturity to be offered an equal voice with adults. I disagree and have taken it on as one of my responsibilities as a researcher to empower the voices of youth. I have come to believe, since completing this research, that to achieve that empowerment, young people must be equal-status collaborators in research concerning them. Since I came to this realization late, my best effort at respecting students' voices in this book was to print long, contextualized passages from my interviews with them. It was my hope that this would allow readers to best judge if I interpreted the students' narratives well or missed something.

Resonance

In my mind, the effort to grasp the "native point of view" is closely tied to the issue of resonance. I have assumed that the closer I approximate a "good" documentation and interpretation of school life and students' experiences and identities, the greater the chance that this work will resonate with young people and adults who have had similar experiences in high school. I have gotten some confirmation of resonance from undergraduate students in classes I've taught or guest-lectured. Several recent studies I've already mentioned have made observations and analyses similar to mine, and I find those comforting. From where I stand now, writing this book in preparation for publication, I can only say that the rest remains to be seen!

Notes

Introduction

1 As a participant observer, I attended class with students, hung out with them during lunch and school breaks, worked with them on school committees or in after-school activities, attended school games, rallies, and other events, and chaperoned the Junior Prom and Senior Balls of each school. For a more in-depth discussion of my methods and my reflections on my role and influence as a researcher among youth, see the appendix.

2 I use the term *racial-ethnic* with some hesitation. At their core, *race* and *ethnicity* are two very different concepts. Racial groups tend to be marked by phenotypical characteristics that locate them within a power hierarchy that privileges "white" people. Ethnic groups tend to be bound by a sense of shared culture, religion, or history, and will not necessarily be in power relationships with other ethnic groups. Moreover, people of different ethnicities can be categorized as one race. Nonetheless, in common usage and popular common sense, the two concepts have become quite fused. As well, through shared experiences of oppression, culturally heterogeneous peoples can develop common cultures and a sense of peoplehood. I believe this can be said of African Americans in the United States. In his article "New Ethnicities" (in *Stuart Hall: Critical Dialogues in Cultural Studies*, ed. Morley and Chen [London: Routledge, 1996], 441–59), Stuart Hall makes a brilliant argument for decoupling ethnicity from race and recoding ethnicity to take on broader meanings that might take us beyond "race." For the time being, I have simply adopted the term "racial-ethnic." For a closer examination of this argument, see Philomena Essed, *Diversity: Gender, Color, and Culture* (Amherst: University of Massachusetts Press, 1996).

3 Barrie Thorne's work, *Gender Play* (New Brunswick: Rutgers University Press, 1993), argues this well and from early on influenced the analytical and methodological foci of my research. See also Gloria Anzaldúa, *Borderlands / La Frontera: The New Mestiza* (San Francisco: Spinsters / Aunt Lute Book Company, 1987); Paul Gilroy, *"There Ain't No Black in the Union Jack": The Cultural Politics of Race and Nation* (Chicago: University of Chicago Press,

1991); Steven Gregory, *Black Corona: Race and the Politics of Place in an Urban Community* (Princeton: Princeton University Press, 1998); Stuart Hall, "Ethnicity: Identity and Difference," *Radical America* 23, no. 4 (1991): 9–20; John Hartigan Jr., *Racial Situations: Class Predicaments of Whiteness in Detroit* (Princeton: Princeton University Press, 1999); bell hooks, *Black Looks: Race and Representation* (Boston: South End Press, 1992); bell hooks, *Yearning: Race, Gender, and Cultural Politics* (Boston: South End Press, 1990); Renato Rosaldo, *Culture and Truth: The Remaking of Social Analysis* (Boston: Beacon Press, 1989); Jonathan Rutherford, *Identity: Community, Culture, Difference* (London: Lawrence and Wishart, 1990); Howard Winant, *Racial Conditions: Politics, Theory, Comparisons* (Minneapolis: University of Minnesota Press, 1994).

4 Tomas Almaguer, *Racial Fault Lines: The Historical Origins of White Supremacy in California* (Berkeley: University of California Press, 1994); George Fredrickson, *White Supremacy: A Comparative Study in American and South African History* (Oxford: Oxford University Press, 1981); David Theo Goldberg, *Racist Culture: Philosophy and the Politics of Meaning* (Cambridge, Mass.: Blackwell, 1993); Michael Omi and Howard Winant, *Racial Formation in the United States: From the 1960s to the 1980s* (New York: Routledge, 1986); Alexander Saxton, *The Rise and Fall of the White Republic* (New York: Verso, 1990); William J. Wilson, *The Declining Significance of Race: Blacks and Changing American Institutions* (Chicago: University of Chicago Press, 1980); Winant, *Racial Conditions*.

5 Hartigan Jr., *Racial Situations*; Lorraine Delia Kenny, "Doing My Homework: The Autoethnography of a White Teenage Girl," in *Racing Research, Researching Race: Methodological Dilemmas in Critical Race Studies*, ed. France Winddance Twine and Jonathan Warren (New York: New York University Press, 2000), 111–33; Howard Pinderhughes, *Race in the Hood: Conflict and Violence Among Urban Youth* (Minneapolis: University of Minnesota Press, 1997); France Winddance Twine, "Brown-Skinned White Girls: Class, Culture, and the Construction of White Identity in Suburban Communities," in *Displacing Whiteness: Essays in Social and Cultural Criticism*, ed. Ruth Frankenberg (Durham: Duke University Press, 1997), 214–43.

6 For whiteness in literature, art, and popular culture, see Richard Delgado and Jean Stefancic, ed., *Critical White Studies: Looking Behind the Mirror* (Philadelphia: Temple University Press, 1997); Richard Dyer, *White* (New York: Routledge, 1997); Mike Hill, ed., *Whiteness: A Critical Reader* (New York: New York University Press, 1997); hooks, *Black Looks*; Toni Morrison, *Playing in the Dark: Whiteness in the Literary Imagination* (New York: Random House, 1993); Fred Pfeil, *White Guys: Studies in Postmodern Domi-*

nation and Difference (New York: Verso, 1995). For whiteness in work and educational structures, see Philomena Essed, *Diversity*; Michelle Fine et al., eds., *Off White: Readings on Race, Power, and Society* (New York: Routledge, 1997). For issues concerning whiteness and pedagogy, see Henry Giroux, "Rewriting the Discourse of Racial Identity: Towards a Pedagogy and Politics of Whiteness," *Harvard Educational Review* 67, no. 2 (1997): 285–320; Joe L. Kincheloe et al., eds., *White Reign: Deploying Whiteness in America* (New York: St. Martin's Press, 1998); Cameron McCarthy and Warren Crichlow, eds., *Race, Identity, and Representation in Education* (New York: Routledge, 1993).

There are some very interesting works on law, property rights, and whiteness. See Ian F. Haney Lopez, *White by Law: The Legal Construction of Race* (New York: New York University Press, 1996); Cheryl Harris, "Whiteness as Property," *Harvard Law Review* 106 (1993): 1707–91; George Lipsitz, "The Possessive Investment in Whiteness: Racialized Social Democracy and the 'White' Problem in American Studies," *American Quarterly* 47, no. 3 (1995): 369–87.

For interrogations into the values and identities of whites in the historical past, see Theodore Allen, *The Invention of the White Race*, vol. 1, *Racial Oppression and Social Control* (London: Verso, 1994); Almaguer, *Racial Fault Lines*; Goldberg, *Racist Culture*; Noel Ignatiev, *How the Irish Became White* (New York: Routledge, 1995); Matthew Frye Jacobson, *Whiteness of a Different Color: European Immigrants and the Alchemy of Race* (Cambridge: Harvard University Press, 1998); Eric Lott, *Love and Theft: Blackface Minstrelsy and the American Working Class* (New York: Oxford University Press, 1993); David Roediger, *Wages of Whiteness: Race and the Making of the American Working Class* (New York: Verso, 1991); David Roediger, *Towards the Abolition of Whiteness* (New York: Verso, 1994); Alexander Saxton, *The Rise and Fall of the White Republic* (New York: Verso, 1990); Vron Ware, *Beyond the Pale: White Women, Racism, and History* (New York: Verso, 1992).

For investigations of white identities in the historical present, see Ruth Frankenberg, *White Women, Race Matters: The Social Construction of Whiteness* (Minneapolis: University of Minnesota Press, 1993); Ruth Frankenberg, ed., *Displacing Whiteness: Essays in Social and Cultural Criticism* (Durham: Duke University Press, 1997); Charles A. Gallagher, "White Reconstruction in the University," *Socialist Review* 24, no. 1 & 2 (1995): 165–87; Charles A. Gallagher, "White Racial Formation: Into the Twenty-First Century," in *Critical White Studies: Looking Behind the Mirror*, ed. Richard Delgado and Jean Stefancic (Philadelphia: Temple University Press, 1997), 6–11; John Hartigan Jr., "Locating White Detroit," in *Displacing*

Whiteness: Essays in Social and Cultural Criticism, ed. Ruth Frankenberg (Durham: Duke University Press, 1997), 180–213; Hartigan Jr., *Racial Situations*; Lorraine Delia Kenny, *Daughters of Suburbia: Growing Up White, Middle Class, and Female* (New Brunswick: Rutgers University Press, 2000); Peggy McIntosh, "White Privilege: Unpacking the Invisible Knapsack," *Peace and Freedom*, July/August 1989: 10–12; Pamela Perry, "White Means Never Having to Say You're Ethnic: White Youth and the Construction of 'Cultureless' Identities," *Journal of Contemporary Ethnography* 30, no.1 (2001): 56–91; Mab Segrest, *Memoirs of a Race Traitor* (Boston: South End Press, 1994); David Wellman, *Portraits of White Racism* (Cambridge: Cambridge University Press, 1977); Matt Wray and Annalee Newitz, eds., *White Trash: Race and Class in America* (New York: Routledge, 1997).

7   Hartigan Jr., *Racial Situations*.

8   See, for example, Lawrence Bobo et al., "Laissez-Faire Racism: The Crystalization of a 'Kinder, Gentler' Anti-Black Ideology," in *Racial Attitudes in the 1990s: Continuity and Change*, ed. Steven A. Tuch and Jack K. Martin (Westport: Praeger, 1997), 15–42; Howard Schuman et al., *Racial Attitudes in America: Trends and Interpretations* (Cambridge: Harvard University Press, 1997); David R. Williams et al., "Traditional and Contemporary Prejudice and Urban Whites' Support for Affirmative Action and Government Help," *Social Problems* 46, no. 4 (1999): 548–71.

9   See Leslie G. Roman, "White Is a Color! White Defensiveness, Postmodernism, and Anti-Racist Pedagogy," in *Race, Identity, and Representation in Education*, ed. Cameron McCarthy and Warren Crichlow (New York: Routledge, 1993). Roman points out that this is an imperfect term because it implies that white people are not themselves a "race," and in so doing it reproduces the invisible power of whiteness. For the time being, however, I prefer it to "minorities," though I use that term occasionally, and "subordinated people" or "nonwhites" unless I want to convey the oppressive social locations of African Americans, Latinos, Asian Americans, and Native Americans in the United States.

10   Dalton Conley, *Being Black, Living in the Red: Race, Wealth, and Social Policy in America* (Berkeley: University of California Press, 1999).

11   Kwame Anthony Appiah, "Race, Culture, Identity: Misunderstood Connections" (unpublished manuscript, 2000); William E. Cross, *Shades of Black: Diversity in African-American Identity* (Philadelphia: Temple University Press, 1991); Essed, *Diversity*; Gilroy, *"There Ain't No Black in the Union Jack"*; Hall, "New Ethnicities" and "Ethnicity"; hooks, *Black Looks*.

12   Alastair Bonnett, *Radicalism, Anti-Racism, and Representation* (London: Routledge, 1993).

13 In *Shades of Black*, Cross discusses this in terms of the degree of salience race, as a reference-group orientation, has over other reference-group orientations that are significant to the individual, such as religion, sexual preference, or class status.

14 Ann Phoenix helped me see this distinction. See Ann Phoenix, " 'I'm White! So What?' The Construction of Whiteness for Young Londoners," in *Off White: Readings on Race and Power in Society*, ed. Michelle Fine, Linda C. Powell, Lois Weis, and L. Mun Wong (New York: Routledge, 1997), 187–97.

15 Pamela Perry, "The Politics of Identity: Community and Ethnicity in a Pro-Sandinista Enclave on Nicaragua's Atlantic Coast," *Berkeley Journal of Sociology* 36 (1991): 115–36.

16 Richard Dyer, "White," *Screen* 29, no. 4 (1988): 44–64; Frankenberg, *White Women, Race Matters*; Roman, "White Is a Color!"

17 Russell J. Dalton and Manfred Kuechler, eds., *Challenging the Political Order: New Social Movements in Western Democracies* (New York: Oxford University Press, 1990); Omi and Winant, *Racial Formation in the United States*.

18 Examples include Bob Blauner, *Black Lives, White Lives: Three Decades of Race Relations in America* (Berkeley: University of California Press, 1989); Andrew Hacker, *Two Nations: Black and White, Separate, Hostile, Unequal* (New York: Ballantine Books, 1992); Harry Kitano and R. Daniels, *American Racism: Exploration of the Nature of Prejudice* (Engelwood Cliffs: Prentice-Hall, 1970); Robert Miles, *Racism* (New York: Routledge, 1989); Paul M. Sniderman and Thomas Leonard Piazza, *The Scar of Race* (Cambridge: Belknap Press of Harvard University Press, 1993); Studs Terkel, *Race: How Blacks and Whites Think and Feel About the American Obsession* (New York: New Press, 1992); Steven A. Tuch and Jack K. Martin, eds., *Racial Attitudes in the 1990s: Continuity and Change* (Westport: Praeger, 1997).

19 Omi and Winant, *Racial Formation in the United States*, 116.

20 Gallagher, "White Reconstruction" and "White Racial Formation"; Jeffrey Prager, "American Political Culture and the Shifting Meaning of Race," *Ethnic and Racial Studies* 10, no. 1 (1987): 62–81; Wellman, *Portraits of White Racism*; Winant, *Racial Conditions*; Howard Winant, "Behind Blue Eyes: Whiteness and Contemporary U.S. Racial Politics," in *Off White: Readings on Race, Power, and Society*, ed. Michelle Fine et al. (New York: Routledge, 1997), 40–53.

21 Nadine Dolby, "Youth and the Global Popular: The Politics and Practices of Race in South Africa," *European Journal of Cultural Studies* 2 (1999): 291–310, and "The Shifting Ground of Race: The Role of Taste in Youth's Production of Identities," *Race, Ethnicity, and Education* 3, no. 1 (2000): 7–

23; Frankenberg, *White Women, Race Matters*; Frankenberg, *Displacing Whiteness*; John Hartigan Jr., "Establishing the Fact of Whiteness," *American Anthropologist* 99, no. 3 (1997): 495–505; Hartigan Jr., *Racial Situations.*

22 Jean-Claude Deschamps and Thierry Devos, "Regarding the Relationship Between Social Identity and Personal Identity," in *Social Identity: International Perspectives*, ed. Stephen Worchel et al. (London: Sage, 1998), 1–12; Henri Tajfel, "Cognitive Aspects of Prejudice," *Journal of Social Issues* 25, no. 4 (1969): 79–97; Henri Tajfel and John C. Turner, *The Social Identity Theory of Intergroup Behavior* (Monterey: Brooks-Cole, 1986).

23 Herbert Blumer, "Race Prejudice as a Sense of Group Position," *Pacific Sociological Review* 1, no. 1 (1958): 3–7; Herbert Blumer and Troy Duster, "Theories of Race and Social Action," in *Sociological Theories: Race and Colonialism* (Paris: UNESCO, 1980), 211–38; Hall, "Ethnicity" and "New Ethnicities."

24 Hall and du Gay, "Introduction."

25 Hall and du Gay, "Introduction," 5.

26 Erik H. Erikson, *Identity: Youth and Crisis* (New York: Norton, 1968).

27 Marcel Danesi, *Cool: The Signs and Meanings of Adolescence* (Toronto: University of Toronto Press, 1994); Simon Frith, *Sound Effects: Youth, Leisure, and the Politics of Rock 'n' Roll* (New York: Pantheon, 1981); Stuart Hall and Tony Jefferson, eds., *Resistance Through Rituals: Youth Subcultures in Post-War Britain* (London: Routledge, 1996); Grace Palladino, *Teenagers: An American History* (New York: Basic Books, 1996).

28 For different discussions about the social and cultural reproduction of socioeconomic class in education, including studies that challenge the determinism of earlier works, see Basil B. Bernstein, *Class, Codes, and Control*, vol. 3, *Towards a Theory of Educational Transmissions* (London: Routledge and Kegan Paul, 1971); Pierre Bourdieu and J. C. Passeron, *Reproduction in Education, Society, and Culture* (Beverly Hills: Sage, 1977); Samuel Bowles and Herbert Gintis, *Schooling in Capitalist America: Educational Reform and the Contradictions of Economic Life* (New York: Basic Books, 1976); Penelope Eckert, *Jocks and Burnouts: Social Categories and Identity in High School* (New York: Teachers College Press, 1989); Douglas E. Foley, *Learning Capitalist Culture: Deep in the Heart of Tejas* (Philadelphia: University of Pennsylvania Press, 1990); Shirley Brice Heath, *Ways with Words: Language, Life, and Work in Communities and Classrooms* (Cambridge: Cambridge University Press, 1983); Annette Lareau, "Social Class Differences in Family-School Relationships: The Importance of Cultural Capital," *Sociology of Education* 60 (April 1987): 73–85; Jay MacLeod, *Ain't No Makin' It* (Boulder: Westview Press, 1987); Jeannie Oakes, *Keeping Track: How Schools Structure Inequality*

(New Haven: Yale University Press, 1985); Paul Willis, *Learning to Labor: How Working-Class Kids Get Working-Class Jobs* (New York: Columbia University Press, 1977).

For gender, see American Association of University Women, *How Schools Shortchange Girls: The A.A.U.W. Report: Action Guide* (Washington, D.C.: American Association of University Women Educational Foundation, 1992); Donna Eder, *School Talk: Gender and Adolescent Culture* (New Brunswick: Rutgers University Press, 1995); Thorne, *Gender Play*.

For a range of research on the reproduction of racial and ethnic identities and inequalities, see Lisa A. Delpit, "The Silenced Dialogue: Power and Pedagogy in Educating Other People's Children," *Harvard Educational Review* 58, no. 3 (1988): 280–98; Fine et al, *Off White*; Signithia Fordham, *Blacked Out: Dilemmas of Race, Identity, and Success at Capital High* (Chicago: University of Chicago Press, 1996); McCarthy and Crichlow, *Race, Identity and Representation*; John Ogbu, "Minority Status and Schooling in Plural Societies," *Comparative Educational Review* 17, no. 2 (1983): 168–90; John Ogbu, "Cultural Discontinuities in Schooling," *Anthropology and Education Quarterly* 13, no. 4 (1982): 290–307; Laurie Olsen, *Made in America: Immigrant Students in Our Public Schools* (New York: New Press, 1997); Angela Valenzuela, *Subtractive Schooling: U.S.-Mexican Youth and the Politics of Caring* (Albany: State University of New York Press, 1999).

Other relevant works include Michael W. Apple, *Education and Power* (New York: Routledge, 1995); Michael W. Apple, *Ideology and Curriculum*, 2d ed. (New York: Routledge, 1990); Henry A. Giroux and Peter McLaren, *Critical Pedagogy, the State, and Cultural Struggle* (Albany: SUNY Press, 1989).

29 Bourdieu and Passeron, *Reproduction in Education, Society and Culture*; Heath, *Ways With Words*; Valenzuela, *Subtractive Schooling*.

30 AAUW, "How Schools Shortchange Girls"; MacLeod, *Ain't No Makin' It*; Claude M. Steele and Joshua Aronson, "Stereotype Threat and the Test Performance of Academically Successful African Americans," in *The Black-White Test Score Gap*, ed. Christopher Jencks and Meredith Phillips (Washington, D.C.: Brookings Institution Press, 1998), 401–27.

31 Fordham, *Blacked Out*; Ogbu, "Minority Status and Schooling in Plural Societies"; Ogbu, "Cultural Discontinuities in Schooling"; Willis, *Learning to Labor*.

32 Reuben Baron et al., "Social Class, Race, and Teacher Expectations," in *Teacher Expectancies*, ed. Jerome B. Dusek (Hillsdale, N.J.: Erlbaum, 1985); Donna Eder, "Ability Grouping as a Self-Fulfilling Prophecy: A Micro-Analysis of Teacher-Student Interaction," *Sociology of Education* 54, no. 3

(1981): 151–62; Ronald F. Ferguson, "Teachers' Perceptions and Expectations and the Black-White Test Score Gap," in *The Black-White Test Score Gap*, ed. Christopher Jencks and Meredith Phillips (Washington, D.C.: Brookings Institutute Press, 1998), 318–74; Sara Lawrence Lightfoot, *Worlds Apart: Relationships Between Families and Schools* (New York: Basic Books, 1978); Ray C. Rist, "Student Social Class and Teacher Expectations: The Self-Fulfilling Prophecy in Ghetto Education," *Harvard Educational Review* 40, no. 3 (1970): 411–51; Steele and Aronson, "Stereotype Threat."

33 Joyce Canaan, "A Comparative Analysis of American Suburban Middle Class, Middle School, and High School Teenage Cliques," in *Interpretive Ethnography of Education: At Home and Abroad*, ed. George Spindler and Louise Spindler (Hillsdale, N.J.: Erlbaum, 1987), 385–406; Eckert, *Jocks and Burnouts*; Thorne, *Gender Play*.

34 Ann Locke Davidson, *Making and Molding Identity in Schools: Student Narratives on Race, Gender, and Academic Engagement* (Albany: SUNY Press, 1996); Perry, "White Means Never Having to Say You're Ethnic."

35 Historical data on "Valley Groves" was drawn from written and oral histories procured from the local historical society and newspaper clippings. Citing exact references would betray a pledge of anonymity.

36 This census data was taken from *CensusCD* [1990 U.S. Census STF 3-A, B,C, and D] (East Brunswick, N.J.: Geolytics, 1996). Unfortunately, California 2000 census data on income was not yet available at the time this book went to press.

37 Kenneth Jackson, *Crabgrass Frontier: The Suburbanization of the United States* (New York: Oxford University Press, 1985); Lipsitz, "The Possessive Investment in Whiteness"; Douglas S. Massey and Nancy A. Denton, *American Apartheid: Segregation and the Making of the Underclass* (Cambridge: Harvard University Press, 1993).

38 These figures are drawn from U.S. census figures, and "white" in these periods included whites with Hispanic origins.

39 For consistency, these are the figures for "whites" that include those with Hispanic origins. The non-Hispanic white populations for Valley Groves and Rancho Nuevo in 1990 were 77 percent and 89 percent, respectively. By 2000, non-Hispanic whites dropped to 61 percent of the population of Valley Groves.

40 The 2000 census population statistics were just coming out as this book was going to press, so some figures, such as the population of Rancho Nuevo in 2000 were not yet available.

41 Christopher Rhomberg, "Social Movements in a Fragmented Society:

Ethnic, Class and Racial Mobilization in [Clavey], CA, 1920–1970." Ph.D. diss., University of California, 1999.

42 Don McCormack, ed., *McCormack's Guides* (Martinez, Cal.: Donnan Publications, 1999).

43 From "Neighborhood Profiles," a project of the "Clavey" Citizen's Committee for Urban Renewal Community Information Service, 1998.

44 Local newspaper, 3 July 1957.

45 Local newspaper, 6 January 1961.

46 Magnet academies are schools within schools. Students take standard core courses but with a special emphasis on a certain field, such as teacher education or performing arts. Entry is based on an application and open to youth outside of the magnet school's district. The goals of most magnet programs are to provide students with focused vocational skills while also decreasing racial isolation and reducing overcrowding at certain schools.

47 It was important that the two schools in the study be in the same general region in order to control for regional differences in white racial identity. However, that limited me to doing a suburban-urban comparison because I was unable to find the demographics I wanted in two different suburbs or cities within the same region.

48 Recently published or soon-to-be published studies in high schools where the researchers made observations and analyses stunningly similar to mine include Prudence L. Carter, "Balancing Acts: Issues of Identity and Cultural Resistance in the Social and Educational Behaviors of Minority Youth" (Ph.D. diss., Columbia University, 1999); Dolby, "The Shifting Ground of Race" and "Youth and the Global Popular"; Kenny, *Daughters of Suburbia*; and Twine, "Brown-Skinned White Girls."

49 The primary role of interracial association, or, in other terms, the necessity of an "outgroup" in the construction of racial identities, is argued widely in anthropology, symbolic interaction theory, cultural studies, critical race theory, and social psychology. See, for example, Fredrik Barth, "Introduction," in *Ethnic Groups and Boundaries: The Social Organization of Culture Difference*, ed. Fredrik Barth (Boston: Little, Brown, 1969), 9–38; Herbert Blumer, "Race Prejudice as a Sense of Group Position," *Pacific Sociological Review* 1 (1): 3–7; Herbert Blumer and Troy Duster, "Theories of Race and Social Action," in *Sociological Theories: Race and Colonialism* (Paris: UNESCO, 1980), 211–38; Hall, "Ethnicity"; Henri Tajfel, *Social Identity and Intergroup Relations* (Cambridge: Cambridge University Press, 1982); Margaret Wetherell and Jonathan Potter, *Mapping the Language of Racism: Discourse and the Legitimation of Exploitation* (New York: Harvester Wheatsheaf, 1992).

50 My parentheses around *white* in this statement point to the awkwardness of imposing categorical ascription on people who do not themselves identify with the ascription. Throughout this book I make racial-ethnic categorizations, calling youth "white," "black" or "African American," "Asian" or "Asian American," "Latino," and so forth. I wish to acknowledge a tension in doing this. Racial categorizations are inherently arbitrary and violent. They arose out of social-political machinations and are not intrinsically "real" differences between peoples, but to this day they continue to reduce the whole of a person's humanity to a singular fiction that has real consequences for one's status and life chances within the U.S. racial hierarchy. When I had the opportunity, I would ask my participants how they identified themselves racial-ethnically, and I would honor their self-definition. Much of the time, however, especially when I surveyed classrooms or public spaces for their racial composition, I guessed people's racial-ethnic identities, relying on my knowledge of what phenotypes, clothing, and language styles tend to mark different racial-ethnic groups. Doing that and asserting those categories in this text frequently felt as if I were perpetuating notions of the self-evidence of race and participating in its social, economic, and spiritual violence.

On the other hand, I am compelled to speak in categorical racial terms because "color-blindness" produces its own kind of violence. Because people's life chances are still very much affected by their racial ascription, we *must* talk about race and acknowledge that the ways people look and act have a significant bearing on how society treats them. To do otherwise only hides and perpetuates the injustices and inequalities. On this front, I have felt a political obligation to counterpose the neoconservative "color-blind" ideology and identify people by the ways I felt they would most likely be "raced." I cannot say, however, that I have happily reconciled the tension between this issue and the other.

51 Blumer, "Race Prejudice"; Blumer and Duster, "Theories of Race"; Hall, "Ethnicity" and "Introduction"; George Herbert Mead, *Mind, Self, and Society* (Chicago: University of Chicago Press, 1934); Joane Nagel, *American Indian Ethnic Renewal* (New York: Oxford University Press, 1996).

52 James Baldwin, "Here Be Dragons," in *The Price of the Ticket* (New York: St. Martin's Press, 1985), 677–90, 690.

53 Here Blumer's argument that racial identities stem from a "sense of group position" is relevant. In "Race Prejudice as a Sense of Group Position," Blumer asserts that, through collective, intragroup public discourse, whites define a sense of group position with respect to blacks and other minorities that is based on claims of superiority and entitlement.

Part One: School Life and Social Meaning

1 Richard Alba, *Ethnic Identity: The Transformation of White America* (New Haven: Yale University Press, 1990); Joe R. Feagin, *Racial and Ethnic Relations* (Englewood Cliffs: Prentice Hall, 1989); David Theo Goldberg, *Racist Culture: Philosophy and the Politics of Meaning* (Cambridge: Blackwell, 1993); Joe L. Kincheloe et al., eds., *White Reign: Deploying Whiteness in America* (New York: St. Martin's Press, 1998); Robert Ezra Park, *Race and Culture* (New York: The Free Press, 1950).

2 Penelope Eckert, *Jocks and Burnouts: Social Categories and Identity in High School* (New York: Teachers College Press, 1989); Joyce Canaan, "A Comparative Analysis of American Suburban Middle Class, Middle School, and High School Teenage Cliques," in *Interpretive Ethnography of Education: At Home and Abroad*, ed. George Spindler and Louise Spindler (Hillsdale, N.J.: Erlbaum, 1987), 385–406; R. W. Connell, *Making the Difference: Schools, Families, and Social Division* (Sydney: Allen and Unwin, 1984); Jay MacLeod, *Ain't No Makin' It* (Boulder: Westview, 1987); Barrie Thorne, *Gender Play: Girls and Boys in School* (New Brunswick: Rutgers University Press, 1993); Paul Willis, *Learning to Labor: How Working Class Kids Get Working Class Jobs* (New York: Columbia University Press, 1977).

3 Howard Pinderhughes, *Race in the Hood: Conflict and Violence Among Urban Youth* (Minneapolis: University of Minnesota Press, 1997).

4 Eckert, *Jocks and Burnouts*, 12.

Chapter 1: Valley Groves "Normal. I'd say I'm just . . . normal."

1 It's worth mentioning that the Gap is arguably an icon of white identity. As a case in point, in a 1998 television episode of *Seinfeld*, Elaine and her current "date" figured out that they each had thought the other was a person of color. When they realized that they were both "white," after surviving a moment of disillusionment and confusion over what they might do together, Elaine said, "Well, you wanna go to the Gap?," to which her date enthusiastically responded "OK!"

2 This is a little different from what Joyce Canaan found in her study "A Comparative Analysis of American Suburban Middle Class, Middle School, and High School Teenage Cliques," in *Interpretive Ethnography of Education: At Home and Abroad,* ed. George and Louise Spindler (Hillsdale, N.J.: Erlbaum, 1987), 385–406. She argues that "jocks" (similar to my "popular" kids) drink and party on weekends but conform to adult values at school. This

makes jocks "masters" of conformist and nonconformist behavior, and that mastery is part of what makes jocks "cool."

3 Canaan, "A Comparative Analysis"; Penelope Eckert, *Jocks and Burnouts: Social Categories and Identity in High School* (New York: Teachers College Press, 1989).

4 Several scholars have done excellent research on class identities in school. See, for example, Julie Bettie, "Women Without Class: *Chicas, Cholas, Trash,* and the Presence/Absence of Class Identity," *Signs: Journal of Women in Culture and Society* 26, no. 1 (2000): 20–35; Joyce Canaan, "A Comparative Analysis"; Eckert, *Jocks and Burnouts*; Paul Willis, *Learning to Labor: How Working Class Kids Get Working Class Jobs* (New York: Columbia University Press, 1977).

5 Sherry B. Ortner, "Identities: The Hidden Life of Class," *Journal of Anthropological Research* 54, no. 1 (1998): 1–17, 8.

6 By this, I refer to certain hand and body gestures that "speak" black identity or identification. I elaborate more on this in the next chapter.

7 Extracted from the flyer, Valley Groves Student Planning Guide.

8 William Beeman asserts that "the meaningfulness of a spectacle is usually proportionate to the degree to which the elements displayed to the public seem to represent key elements in the public's cultural and emotional life. . . . Public events, by means of their structure and enactment, reconstitute the whole community." See William O. Beeman, "The Anthropology of Theater and Spectacle," *Annual Review of Anthropology* 22 (1993): 369–93, 380.

9 John Hartigan Jr., *Racial Situations: Class Predicaments of Whiteness in Detroit* (Princeton: Princeton University Press, 1999); John Hartigan Jr., "Locating White Detroit," in *Displacing Whiteness: Essays in Social and Cultural Criticism*, ed. Ruth Frankenberg (Durham: Duke University Press, 1997), 180–213; Thandeka, "The Cost of Whiteness," *Tikkun* 14, no. 3 (1999): 33–38; Matt Wray and Annalee Newitz, eds., *White Trash: Race and Class in America* (New York: Routledge, 1997).

10 Hazel Carby, *Reconstructing Womanhood: The Emergence of the Afro-American Woman Novelist* (New York: Oxford University Press, 1987); Jacquelyn Dowd Hall, " 'The Mind That Burns in Each Body': Women, Rape, and Racial Violence," in *Powers of Desire: The Politics of Sexuality*, ed. Ann Snitow et al. (New York: Monthly Review Press, 1983), 328–49.

11 Eckert, *Jocks and Burnouts*; Lorraine Delia Kenny, *Daughters of Suburbia: Growing Up White, Middle Class, and Female* (New Brunswick: Rutgers University Press, 2000); France Winddance Twine, "Brown-Skinned White Girls: Class, Culture, and the Construction of White Identity in Suburban

Communities," in *Displacing Whiteness: Essays in Social and Cultural Criticism*, ed. Ruth Frankenberg (Durham: Duke University Press, 1997), 214–43.

12 Raymond Williams, "Base and Superstructure in Marxist Cultural Theory," in *Schooling and Capitalism: A Sociological Reader*, ed. Roger Dale (London: Routledge and Kegan Paul, 1976), 202–10, 204–05.

Chapter 2: Clavey High
"There aren't enough white kids here to have many skaters."

1 See, for example, Dennis Carlson, "Stories of Colonial and Postcolonial Education," in *Off White: Readings on Race, Power, and Society*, ed. Michelle Fine et al. (New York: Routledge, 1997), 137–48; and Lorraine Delia Kenny, "Doing My Homework: The Autoethnography of a White Teenage Girl," in *Racing Research, Researching Race: Methodological Dilemmas in Critical Race Studies*, ed. France Winddance Twine and Jonathan Warren (New York: New York University Press, 2000), 111–33.

2 John Clarke argues that working-class, subversive style can be coopted and generalized to make a "generational" style that tries to deny class differences; see his article "Style," in *Resistance Through Rituals: Youth Subcultures in Post-War Britain*, ed. Stuart Hall and Tony Jefferson (London: Routledge, 1975). I suggest a similar thing happened with black, urban style at Clavey; elements of it became a "generational" style that dropped the previous racial element (and black identity statement).

3 Julie Bettie, "Women Without Class: *Chicas, Cholas*, Trash, and the Presence/Absence of Class Identity," *Signs: Journal of Women in Culture and Society* 26, no. 1 (2000): 20–35. Bettie's research on class identities among working-class white and Mexican-American girls excellently illustrates the distinction between class "origin" and "performance" and makes the point that not only are girls "classed" subjects, but through class performance girls actively shape their peer-group relations and class futures. See also her book, *Women Without Class: Race, Identity, and Performance Among White and Mexican American Youth* (Berkeley: University of California Press, in press).

4 Other scholars who have also found that youth in integrated schools tend principally to differentiate and organize themselves by race and ethnicity include Prudence L. Carter, "Balancing Acts: Issues of Identity and Cultural Resistance in the Social and Educational Behaviors of Minority Youth" (Ph.D. diss., Columbia University, 1999); Mark Gottdiener, *Postmodern Semiotics: Material Culture and the Forms of Postmodern Life* (Cambridge: Blackwell, 1995); Carolyn Jew and Marta Tienda, "Selective Sorting in High Schools: Racial and Ethnic Effects on Friendship Formation," Toronto:

American Sociological Association Annual Meetings, 1997; Wesley Shrum et al., "Friendship in School: Gender and Racial Homophily," *Sociology of Education* 61, no. 4 (1988): 227–39; Maureen T. Hallinan and Richard A. Williams, "Interracial Friendship Choices in Secondary Schools," *American Sociological Review* 54, no. 1 (1989): 67–78. Similar findings have been made outside the United States; see Nadine Dolby, *Constructing Race: Youth, Identity, and Popular Culture in South Africa* (Albany: SUNY Press, 2001) and "The Shifting Ground of Race: The Role of Taste in Youth's Production of Identities," *Race, Ethnicity, and Education* 3, no. 1 (2000): 7–23.

5 Several studies have found similar codes for white identity: Signithia Fordham and John Ogbu, "Black Students' School Success: Coping with the "Burden of 'Acting White'," *The Urban Review* 18, no. 3 (1986): 176–206; and Carter, "Balancing Acts." Carter outlines three main dimensions of acting white: "speech differences and interactional style; behaviors which suggest that one is being stuck up and trying to be better than another; and primary social interaction at school with Whites" (43).

6 For a wider discussion concerning this topic, specifically the sanctions for "acting white" or "acting black," see Carter, "Balancing Acts"; and Fordham and Ogbu, "Black Students' School Success." Carter argues against Fordham and Ogbu's assertion that minority youth avoid academic achievement because they equate it with "acting white." Carter instead asserts that minority youth are likely to disengage from schools as a form of resistance to cultural expectations.

7 Nadine Dolby made very similar findings in her work examining youth cultures and white identities in a multiracial high school in South Africa. In particular, she writes about a white girl, "Shirley," who was accepted as "coloured" by many students because of the way she adopted the practices of a coloured identity. See Nadine Dolby, *Constructing Race.*

8 This might be explained in part by what bell hooks describes as "interracial homo-social patriarchal bonding" between black and white men in *Killing Rage: Ending Racism* (New York: Henry Holt, 1995), 2. Her point is that this "bonding" excludes women from discourse about race; I suggest that it could also exclude them from certain entitlements to styles.

9 I touch on this subject again in chapter 4. For arguments along these lines, see Mike Brake, *The Sociology of Youth Culture and Youth Subcultures: Sex and Drugs and Rock 'n' Roll?* (Boston: Routledge and Kegan Paul, 1980); Stuart Hall and Tony Jefferson, eds., *Resistance Through Rituals: Youth Subcultures in Post-War Britain* (London: Routledge, 1996); Janet K. Mancini, *Strategic Styles: Coping in the Inner City* (Hanover: University Press of New England, 1980).

10 Signithia Fordham, "Racelessness as a Factor in Black Students' School Success: Pragmatic Strategy or Pyrrhic Victory?," *Harvard Educational Review* 58, no. 1 (1988): 54–84, 56. See also Carter, "Balancing Acts."

11 Donna Eder, "Ability Grouping as a Self-Fulfilling Prophecy: A Micro-Analysis of Teacher-Student Interaction," *Sociology of Education* 54, no. 3 (1981): 151–62; Reuben Baron et al., "Social Class, Race and Teacher Expectations," in *Teacher Expectancies*, ed. Jerome B. Dusek (Hillsdale, N.J.: Erlbaum, 1985); Ronald F. Ferguson, "Teachers' Perceptions and Expectations and the Black-White Test Score Gap," in *The Black-White Test Score Gap*, ed. Christopher Jencks and Meredith Phillips (Washington, D.C.: Brookings Institution Press, 1998), 318–74; Sara Lawrence Lightfoot, *Worlds Apart: Relationships between Families and Schools* (New York: Basic Books, 1978); Claude M. Steele and Joshua Aronson, "Stereotype Threat and the Test Performance of Academically Successful African Americans," in *The Black-White Test Score Gap*, ed. Jencks and Phillips, 401–27.

12 Only relatively few Asian Americans actually meet the "model minority" stereotype, but as a hegemonic device the stereotype goes far in maintaining white racial dominance. It eclipses the problems of poverty, illiteracy, discrimination, and racism that many Asian Americans face, while asserting that "race" has no bearing on economic mobility, only "hard work" does. This not only denies the role of racism and white dominance in perpetuating racial inequalities in the United States, but drives a wedge between Asians and other minorities who might otherwise effectively join together and organize for racial justice. See Stacey J. Lee, *Unraveling the "Model Minority" Stereotype: Listening to Asian American Youth* (New York: Teachers College Press, 1996), for an elaboration of this argument, as well as convincing evidence that Asian youth not only fail to categorically fit the model minority stereotype but also can be adversely affected by it.

13 Ferguson, "Teachers' Perceptions and Expectations and the Black-White Test Score Gap"; Steele and Aronson, "Stereotype Threat and the Test Performance of Academically Successful African Americans."

14 Glenn Loury, referring to the ways low expectations of and stereotypes about African Americans become self-fulfilling prophesies, used this term in a W.E.B. DuBois Lecture Series at Harvard University titled "The Economics and Ethics of Racial Classification," April 2000.

15 In his study of Latinos in high school, Gil Conchas found that students "made strong links between the racial composition of the different academic programs and the racial stigmas associated with each" and were aware of how school programs "reinforced racial and ethnic stereotypes." Gilberto Q. Conchas, "Structuring Failure and Success: Understanding the

Variability in Latino School Engagement," *Harvard Educational Review* (2001). See also Laurie Olsen, *Made in America: Immigrant Students in Our Public Schools* (New York: New Press, 1997).

16 The intervention of parents in the placement of their children also raises the role of class privilege in tracking. Middle-class parents with postsecondary education know how to work the system in ways that working-class parents do not. In U.S. society today, race and class are tightly intermeshed. They unravel, if temporarily, precisely in situations like the one described above, when a middle-class, black youth with an "A" average is guided away from accelerated classes. See Annette Lareau, "Social Class Differences in Family-School Relationships: The Importance of Cultural Capital," *Sociology of Education* 60 (April 1987): 73–85.

17 In her study of a multicultural high school, Olsen (*Made in America*) found that the "majority of [white students'] references to race were about black-white relations" (71–72). As with the whites I spoke to at Clavey, the analyses and comments of her white participants about race and racial unfairness focused mostly on blacks and less on Latino or Asians.

18 See Joyce Canaan, "A Comparative Analysis of American Suburban Middle Class, Middle School, and High School Teenage Cliques," in *Interpretive Ethnography of Education: At Home and Abroad*, ed. George Spindler and Louise Spindler (Hillsdale, N.J.: Erlbaum, 1987), 385–406. There are other possible explanations for the persistence of a white-black racial paradigm in the face of broad racial and ethnic diversity that reach into symbolic structures beyond the school. First, to the extent that race-ethnic difference is organized around a "pigmentocracy," the lighter one's skin color, the greater one's ability to claim a "white" identity and receive the assigned privileges. Connected to that is the ways racial dualities sustain class dualities, where *white* stands for "middle-class" and "elite," and *black* stands for "working-class" and/or "poor." Third, the persistence can be explained by ongoing (white) obsession with the values attached to the concepts of *white* (purity, order, goodness) and *black* (impurity, disorder, evil). Finally, I think that the particular relationship between whites and blacks themselves has an ongoing bearing on the persistence of a white-black paradigm. Long-standing political and historical antagonisms coupled with a deep-seated interdependence in terms of identity makes the white-black bond particularly durable and significant. On this latter point, see Lawrence Bobo and Vincent L. Hutchings, "Perceptions of Racial Competition in a Multiracial Setting," *American Sociological Review* 61, no. 6 (1996): 951–72.

19 For a similar argument about the ways kids in elementary school perform

gender differences, see Barrie Thorne, *Gender Play: Girls and Boys in School* (New Brunswick: Rutgers University Press, 1993).

20 Others who have found similar stereotypes of white youth are Jew and Tienda, "Selective Sorting in High Schools," and Carter, "Balancing Acts."

21 Racialized social spaces on some high school campuses have become commonplace. In a 1995 PBS documentary titled "School Colors," filmed at Berkeley High School, youth coined spaces "Europe," "Africa," and "China" to designate where whites, African American, and Asian American youth respectively hung out. Also, see Mary Bucholtz, "Borrowing Blackness: African American Vernacular English and European American Youth Identities" (Ph.D. diss., University of California, 1997).

22 Thomas Kochman, *Black and White Styles in Conflict* (Chicago: University of Chicago Press, 1981), 18.

23 Stuart Hall defines three "repertoires" that are distinctive of black diasporic culture: (1) *style* as the "subject of what is going on"; (2) *music* as the "deep structure of [black] cultural life"; and (3) the *body* as "canvasses of representation." Stuart Hall, "What is the 'Black' in Black Popular Culture?," in *Black Popular Culture*, ed. Michelle Wallace and Gina Dent (Seattle: Bay Press, 1992), 21–33, 27. Paul Gilroy adds that the body in black culture carries "potent meanings" because it rests at the core of historical efforts of blacks to assert their humanity, in *"There Ain't No Black in the Union Jack": The Cultural Politics of Race and Nation* (Chicago: University of Chicago Press, 1991), 226. See also Paul Gilroy, *The Black Atlantic: Modernity and Double Consciousness* (Cambridge: Harvard University Press, 1993); Tricia Rose, *Black Noise: Rap Music and Black Culture in Contemporary America* (Hanover: Wesleyan University Press, 1994); Wallace and Dent, eds., *Black Popular Culture*.

24 For more on the ways white people construct whiteness among themselves see John Hartigan Jr., *Racial Situations: Class Predicaments of Whiteness in Detroit* (Princeton: Princeton University Press, 1999), and Thandeka, *Learning to Be White: Money, Race, and God in America* (New York: Continuum, 1990) and "The Cost of Whiteness," *Tikkun* 14, no. 3 (1999): 33–38.

25 Olsen similarly found that "in the midst of intense racial sorting, white identity has lost its transparency for white students who no longer see themselves as raceless" (*Made in America*, 67).

Part Two: Identity and Culture

1 Becky Thompson and Sangeeta Tyagi, eds., *Names We Call Home* (New York: Routledge, 1996).

2   Stuart Hall argues that "the concept of identity does *not* signal that stable core of the self," but a strategic and positioned self. See Stuart Hall, "Introduction: Who Needs Identity?," in *Questions of Cultural Identity*, ed. Stuart Hall and Paul du Gay (London: Sage, 1996), 1–17, 3.

3   Hall, "Introduction," 6.

Chapter 3: Situated Meanings of "White" as a Cultural Identity

1   See, for example, Richard Alba, *Ethnic Identity: The Transformation of White America* (New Haven: Yale University Press, 1990); Herbert J. Gans, "Symbolic Ethnicity: The Future of Ethnic Groups and Cultures in America," *Ethnic and Racial Studies* 2, no. 1 (1979): 1–20; Stephen Steinberg, *The Ethnic Myth: Race, Ethnicity, and Class in America* (Boston: Beacon Press, 1981); Mary C. Waters, *Ethnic Options: Choosing Identities in America* (Berkeley: University of California Press, 1990).

2   Barry's narrative resonates somewhat with W. J. Wilson's argument in *The Declining Significance of Race* (Chicago: University of Chicago Press, 1980) that economic class is more important than race in determining one's life chances.

3   Waters, *Ethnic Options.*

4   Herbert Gans was the first to coin this term. In "Symbolic Ethnicity" Gans argues that, because of acculturation and assimilation, third- or fourth-generation European immigrant groups are less interested in sustaining traditional cultures than in merely sustaining an ethnic identity through ways of "feeling and expressing that identity in a suitable way" (7–8). In this respect, he argues, ethnic identity for many of European origin is less an ascriptive identity than a voluntary one, maintained by as little as "feeling" ethnic. See also Stephen Steinberg, *The Ethnic Myth.*

5   Waters, *Ethnic Options*; Alba, *Ethnic Identity.*

6   See Philomena Essed, *Diversity: Gender, Color, and Culture* (Amherst: University of Massachusetts Press, 1996).

7   Renato Rosaldo, *Culture and Truth: The Remaking of Social Analysis* (Boston: Beacon Press, 1989).

8   See George A. De Vos et al., *Ethnic Identity: Cultural Continuities and Change* (Palo Alto: Mayfield, 1975); Pamela Perry, "The Politics of Identity: Community and Ethnicity in a Pro-Sandinista Enclave on Nicaragua's Atlantic Coast," *Berkeley Journal of Sociology* 36 (1991): 115–36.

9   Rosaldo, *Culture and Truth.* For a similar argument that high-status, dominant groups place less emphasis on the importance of a collective cultural identity than on the importance of the autonomy of the individual, see

Dario Paez et al., "Constructing Social Identity: The Role of Status, Collective Values, Collective Self-Esteem, Perception and Social Behavior," in *Social Identity: International Perspectives*, ed. Stephen Worchel et al. (London: Sage, 1998), 211–29.

10 Joe R. Feagin, *Racial and Ethnic Relations* (Englewood Cliffs, N.J.: Prentice-Hall, 1989).

11 John Rundell and Stephen Mennell, eds., *Classical Readings in Culture and Civilization* (London: Routledge, 1998).

12 Kenneth J. Gergen, *The Saturated Self: Dilemmas of Identity in Contemporary Life* (New York: Basic Books, 1991). Also see Anne Carolyn Klein, *Meeting the Great Bliss Queen: Buddhists, Feminists, and the Art of the Self* (Boston: Beacon Press, 1995).

13 For a wider elaboration of this argument, see Pamela Perry, "White Means Never Having to Say You're Ethnic: White Youth and the Construction of 'Cultureless' Identities," *Journal of Contemporary Ethnography* 30, no. 1 (2001): 56–91.

14 In *Culture and Truth* Rosaldo argues that "as the Other becomes more culturally visible, the self becomes correspondingly less so" (202). For a similar argument, see Lorraine Delia Kenny, "Doing My Homework: The Autoethnography of a White Teenage Girl," in *Racing Research, Researching Race: Methodological Dilemmas in Critical Race Studies*, ed. France Winddance Twine and Jonathan Warren (New York: New York University Press, 2000), 111–33. Kenny shows how "teaching tolerance" and other superficial multicultural practices teach whites how "not to notice their own whiteness and their own positions of relative privilege."

15 This "genetic" conceptualization of *culture* stems from two social-historical processes. It has roots in the turn from biological explanations of race to "cultural" explanations, but has contemporary reinforcement in mainstream discourses about multiculturalism and multicultural education, which students at Clavey were daily subject to. Moreover, group identities tend to take on the appearance of fixity and of carrying essential qualities under conditions of political threat or domination. See Stuart Hall, "New Ethnicities," in *Stuart Hall: Critical Dialogues in Cultural Studies*, ed. David Morley and Kuan-Hsing Chen (London: Routledge, 1996), 441–59; Stuart Hall, "Introduction: Who Needs Identity?"; Nicholas B. Dirks et al., *Culture / Power / History: A Reader in Contemporary Social Theory* (Princeton: Princeton University Press, 1994).

16 For a similar argument—but with respect to the experience of gender in different gendered relationships—see Nancy Chodorow, "Gender as a Personal and Cultural Construction," *Signs* (spring 1995): 516–44.

17 See Institute for the Study of Social Change and Troy Duster (P.I.), "Diversity Project Final Report," Berkeley: University of California, 1991. The report made a similar observation of white students who had more association with students of color than other whites.

18 Social psychologists have argued that when one's social identity is on the defensive, in-group and out-group categorizing and stereotyping come most into play. See, for example, Henri Tajfel, "Cognitive Aspects of Prejudice," *Journal of Social Issues* 25, no. 4 (1969): 79–97; Paez et al., "Constructing Social Identity."

19 See Bob Blauner, *Black Lives, White Lives: Three Decades of Race Relations in America* (Berkeley: University of California Press, 1989). Blauner similarly found that whites and blacks in his study had different perspectives on contemporary race relations. African Americans tended to have a more long-term historical outlook whereas whites tended to want to look more optimistically forward and put racial issues of the past behind.

20 Charles A. Gallagher, "White Reconstruction in the University," *Socialist Review* 24, no. 1 and 2 (1995): 165–87.

Chapter 4: Doing Identity in Style

1 The main argument is that, through a process beginning with mandatory schooling and deindustrialization, both of which helped to create a space and identity for young people outside of the home, and coming to full fruition during the economic boom of the 1950s, which presented youth with yet more free time and disposable capital, young people increasingly became a distinct and lucrative consumer market. Products geared toward "teenagers" effectively constructed the category and teenage needs, behaviors, and identities. For more elaboration of this argument, see, for example, Marcel Danesi, *Cool: The Signs and Meanings of Adolescence* (Toronto: University of Toronto Press, 1994); Todd Gitlin, *The Sixties: Years of Hope, Days of Rage* (New York: Bantam Books, 1993); Stuart Hall and Tony Jefferson, eds., *Resistance Through Rituals: Youth Subcultures in Post-War Britain* (London: Routledge, 1996); Grace Palladino, *Teenagers: An American History* (New York: Basic Books, 1996).

2 Simon Frith, *Sound Effects: Youth, Leisure, and the Politics of Rock 'n' Roll* (New York: Pantheon, 1981).

3 Some recent works that masterfully theorize and illuminate the relationships between youth, popular culture, and race, class, gender identities include Andy Bennett, *Popular Music and Youth Culture: Music, Identity and Place* (New York: St. Martin's Press, 2000); Cameron McCarthy, *Sound

Identities: Popular Music and the Cultural Politics of Education (New York: Peter Lang, 1999); Andrew Ross and Tricia Rose, *Microphone Fiends: Youth Music and Youth Culture* (New York: Routledge, 1994).

4 Glenn M. Hudak, "The 'Sound' Identity: Music-Making and Schooling," in *Sound Identities: Popular Music and the Cultural Politics of Education*, ed. Cameron McCarthy (New York: Peter Lang, 1999), 447–72.

5 Toni Morrison argues that the "black idiom and the sensibilities it has come to imply are appropriated for the associative value they lend to modernism—to being hip, sophisticated, ultra urbane." *Playing in the Dark: Whiteness in the Literary Imagination* (New York: Random House, 1993), 52.

6 By the time this book went to press, sayings like "Y'know wha' I'm sayin'?" and "Whatsup!" had become so generalized that you might hear my seventy-five-year-old mother saying them. At the time of this research, however, and at this site, they were still quite marked as urban black slang.

7 Mark Gottdiener, *Postmodern Semiotics: Material Culture and the Forms of Postmodern Life* (Cambridge: Blackwell, 1995), 12. This notion of the icon is derived from the work of Charles Peirce.

8 hooks and others have emphasized how racist stereotypes about "unbridled and virulent" black male masculinity make their way into the associations that white (and some black) males place on black cultural forms. See bell hooks, *Killing Rage: Ending Racism* (New York: Henry Holt, 1995).

9 Junior high school seems to be a key time when students of different racial-ethnic ascriptions self-segregate into friendship groups of "like kind." See Wesley Shrum et al., "Friendship in School: Gender and Racial Homophily," *Sociology of Education* 61, no. 4 (1988): 227–39. This focused study of gender and racial homophily of friendship groups in a southern California community found that racial segregation and preferences are minimal in elementary school and then increase through grade seven. In middle school, whites, especially, turn to in-group preferences.

10 Pierre Bourdieu, *Distinction: A Social Critique of the Judgment of Taste* (Cambridge: Harvard University Press, 1984), 56. Bourdieu argues, "tastes (i.e. manifested preferences) are the practical affirmation of an inevitable difference. It is no accident that, when they have to be justified, they are asserted purely negatively, by the refusal of other tastes. In matters of taste . . . all determination is negation; and tastes are perhaps first and foremost distastes, disgust provoked by horror or visceral intolerance ('sick-making'), of the tastes of others."

11 This understanding of tastes is fundamentally shaped by Bourdieu in *Distinction*. Chris Richards and Nadine Dolby advance Bourdieu by illuminating tastes as a relational strategy that implicates social identities other than

class. See Chris Richards, "Live Through This: Music, Adolescence, and Autobiography," in *Sound Identities: Popular Music and the Cultural Politics of Education*, ed. Cameron McCarthy (New York: Peter Lang, 1999), 255–88; and Nadine Dolby, "The Shifting Ground of Race: The Role of Taste in Youth's Production of Identities," *Race, Ethnicity, and Education* 3, no. 1 (2000): 7–23.

12   Paul Willis, *Profane Culture* (London: Routledge, 1978).

13   British punk, from which American punk originally sprang in the 1970s, was predominantly associated with working-class youth, whereas contemporary commercial (softcore) American punk tends to be most appreciated by middle-class youth. On British punk rock, read Dick Hebdige, *Subculture: The Meaning of Style* (London: Methuen, 1979).

14   See Sherry B. Ortner, "Identities: The Hidden Life of Class," *Journal of Anthropological Research* 54, no. 1 (1998): 1–17.

15   Troy Duster argues that in-group members, regardless of race or ethnicity, tend to see their group as heterogeneous and out-group members as homogeneous. See Troy Duster, "The Diversity of California Berkeley: An Emerging Reformulation of 'Competence' in an Increasingly Multicultural World," in *Beyond a Dream Deferred: Multicultural Education and the Politics of Excellence*, ed. Becky Thompson and Sangeeta Tyagi (Minneapolis: University of Minnesota Press, 1993), 231–55.

16   Lawrence Grossberg, "Rock and Roll in Search of an Audience," in *Popular Music and Communication*, ed. James Lull (Newbury Park: Sage, 1987).

17   See Susan McClary, "Same As It Ever Was: Youth Culture and Music," in *Microphone Fiends: Youth Music and Youth Culture*, ed. Andrew Ross and Tricia Rose (New York: Routledge, 1994), 29–40.

18   Simon Frith, "Music and Identity," in *Questions of Cultural Identity*, ed. Stuart Hall and Paul du Gay (London: Sage, 1996), 108–27.

19   Read Hudak, "The 'Sound' Identity," for a theorization of how the coordination between performers and audience of the temporal order of music constructs a musical "We."

20   Rap music, performed by African American artists, sells widely and profitably to white audiences. Still, white rap and r & b bands are growing and being mainstaged on TV shows like MTV.

21   Hudak, "The 'Sound' Identity."

22   Frith, "Music and Identity," 121.

23   For very similar findings and analysis, but in a radically different context—South Africa—read Dolby, "The Shifting Ground of Race." Dolby argues that white South Africans in a multiracial high school in which she did ethnographic research actively constructed collective racial selves through

the "selection, arrangement and presentation of clothing, and individual's taste in music" (13).

24   Herbert Blumer and Troy Duster, "Theories of Race and Social Action," in *Sociological Theories: Race and Colonialism* (Paris: UNESCO, 1980), 211–38, 231.

25   John Clarke, "Style," in *Resistance Through Rituals: Youth Subcultures in Post-War Britain*, ed. Stuart Hall and Tony Jefferson (London: Routledge, 1996).

26   Rock critic Bill Adler, quoted in David Samuels, "The Rap on Rap: The 'Black Music' That Isn't Either," in *Rap on Rap: Straight-up Talk on Hip-Hop Culture*, ed. Adam Sexton (New York: Delta, 1995), 241–53, 244–45.

27   Samuels, "The Rap on Rap."

28   Zora Neale Hurston, quoted in powell, p. 1492. Originally in Zora Neale Hurston, "How It Feels To Be Coloured Me," in *I Love Myself When I am Laughing . . . and Then Again When I am Looking Mean and Impressive: A Zora Neale Hurston Reader*, ed. Alice Walker (Old Westbury: The Feminist Press, 1979), 152–53.

29   Frith, "Music and Identity"; Paul Gilroy, *"There Ain't No Black in the Union Jack": The Cultural Politics of Race and Nation* (Chicago: University of Chicago Press, 1991); bell hooks, *Black Looks: Race and Representation* (Boston: South End Press, 1992).

30   Stuart Hall, "What Is the 'Black' in Black Popular Culture?," in *Black Popular Culture*, ed. Michelle Wallace and Gina Dent (Seattle: Bay Press, 1992), 21–33, 27.

31   Hall, "What Is the 'Black' in Black Popular Culture?"; Tricia Rose, *Black Noise: Rap Music and Black Culture in Contemporary America* (Hanover: Wesleyan University Press, 1994).

32   Since 1979, when Stuart Hall and Tony Jefferson first published *Resistance Through Rituals*, the premise that youth cultures symbolically solve contradictions and problems in young people's lives has been widely embraced. See, for example, Mike Brake, *The Sociology of Youth Culture and Youth Subcultures: Sex and Drugs and Rock 'n' Roll?* (Boston: Routledge and Kegan Paul, 1980); Rachel Felder, *Manic Pop Thrill* (Hopewell, N.J.: Ecco Press, 1993); Frith, *Sound Effects*; and Janet K. Mancini, *Strategic Styles: Coping in the Inner City* (Hanover: University Press of New England, 1980). Recently, scholars have begun to challenge this claim; see Andrew Ross, "Introduction," in *Microphone Fiends: Youth Music and Youth Culture*, ed. Andrew Ross and Tricia Rose (New York: Routledge, 1994), 1–13.

33   Danesi, *Cool*, 37.

34   In different ways rap music and video have been massaged to appeal to white audiences; see Stephen Rodrick, "Hip-Hop Flop: The Failure of

Liberal Rap," in *Rap on Rap: Straight-up Talk on Hip-Hop Culture*, ed. Adam Sexton (New York: Delta, 1995), 113–17; Samuels, "The Rap on Rap."

35 Medria L. Connolly and Debra A. Noumair, "The White Girl in Me, the Colored Girl in You, and the Lesbian in Us: Crossing Boundaries," in *Off White: Readings on Race, Power, and Society*, ed. Michelle Fine et al. (New York: Routledge, 1997), 326.

Part Three: Identity and Group Position

1 Herbert Blumer, "Race Prejudice as a Sense of Group Position," *Pacific Sociological Review* 1, no. 1 (1958): 3–7.

Chapter 5: The Million Man March

1 Mark Fuhrman was one of the LAPD detectives on the O.J. Simpson case and a witness for the prosecution. Defense attorneys brought evidence of Fuhrman using blatantly racist language on the job and tried to cast doubt on his testimony through raising the possibility that Fuhrman was part of a conspiracy to frame O.J. for the murders of Nicole Brown Simpson and Ron Goldman.

2 For other ethnographies of the structured silences and evasions of race and whiteness in suburban schools, see Lorraine Delia Kenny, *Daughters of Suburbia: Growing Up White, Middle Class, and Female* (New Brunswick: Rutgers University Press, 2000); France Winddance Twine, "Brown-Skinned White Girls: Class, Culture, and the Construction of White Identity in Suburban Communities," in *Displacing Whiteness: Essays in Social and Cultural Criticism*, ed. Ruth Frankenberg (Durham: Duke University Press, 1997), 214–43.

3 See John Hartigan Jr., *Racial Situations: Class Predicaments of Whiteness in Detroit* (Princeton: Princeton University Press, 1999). Hartigan argues, among other things, that socioeconomic class inflects the significance of white racialness by virtue of placing whites in close association with people of color, by whom whites are themselves raced. On the silencing and sanctioning of minority groups in schools, see, for example, Ann Locke Davidson, *Making and Molding Identity in Schools: Student Narratives on Race, Gender, and Academic Engagement* (Albany: SUNY Press, 1996); Michelle Fine, "Silencing and Nurturing Voice in an Improbable Context: Urban Adolescents in Public School," in *Critical Pedagogy, the State, and Cultural Struggle*, ed. Henry Giroux and Peter McLaren (Albany: SUNY Press, 1989), 152–

73; Laurie Olsen, *Made in America: Immigrant Students in Our Public Schools* (New York: New Press, 1997); and Angela Valenzuela, *Subtractive Schooling: U.S.-Mexican Youth and the Politics of Caring* (Albany: SUNY Press, 1999).

4 Lawrence Bobo and Vincent L. Hutchings, "Perceptions of Racial Competition in a Multiracial Setting," *American Sociological Review* 61, no. 6 (1996): 951–72, 956.

Chapter 6: The Social Implications of White Identity

1 See the methodological appendix for my reflections on which groups of kids I did not manage to interact with and why.

2 Howard Winant similarly observes that "from the late 1960s on, white identity has been reinterpreted, rearticulated in a dualistic fashion: on the one hand egalitarian, on the other hand privileged." Howard Winant, "Behind Blue Eyes: Whiteness and Contemporary U.S. Racial Politics," in *Off White: Readings on Race, Power, and Society*, ed. Michelle Fine, Lois Weis, Linda Powel, and L. Mun Wong (New York: Routledge, 1997), 40–53.

3 Prudence L. Carter, "Balancing Acts: Issues of Identity and Cultural Resistance in the Social and Educational Behaviors of Minority Youth" (Ph.D. diss., Columbia University, 1999); Tricia Rose, *Black Noise: Rap Music and Black Culture in Contemporary America* (Hanover: Wesleyan University Press, 1994).

4 Rose, *Black Noise,* 38.

5 For examinations of the ways whites project their "racist" fears unto other, usually working-class, whites, see John Hartigan Jr., *Racial Situations: Class Predicaments of Whiteness in Detroit* (Princeton: Princeton University Press, 1999); Matt Wray and Annalee Newitz, eds., *White Trash: Race and Class in America* (New York: Routledge, 1997).

6 Herbert Blumer, "Race Prejudice as a Sense of Group Position," *Pacific Sociological Review* 1, no. 1 (1958): 3–7, 6.

7 Nancy Chodorow, *The Reproduction of Mothering: Psychoanalysis and the Sociology of Gender* (Berkeley: University of California Press, 1978); Carol Gilligan, *In a Different Voice: Psychological Theory and Women's Development* (Cambridge: Harvard University Press, 1982).

8 American Association of University Women, *How Schools Shortchange Girls: The A.A.U.W. Report: Action Guide* (Washington, D.C.: American Association of University Women Educational Foundation, 1992).

9 Henri Tajfel, "Cognitive Aspects of Prejudice," *Journal of Social Issues* 25, no.

4 (1969): 79–97; John C. Turner, "Henri Tajfel: An Introduction," in *Social Groups and Identities: Developing the Legacy of Henri Tajfel*, ed. W. Peter Robinson (Oxford: Butterworth-Heinemann, 1996), 1–24.

10 I am not saying that there is no basis for a positive white identity. I was once quoted in a newspaper as saying, "White youth don't have anything to be proud of." Taken out of context, this quote admittedly sounds strange; I was basically trying to say what I'm saying here, that there aren't discursive resources out there for white youth to construct a positive collective identity. I received hate mail for that statement from some white supremacists, including one who told me I should be "dragged through the streets of the town in which [I was] born and hung by the neck until [I] died."

11 Also defined as "aversive racism," "symbolic racism," "laissez-faire racism." See Lawrence Bobo et al., "Laissez-Faire Racism: The Crystalization of a 'Kinder, Gentler' Anti-Black Ideology," in *Racial Attitudes in the 1990s: Continuity and Change*, ed. Steven A. Tuch and Jack K. Martin (Westport: Praeger, 1997), 15–42; Joel Kovel, *White Racism: A Psychohistory* (New York: Columbia University Press, 1970); Thomas F. Pettigrew, "The Nature of Modern Racism in the United States," *Revue Internationale de Psychologie Sociale* 2 (1989): 291–303; Howard Schuman et al., *Racial Attitudes in America: Trends and Interpretations* (Cambridge: Harvard University Press, 1997); David O. Sears, "Symbolic Racism," in *Eliminating Racism: Profiles in Controversy*, ed. Dalmas A. Taylor and Phyllis A. Katz (New York: Plenum Press, 1988), 53–84; David R. Williams et al., "Traditional and Contemporary Prejudice and Urban Whites' Support for Affirmative Action and Government Help," *Social Problems* 46, no. 4 (1999): 548–71.

Conclusion: Beyond Whiteness

1 Herbert Blumer, "Race Prejudice as a Sense of Group Position," *Pacific Sociological Review* 1, no. 1 (1958): 3–7, 3.

2 Stuart Hall, "Ethnicity: Identity and Difference," *Radical America* 23, no. 4 (1991): 9–20; Fredrik Barth, "Introduction," in *Ethnic Groups and Boundaries: The Social Organization of Culture Difference*, ed. Fredrik Barth (Boston: Little, Brown, 1969), 9–38; Herbert Blumer and Troy Duster, "Theories of Race and Social Action," in *Sociological Theories: Race and Colonialism* (Paris: UNESCO, 1980), 211–38.

3 Barth, "Introduction"; Blumer, "Race Prejudice as a Sense of Group Position"; Henri Tajfel, *Social Identity and Intergroup Relations* (Cambridge: Cambridge University Press, 1982); Henri Tajfel and John C. Turner, *The Social Identity Theory of Intergroup Behavior* (Monterey: Brooks-Cole, 1986).

4   Blumer and Duster, "Theories of Race and Social Action," 231.

5   Barth, "Introduction"; Blumer, "Race Prejudice as a Sense of Group Posi-
    tion"; Joane Nagel, *American Indian Ethnic Renewal* (New York: Oxford
    University Press, 1996); Margaret Wetherell and Jonathan Potter, *Mapping
    the Language of Racism: Discourse and the Legitimation of Exploitation* (New
    York: Harvester Wheatsheaf, 1992).

6   Ruth Frankenberg, ed., *Displacing Whiteness: Essays in Social and Cultural
    Criticism* (Durham: Duke University Press, 1997).

7   In "Race Prejudice as a Sense of Group Position," Blumer argues that one of
    four basic feelings associated with race prejudice is the "fear or apprehen-
    sion that the subordinate racial group is threatening, or will threaten, the
    position of the dominant group" (4). William J. Wilson believes that this is
    the defining feature of race prejudice (from a lecture at Harvard University,
    spring 2000).

8   Nancy Chodorow, "Gender as a Personal and Cultural Construction," *Signs*
    (spring 1995): 516–44.

9   Ibid., 538.

10 Hazel V. Carby, "White Woman Listen! Black Feminism and the Bound-
    aries of Sisterhood," in *The Empire Strikes Back: Race and Racism in 70s Britain*,
    ed. University of Birmingham Centre for Contemporary Cultural Studies
    (London: Hutchinson, 1982), 212–35; Patricia Hill Collins, *Black Feminist
    Thought: Knowledge, Consciousness, and the Politics of Empowerment* (London:
    Harper Collins Academic, 1990); Cherríe Moraga and Gloria Anzaldúa,
    This Bridge Called My Back: Writings by Radical Women of Color (Watertown,
    Mass.: Persephone Press, 1981); john a. powell, "Reflections On the Self:
    Exploring Between and Beyond Modernity and Postmodernity," *Minnesota
    Law Review* 81, no. 6 (1997): 1481–520; Renato Rosaldo, *Culture and Truth:
    The Remaking of Social Analysis* (Boston: Beacon Press, 1989).

11 Sherry B. Ortner, "Identities: The Hidden Life of Class," *Journal of Anthro-
    pological Research* 54, no. 1 (1998): 1–17, 8.

12 Works engaging discussion on the unified versus the multiple self include
    Katherine Ewing, "The Illusion of Wholeness: Culture, Self, and the Expe-
    rience of Inconsistency," *Ethos* 18, no. 1 (1990): 251–78; Kenneth J. Ger-
    gen, *The Saturated Self: Dilemmas of Identity in Contemporary Life* (New York:
    Basic Books, 1991); Anthony Giddens, *Modernity and Self-Identity: Self and
    Society in the Late Modern Age* (Stanford: Stanford University Press, 1991);
    Anne Carolyn Klein, *Meeting the Great Bliss Queen: Buddhists, Feminists and
    the Art of the Self* (Boston: Beacon Press, 1995); Scott Lash and Jonathan
    Friedman, eds., *Modernity and Identity* (Cambridge: Blackwell, 1992); and
    powell, "Reflections of the Self."

13 George Herbert Mead, *Mind, Self, and Society* (Chicago: University of Chicago Press, 1934).

14 James Baldwin, *The Price of the Ticket: Collected Nonfiction, 1948–85* (New York: St. Martins's/Marek, 1985); W. E. B. Du Bois, *The Souls of Black Folk* (New York: The Blue Heron Press, 1953); Frantz Fanon, *Black Skin, White Masks* (New York: Grove Weidenfeld, 1967); Zora Neale Hurston, "How It Feels To Be Coloured Me," in *I Love Myself When I am Laughing . . . And Then Again When I am Looking Mean and Impressive: A Zora Neale Hurston Reader*, ed. Alice Walker (Old Westbury: The Feminist Press, 1979).

15 Baldwin, *The Price of the Ticket*, 232.

16 Fanon, *Black Skin, White Masks*; Joel Kovel, *White Racism: A Psychohistory* (New York: Columbia University Press, 1970); powell, "Reflections of the Self."

17 My understanding of the role of structures in constituting subjectivities is fundamentally influenced by Antonio Gramsci, *Selections From the Prison Notebooks* (New York: International Press, 1971); Raymond Williams, *Marxism and Literature* (Oxford: Oxford University Press, 1977); Paul Willis, *Learning to Labor: How Working Class Kids Get Working Class Jobs* (New York: Columbia University Press, 1977); and Pierre Bourdieu, *Outline of a Theory of Practice* (Cambridge: Cambridge University Press, 1977). Gramsci (followed by Williams, then Willis) countered deterministic Marxist structural theories with the argument that material and ideological structures set bounds on but do not determine what is thinkable. Bourdieu developed an understanding of the dialectic between social structures and human agency. In *Distinction: A Social Critique of the Judgment of Taste* (Cambridge: Harvard University Press, 1984), he argues that the "conditions of existence," which include the "hierarchies and classifications inscribed in objects . . . , in institutions (for example, the educational system), or simply in language," become "inscribed in people's minds," whereby people's thought and practices become "structuring" agents themselves, reproducing the conditions of existence (470–71).

18 Michael W. Apple, *Education and Power* (New York: Routledge, 1995); Samuel Bowles and Herbert Gintis, *Schooling in Capitalist America: Educational Reform and the Contradictions of Economic Life* (New York: Basic Books, 1976); Penelope Eckert, *Jocks and Burnouts: Social Categories and Identity in High School* (New York: Teachers College Press, 1989); Jeannie Oakes, *Keeping Track: How Schools Structure Inequality* (New Haven: Yale University Press, 1985), and "More than a Misapplied Technology: A Normative and

Political Response to Hallinan on Tracking," *Sociology of Education* 67, no. 2 (1994): 84–88; Jeannie Oakes and Gretchen Guiton, "Matchmaking: The Dynamics of High School Tracking Decisions," *American Educational Research Journal* 32, no. 1 (1995): 3–33.

19   Basil B. Bernstein, *Class, Codes and Control*, vol. 3: *Towards a Theory of Educational Transmissions* (London: Routledge and Kegan Paul, 1971); Pierre Bourdieu and J. C. Passeron, *Reproduction in Education, Society, and Culture* (Beverly Hills: Sage, 1977); Gilberto Q. Conchas, "Structuring Failure and Success: Understanding the Variability in Latino School Engagement," *Harvard Educational Review* (2001); Ann Locke Davidson, *Making and Molding Identity in Schools: Student Narratives on Race, Gender, and Academic Engagement* (Albany: SUNY Press, 1996); Lisa A. Delpit, "The Silenced Dialogue: Power and Pedagogy in Educating Other People's Children," *Harvard Educational Review* 58, no. 3 (1988): 280–98; Michelle Fine et al., eds., *Off White: Readings on Race, Power, and Society* (New York: Routledge, 1997); Shirley Brice Heath, *Ways with Words: Language, Life, and Work in Communities and Classrooms* (Cambridge: Cambridge University Press, 1983); Laurie Olsen, *Made in America: Immigrant Students in Our Public Schools* (New York: New Press, 1997); Beverly Daniel Tatum, *"Why Are All the Black Kids Sitting Together in the Cafeteria?" and Other Conversations About Race* (New York: Basic Books, 1997).

20   Ien Ang and Joke Hermes, "Gender and/in Media Consumption," in *Mass Media and Society*, ed. James Curran and Michael Gurevitch (New York: Edward Arnold, 1991), 307–28; Howard Pinderhughes, *Race in the Hood: Conflict and Violence Among Urban Youth* (Minneapolis: University of Minnesota Press, 1997); Janice Radway, "Interpretive Communities and Variable Literacies: The Functions of Romance Reading," in *Rethinking Popular Culture*, ed. Chandra Mujerki and Michael Schudson (Berkeley: University of California Press, 1991).

21   See Pinderhughes, *Race in the Hood*. Pinderhughes brilliantly demonstrates the ways cultural, political, social, psychological, and economic factors differently intersect to create interpretive communities that differently make sense of wider cultural, political, and social structures.

22   Gunnar Myrdal, *An American Dilemma: The Negro Problem and Modern Democracy* (New York: Harper and Row, 1962).

23   See Alastair Bonnett, *Radicalism, Anti-Racism, and Representation* (London: Routledge, 1993). Bonnett draws attention to the tension educators face trying to prepare students for participation in a stratified labor market *and* treat them all as equals.

24 Howard Winant, *Racial Conditions: Politics, Theory, Comparisons* (Minneapolis: University of Minnesota Press, 1994).

25 Michael Omi and Howard Winant, *Racial Formation in the United States: From the 1960s to the 1980s* (New York: Routledge, 1986).

26 Antonio Gramsci, *Selections From the Prison Notebooks* (New York: International Press, 1971), 80.

27 Winant, *Racial Conditions*, 29.

28 Clifford Geertz, *The Interpretation of Cultures* (New York: Basic Books, 1973), 144.

29 Paul Willis, *Learning to Labor*, 119.

30 Willis, *Learning to Labor*.

31 For a similar argument, see Bonnett, *Radicalism, Anti-Racism, and Representation*.

32 Pinderhughes, *Race in the Hood*.

33 See Nadine Dolby, "Youth and the Global Popular: The Politics and Practices of Race in South Africa," *European Journal of Cultural Studies* 2 (1999): 291–310, and "The Shifting Ground of Race: The Role of Taste in Youth's Production of Identities," *Race, Ethnicity, and Education* 3, no. 1 (2000): 7–23.

34 John Hartigan Jr., *Racial Situations: Class Predicaments of Whiteness in Detroit* (Princeton: Princeton University Press, 1999), 279.

35 Gary Orfield et al. "The Growth of Segregation in American Schools: Changing Patterns of Separation and Poverty Since 1968" (Cambridge: Harvard Project on School Desegregation, 1993).

36 Martin Luther King Jr., "The Ethical Demands for Integration," in *A Testament of Hope: The Essential Writings and Speeches of Martin Luther King Jr.*, ed. James Melvin Washington (San Francisco: Harper, 1962).

37 See Orfield, "The Growth of Segregation in American Schools." See also Massey and Denton, *American Apartheid: Segregation and the Making of the Underclass* (Cambridge: Harvard University Press, 1993); and William J. Wilson, *The Truly Disadvantaged: The Inner City, the Underclass, and Public Policy* (Chicago: University of Chicago Press, 1987).

38 Jomills H. Braddock, "The Perpetuation of Segregation Across Levels of Education: A Behavioral Assessment of the Contact-Hypothesis," *Sociology of Education* 53, no. 3 (1980): 178–86; Douglas S. Massey and Nancy A. Denton, *American Apartheid*; Amy S. Wells and Robert L. Crain, "Perpetuation Theory and the Long-Term Effects of School Desegregation," *Review of Educational Research* 96, no. 4 (1994): 691–706.

39 Samuel Lucas' recent study, *Tracking Inequality: Stratification and Mobility in American High Schools* (New York: Teachers College Press, 1999), expresses

this conundrum well. See also Maureen Hallinan and Jeannie Oakes, "Exchange," *Sociology of Education* 67, no. 2 (1994): 79–91.

40 Some of the few arguments along these lines include Conchas, "Structuring Failure and Success"; Ann Locke Davidson, *Making and Molding Identity in Schools: Student Narratives on Race, Gender, and Academic Engagement* (Albany: SUNY Press, 1996); Michelle Fine, "Witnessing Whiteness," in *Off White: Readings on Race, Power and Society*, ed. Michelle Fine et al. (New York: Routledge, 1997), 57–65; Michelle Fine et al., "Communities of Difference: A Critical Look at Desegregated Spaces Created For and By Youth," *Harvard Educational Review* 67, no. 2 (1997): 247–84; Oakes, *Keeping Track* and "More than a Misapplied Technology."

41 Peter McLaren coins these terms in "White Terror and Oppositional Agency: Towards a Critical Multiculturalism," in *Multiculturalism: A Critical Reader*, ed. David Theo Goldberg (Cambridge: Blackwell, 1994), 45–74.

42 McLaren, "White Terror and Oppositional Agency," 49.

43 McLaren, "White Terror and Oppositional Agency," 51.

44 Stuart Hall, "New Ethnicities," in *Stuart Hall: Critical Dialogues in Cultural Studies*, ed. David Morley and Kuan-Hsing Chen (London: Routledge, 1996), 441–59, 447.

45 My thoughts on this new multiculturalism are most influenced by Stuart Hall's concept of "new ethnicity" (in Hall, "New Ethnicities"). For similar discussions on critical multiculturalism, also see David Theo Goldberg, ed., *Multiculturalism: A Critical Reader* (Boston: Blackwell, 1994); Cameron McCarthy, "After the Canon: Knowledge and Ideological Representation in the Multicultural Discourse on Curriculum Reform," in *Race, Identity, and Representation in Education*, ed. Cameron McCarthy and Warren Crichlow (New York: Routledge, 1993), 289–305.

46 Henry Giroux, "Rewriting the Discourse of Racial Identity: Towards a Pedagogy and Politics of Whiteness," *Harvard Educational Review* 67, no. 2 (1997): 285–320, 293.

47 Fine et al., "Communities of Difference."

48 Fine et al., "Communities of Difference," quoting S. S. Brehm and S. M. Kassim, *Social Psychology* (Boston: Houghton Mifflin, 1996), 248–49. See also Robert Slavin, "Enhancing Intergroup Relations in Schools: Cooperative Learning and Other Strategies," in *Toward a Common Destiny: Improving Race and Ethnic Relations in America*, ed. W. D. Hawley and A. W. Jackson (San Francisco: Jossey-Bass, 1995), 291–314.

49 Fine et al., "Communities of Difference," 251.

50 Fine et al., "Communities of Difference," 249.

Appendix: Methods and Reflections

1 Statistics for students on AFDC at Clavey were 4 percent compared to 3.4 percent at Valley Groves. Statistics for those on a free or reduced lunch program were 14 percent at Clavey and 8 percent at Valley Groves. In the school district in which Clavey High was located, the next lowest AFDC and free/reduced lunch statistics were 29 percent and 39 percent, respectively. The California Learning Assessment System (CLAS) rated the socioeconomic index for Clavey sophomores in 1994 at 3.03, indicating that the parents of Clavey sophomores had, on the average, "some college." The norm for parental education in the district was 2.52 (between "high school" and "some college").

2 Julie Bettie, "Women Without Class: *Chicas, Cholas*, Trash, and the Presence/Absence of Class Identity," *Signs: Journal of Women in Culture and Society* 26, no. 1 (2000): 20–35. See also her *Women Without Class* (Berkeley: University of California Press, in press).

3 See Prudence L. Carter, "Balancing Acts: Issues of Identity and Cultural Resistance in the Social and Educational Behaviors of Minority Youth" (Ph.D. diss., Columbia University, 1999); Nadine Dolby, "Youth and the Global Popular: The Politics and Practices of Race in South Africa," *European Journal of Cultural Studies* 2 (1999): 291–310, and "The Shifting Ground of Race: The Role of Taste in Youth's Production of Identities," *Race, Ethnicity, and Education* 3, no. 1 (2000): 7–23, and *Constructing Racialized Selves: Youth, Identity, and Popular Culture in South Africa* (Albany: SUNY Press, in press); Lorraine Delia Kenny, "Doing My Homework: The Autoethnography of a White Teenage Girl," in *Racing Research, Researching Race: Methodological Dilemmas in Critical Race Studies*, ed. France Winddance Twine and Jonathan Warren (New York: New York University Press, 2000), 111–33; France Winddance Twine, "Brown-Skinned White Girls: Class, Culture, and the Construction of White Identity in Suburban Communities," in *Displacing Whiteness: Essays in Social and Cultural Criticism*, ed. Ruth Frankenberg (Durham: Duke University Press, 1997), 214–43.

Bibliography

Alba, Richard. 1990. *Ethnic Identity: The Transformation of White America*. New Haven: Yale University Press.

Allen, Theodore. 1994. *The Invention of the White Race*. Vol. 1. *Racial Oppression and Social Control*. London: Verso.

Almaguer, Tomas. 1994. *Racial Fault Lines: The Historical Origins of White Supremacy in California*. Berkeley: University of California Press.

American Association of University Women. 1992. *How Schools Shortchange Girls: The A.A.U.W. Report: Action Guide*. Washington, D.C.: American Association of University Women Educational Foundation.

Ang, Ien, and Joke Hermes. 1991. "Gender and/in Media Consumption." In *Mass Media and Society*, edited by James Curran and Michael Gurevitch. New York: Edward Arnold, 307–28.

Anzaldúa, Gloria. 1987. *Borderlands/La Frontera: The New Mestiza*. San Francisco: Spinsters/Aunt Lute Book Company.

Appiah, Kwame Anthony. 2000. "Race, Culture, Identity: Misunderstood Connections." Unpublished manuscript.

Apple, Michael W. 1995. *Education and Power*. New York: Routledge.

——. 1990. *Ideology and Curriculum*. 2d ed. New York: Routledge.

Baldwin, James. 1985. *The Price of the Ticket: Collected Nonfiction, 1948–85*. New York: St. Martins's/Marek.

Baron, Reuben, David Y. H. Tom, and Harris M. Cooper. 1985. "Social Class, Race, and Teacher Expectations." In *Teacher Expectancies*, edited by Jerome B. Dusek. Hillsdale, N.J.: Erlbaum.

Barth, Fredrik. 1969. "Introduction." In *Ethnic Groups and Boundaries: The Social Organization of Culture Difference*, edited by Fredrik Barth. Boston: Little, Brown, 9–38.

Beeman, William O. 1993. "The Anthropology of Theater and Spectacle." *Annual Review of Anthropology* 22 (1): 369–93.

Bennett, Andy. 2000. *Popular Music and Youth Culture: Music, Identity, and Place*. New York: St. Martin's Press.

Bernstein, Basil B. 1971. *Class, Codes and Control*. Vol. 3. *Towards a Theory of Educational Transmissions*. London: Routledge and Kegan Paul.

Bettie, Julie. 2000. "Women Without Class: *Chicas, Cholas*, Trash, and the Presence/Absence of Class Identity." *Signs: Journal of Women in Culture and Society* 26 (1): 20–35.

———. in press. *Women Without Class: Race, Identity, and Performance Among White and Mexican American Youth*. Berkeley: University of California Press.

Blauner, Bob. 1989. *Black Lives, White Lives: Three Decades of Race Relations in America*. Berkeley: University of California Press.

Blumer, Herbert. 1958. "Race Prejudice as a Sense of Group Position." *Pacific Sociological Review* 1 (1): 3–7.

Blumer, Herbert, and Troy Duster. 1980. "Theories of Race and Social Action." In *Sociological Theories: Race and Colonialism*. Paris: UNESCO, 211–38.

Bobo, Lawrence, and Vincent L. Hutchings. 1996. "Perceptions of Racial Competition in a Multiracial Setting." *American Sociological Review* 61 (6): 951–72.

Bobo, Lawrence, James R. Kluegel, and Ryan A. Smith. 1997. "Laissez-Faire Racism: The Crystalization of a 'Kinder, Gentler' Anti-Black Ideology." In *Racial Attitudes in the 1990s: Continuity and Change*, edited by Steven A. Tuch and Jack K. Martin. Westport: Praeger, 15–42.

Bonnett, Alastair. 1993. *Radicalism, Anti-Racism, and Representation*. London: Routledge.

Bourdieu, Pierre. 1984. *Distinction: A Social Critique of the Judgment of Taste*. Cambridge: Harvard University Press.

———. 1977. *Outline of a Theory of Practice*. Cambridge: Cambridge University Press.

Bourdieu, Pierre, and J. C. Passeron. 1977. *Reproduction in Education, Society, and Culture*. Beverly Hills: Sage.

Bowles, Samuel, and Herbert Gintis. 1976. *Schooling in Capitalist America: Educational Reform and the Contradictions of Economic Life*. New York: Basic Books.

Braddock, Jomills H. 1980. "The Perpetuation of Segregation Across Levels of Education: A Behavioral Assessment of the Contact-Hypothesis." *Sociology of Education* 53 (3): 178–86.

Brake, Mike. 1980. *The Sociology of Youth Culture and Youth Subcultures: Sex and Drugs and Rock 'n' Roll*. Boston: Routledge and Kegan Paul.

Brehm, S. S., and S. M. Kassim. 1996. *Social Psychology*. 3d ed. Boston: Houghton Mifflin.

Bucholtz, Mary. 1997. "Borrowing Blackness: African American Vernacular

English and European American Youth Identities." Ph.D. Dissertation, University of California.

Canaan, Joyce. 1987. "A Comparative Analysis of American Suburban Middle Class, Middle School, and High School Teenage Cliques." In *Interpretive Ethnography of Education: At Home and Abroad*, edited by George Spindler and Louise Spindler. Hillsdale, N.J.: Erlbaum, 385–406.

Carby, Hazel. 1987. *Reconstructing Womanhood: The Emergence of the Afro-American Woman Novelist*. New York: Oxford University Press.

———. 1982. "White Woman Listen! Black Feminism and the Boundaries of Sisterhood." In *The Empire Strikes Back: Race and Racism in 70s Britain*, edited by University of Birmingham Centre for Contemporary Cultural Studies. London: Hutchinson, 212–35.

Carlson, Dennis. 1997. "Stories of Colonial and Postcolonial Education." In *Off White: Readings on Race, Power, and Society*, edited by Michelle Fine, Lois Weis, Linda C. Powell, and L. Mun Wong. New York: Routledge, 137–48.

Carter, Prudence L. 1999. "Balancing Acts: Issues of Identity and Cultural Resistance in the Social and Educational Behaviors of Minority Youth." Ph.D. Dissertation, Columbia University.

Chodorow, Nancy. 1995. "Gender as a Personal and Cultural Construction." *Signs* (spring): 516–44.

———. 1978. *The Reproduction of Mothering: Psychoanalysis and the Sociology of Gender*. Berkeley: University of California Press.

Clarke, John. 1975. "Style." In *Resistance Through Rituals: Youth Subcultures in Post-War Britain*, edited by Stuart Hall and Tony Jefferson. London: Routledge.

Collins, Patricia Hill. 1990. *Black Feminist Thought: Knowledge, Consciousness, and the Politics of Empowerment*. London: Harper Collins Academic.

Conchas, Gilberto Q. 2001. "Structuring Failure and Success: Understanding the Variability in Latino School Engagement." *Harvard Educational Review*.

Conley, Dalton. 1999. *Being Black, Living in the Red: Race, Wealth, and Social Policy in America*. Berkeley: University of California Press.

Connell, R. W. 1984. *Making the Difference: Schools, Families, and Social Division*. Sydney: George Allen and Unwin.

Connolly, Medria L., and Debra A. Noumair. 1997. "The White Girl in Me, the Colored Girl in You, and the Lesbian in Us: Crossing Boundaries." In *Off White: Readings on Race, Power, and Society*, edited by Michelle Fine, Lois Weis, Linda C. Powell, and L. Wun Wong. New York: Routledge.

Cross, William E. 1991. *Shades of Black: Diversity in African-American Identity*. Philadelphia: Temple University Press.

Dalton, Russell J., and Manfred Kuechler, eds. 1990. *Challenging the Political*

Order: New Social Movements in Western Democracies. New York: Oxford University Press.

Danesi, Marcel. 1994. *Cool: The Signs and Meanings of Adolescence*. Toronto: University of Toronto Press.

Davidson, Ann Locke. 1996. *Making and Molding Identity in Schools: Student Narratives on Race, Gender, and Academic Engagement*. Albany: SUNY Press.

De Vos, George A., Lola Romanucci-Ross, and Wenner-Gren Foundation for Anthropological Research. 1975. *Ethnic Identity: Cultural Continuities and Change*. Palo Alto: Mayfield Publishing Company.

Delgado, Richard, and Jean Stefancic, eds. 1997. *Critical White Studies: Looking Behind the Mirror*. Philadelphia: Temple University Press.

Delpit, Lisa A. 1988. "The Silenced Dialogue: Power and Pedagogy in Educating Other People's Children." *Harvard Educational Review* 58 (3): 280–98.

Deschamps, Jean-Claude, and Thierry Devos. 1998. "Regarding the Relationship Between Social Identity and Personal Identity." In *Social Identity: International Perspectives*, edited by Stephen Worchel, J. Francisco Morales, Dario Paez, and Jean-Claude Deschamps. London: Sage, 1–12.

Dirks, Nicholas B., Geoff Eley, and Sherry B. Ortner. 1994. *Culture / Power / History: A Reader in Contemporary Social Theory*. Princeton: Princeton University Press.

Dolby, Nadine. 2001. *Constructing Race: Youth, Identity, and Popular Culture in South Africa*. Albany: SUNY Press.

——. 2000. "The Shifting Ground of Race: The Role of Taste in Youth's Production of Identities." *Race, Ethnicity, and Education* 3 (1): 7–23.

——. 1999. "Youth and the Global Popular: The Politics and Practices of Race in South Africa." *European Journal of Cultural Studies* 2: 291–310.

Dowd Hall, Jacquelyn. 1983. " 'The Mind That Burns in Each Body': Women, Rape, and Racial Violence." In *Powers of Desire: The Politics of Sexuality*, edited by Ann Snitow, Christine Stansell, and Sharon Thompson. New York: Monthly Review Press, 328–49.

Du Bois, W. E. B. 1953. *The Souls of Black Folk*. New York: The Blue Heron Press.

Duster, Troy, and The Institute for the Study of Social Change. 1991. "Diversity Project Final Report." Berkeley: University of California, Berkeley.

Duster, Troy. 1993. "The Diversity of California Berkeley: An Emerging Reformulation of 'Competence' in an Increasingly Multicultural World." In *Beyond a Dream Deferred: Multicultural Education and the Politics of Excellence*, edited by Becky Thompson and Sangeeta Tyagi. Minneapolis: University of Minnesota Press, 231–55.

Dyer, Richard. 1997. *White*. New York: Routledge.

———. 1988. "White." *Screen* 29 (4): 44–64.

Eckert, Penelope. 1989. *Jocks and Burnouts: Social Categories and Identity in High School*. New York: Teachers College Press.

Eder, Donna. 1995. *School Talk: Gender and Adolescent Culture*. New Brunswick: Rutgers University Press.

———. 1981. "Ability Grouping as a Self-Fulfilling Prophecy: A Micro-Analysis of Teacher-Student Interaction." *Sociology of Education* 54 (3): 151–62.

Erikson, Erik H. 1968. *Identity: Youth and Crisis*. New York: Norton.

Essed, Philomena. 1996. *Diversity: Gender, Color, and Culture*. Amherst: University of Massachusetts Press.

Ewing, Katherine. 1990. "The Illusion of Wholeness: Culture, Self, and the Experience of Inconsistency." *Ethos* 18 (1): 251–78.

Fanon, Frantz. 1967. *Black Skin, White Masks*. New York: Grove Weidenfeld.

Feagin, Joe R. 1989. *Racial and Ethnic Relations*. Englewood Cliffs: Prentice-Hall.

Felder, Rachel. 1993. *Manic Pop Thrill*. Hopewell, N.J.: Ecco Press.

Ferguson, Ronald F. 1998. "Teachers' Perceptions and Expectations and the Black-White Test Score Gap." In *The Black-White Test Score Gap*, edited by Christopher Jencks and Meredith Phillips. Washington, D.C.: Brookings Institution Press, 318–74.

Fine, Michelle. 1997. "Witnessing Whiteness." In *Off White: Readings on Race, Power, and Society*, edited by Michelle Fine, Linda C. Powell, Lois Weis, and L. Mun Wong. New York: Routledge, 57–65.

———. 1989. "Silencing and Nurturing Voice in an Improbable Context: Urban Adolescents in Public School." In *Critical Pedagogy, the State, and Cultural Struggle*, edited by Henry Giroux and Peter McLaren. Albany: SUNY Press, 152–73.

Fine, Michelle, Lois Weis, and Linda C. Powell. 1997. "Communities of Difference: A Critical Look at Desegregated Spaces Created for and by Youth." *Harvard Educational Review* 67 (2): 247–84.

Fine, Michelle, Lois Weis, Linda C. Powell, and L. Mun Wong, eds. 1997. *Off White: Readings on Race, Power, and Society*. New York: Routledge.

Foley, Douglas E. 1990. *Learning Capitalist Culture: Deep in the Heart of Tejas*. Philadelphia: University of Pennsylvania Press.

Fordham, Signithia. 1996. *Blacked Out: Dilemmas of Race, Identity, and Success at Capital High*. Chicago: University of Chicago Press.

———. 1988. "Racelessness as a Factor in Black Students' School Success: Pragmatic Strategy or Pyrrhic Victory?" *Harvard Educational Review* 58 (1): 54–84.

Fordham, Signithia, and John Ogbu. 1986. "Black Students' School Success:

Coping with the Burden of 'Acting White'." *The Urban Review* 18 (3): 176–206.

Frankenberg, Ruth. 1993. *White Women, Race Matters: The Social Construction of Whiteness*. Minneapolis: University of Minnesota Press.

——, ed. 1997. *Displacing Whiteness: Essays in Social and Cultural Criticism*. Durham: Duke University Press.

Fredrickson, George. 1981. *White Supremacy: A Comparative Study in American and South African History*. Oxford: Oxford University Press.

Frith, Simon. 1996. "Music and Identity." In *Questions of Cultural Identity*, edited by Stuart Hall and Paul du Gay. London: Sage, 108–27.

——. 1981. *Sound Effects: Youth, Leisure, and the Politics of Rock 'n' Roll*. New York: Pantheon.

Gallagher, Charles A. 1997. "White Racial Formation: Into the Twenty-First Century." In *Critical White Studies: Looking Behind the Mirror*, edited by Richard Delgado and Jean Stefancic. Philadelphia: Temple University Press, 6–11.

——. 1995. "White Reconstruction in the University." *Socialist Review* 24 (1 & 2): 165–87.

Gans, Herbert J. 1979. "Symbolic Ethnicity: The Future of Ethnic Groups and Cultures in America." *Ethnic and Racial Studies* 2 (1): 1–20.

Geertz, Clifford. 1973. *The Interpretation of Cultures*. New York: Basic Books.

Gergen, Kenneth J. 1991. *The Saturated Self: Dilemmas of Identity in Contemporary Life*. New York: Basic Books.

Giddens, Anthony. 1991. *Modernity and Self-Identity: Self and Society in the Late Modern Age*. Stanford: Stanford University Press.

Gilligan, Carol. 1982. *In a Different Voice: Psychological Theory and Women's Development*. Cambridge: Harvard University Press.

Gilroy, Paul. 1993. *The Black Atlantic: Modernity and Double Consciousness*. Cambridge: Harvard University Press.

——. 1991. *"There Ain't No Black in the Union Jack": The Cultural Politics of Race and Nation*. Chicago: University of Chicago Press.

Giroux, Henry. 1997. "Rewriting the Discourse of Racial Identity: Towards a Pedagogy and Politics of Whiteness." *Harvard Educational Review* 67 (2): 285–320.

Giroux, Henry A., and Peter McLaren. 1989. *Critical Pedagogy, the State, and Cultural Struggle*. Albany: SUNY Press.

Gitlin, Todd. 1993. *The Sixties: Years of Hope, Days of Rage*. Revised trade ed. New York: Bantam Books.

Goldberg, David Theo. 1993. *Racist Culture: Philosophy and the Politics of Meaning*. Cambridge: Blackwell.

——, ed. 1994. *Multiculturalism: A Critical Reader*. Boston: Blackwell.

Gottdiener, Mark. 1995. *Postmodern Semiotics: Material Culture and the Forms of Postmodern Life*. Cambridge: Blackwell.

Gramsci, Antonio. 1971. *Selections from the Prison Notebooks*. New York: International Press.

Gregory, Steven. 1998. *Black Corona: Race and the Politics of Place in an Urban Community*. Princeton: Princeton University Press.

Grossberg, Lawrence. 1987. "Rock and Roll in Search of an Audience." In *Popular Music and Communication*, edited by James Lull. Newbury Park: Sage.

Hacker, Andrew. 1992. *Two Nations: Black and White, Separate, Hostile, Unequal*. New York: Ballantine Books.

Hall, Stuart. 1996. "Introduction: Who Needs Identity?" In *Questions of Cultural Identity*, edited by Stuart Hall and Paul du Gay. London: Sage, 1–17.

——. 1996. "New Ethnicities." In *Stuart Hall: Critical Dialogues in Cultural Studies*, edited by David Morley and Kuan-Hsing Chen. London: Routledge, 441–59.

——. 1992. "What Is the 'Black' in Black Popular Culture?" In *Black Popular Culture*, edited by Michele Wallace and Gina Dent. Seattle: Bay Press, 21–33.

——. 1991. "Ethnicity: Identity and Difference." *Radical America* 23 (4): 9–20.

Hall, Stuart, and Tony Jefferson, eds. 1996. *Resistance Through Rituals: Youth Subcultures in Post-War Britain*. London: Routledge.

Hallinan, Maureen, and Jeannie Oakes. 1994. "Exchange." *Sociology of Education* 67 (2): 79–91.

Hallinan, Maureen T., and Richard A. Williams. 1989. "Interracial Friendship Choices in Secondary Schools." *American Sociological Review* 54 (1): 67–78.

Haney Lopez, Ian F. 1996. *White by Law: The Legal Construction of Race*. New York: New York University Press.

Harris, Cheryl. 1993. "Whiteness as Property." *Harvard Law Review* 106: 1707–91.

Hartigan Jr., John. 1999. *Racial Situations: Class Predicaments of Whiteness in Detroit*. Princeton: Princeton University Press.

——. 1997. "Locating White Detroit." In *Displacing Whiteness: Essays in Social and Cultural Criticism*, edited by Ruth Frankenberg. Durham: Duke University Press, 180–213.

——. 1997. "Establishing the Fact of Whiteness." *American Anthropologist* 99 (3): 495–505.

Heath, Shirley Brice. 1983. *Ways with Words: Language, Life, and Work in Communities and Classrooms*. Cambridge: Cambridge University Press.

Hebdige, Dick. 1979. *Subculture: The Meaning of Style*. London: Methuen.

Hill, Mike, ed. 1997. *Whiteness: A Critical Reader*. New York: New York University Press.

hooks, bell. 1995. *Killing Rage: Ending Racism*. New York: Henry Holt.

——. 1992. *Black Looks: Race and Representation*. Boston: South End Press.

——. 1990. *Yearning: Race, Gender, and Cultural Politics*. Boston: South End Press.

Hudak, Glenn M. 1999. "The 'Sound' Identity: Music-Making and Schooling." In *Sound Identities: Popular Music and the Cultural Politics of Education*, edited by Cameron McCarthy. New York: Peter Lang, 447–72.

Hurston, Zora Neale. 1979. "How It Feels to Be Coloured Me." In *I Love Myself When I Am Laughing . . . And Then Again When I Am Looking Mean and Impressive: A Zora Neale Hurston Reader*, edited by Alice Walker. Old Westbury: The Feminist Press.

Ignatiev, Noel. 1995. *How the Irish Became White*. New York: Routledge.

Ignatiev, Noel, and John Garvey, eds. 1996. *Race Traitor*. New York: Routledge.

Jackson, Kenneth. 1985. *Crabgrass Frontier: The Suburbanization of the United States*. New York: Oxford University Press.

Jacobson, Matthew Frye. 1998. *Whiteness of a Different Color: European Immigrants and the Alchemy of Race*. Cambridge: Harvard University Press.

Jew, Carolyn, and Marta Tienda. 1997. "Selective Sorting in High Schools: Racial and Ethnic Effects on Friendship Formation." Toronto: American Sociological Association Annual Meetings.

Kenny, Lorraine Delia. 2000. *Daughters of Suburbia: Growing Up White, Middle Class, and Female*. New Brunswick: Rutgers University Press.

——. 2000. "Doing My Homework: The Autoethnography of a White Teenage Girl." In *Racing Research, Researching Race: Methodological Dilemmas in Critical Race Studies*, edited by France Winddance Twine and Jonathan Warren. New York: New York University Press, 111–33.

Kincheloe, Joe L., Shirley R. Steinberg, Nelson M. Rodriguez, and Ronald E. Chennault, eds. 1998. *White Reign: Deploying Whiteness in America*. New York: St. Martin's Press.

King Jr., Martin Luther. 1962. "The Ethical Demands for Integration." In *A Testament of Hope: The Essential Writings and Speeches of Martin Luther King Jr.*, edited by James Melvin Washington. San Francisco: Harper.

Kitano, Harry, and R. Daniels. 1970. *American Racism: Exploration of the Nature of Prejudice*. Englewood Cliffs: Prentice-Hall.

Klein, Anne Carolyn. 1995. *Meeting the Great Bliss Queen: Buddhists, Feminists and the Art of the Self*. Boston: Beacon Press.

Kochman, Thomas. 1981. *Black and White Styles in Conflict.* Chicago: University of Chicago Press.

Kovel, Joel. 1970. *White Racism: A Psychohistory.* New York: Columbia University Press.

Lareau, Annette. 1987. "Social Class Differences in Family-School Relationships: The Importance of Cultural Capital." *Sociology of Education* 60 (April): 73–85.

Lash, Scott, and Jonathan Friedman, eds. 1992. *Modernity and Identity.* Cambridge: Blackwell.

Lee, Stacey J. 1996. *Unraveling the "Model Minority" Stereotype: Listening to Asian American Youth.* New York: Teachers College Press.

Lightfoot, Sara Lawrence. 1978. *Worlds Apart: Relationships Between Families and Schools.* New York: Basic Books.

Lipsitz, George. 1995. "The Possessive Investment in Whiteness: Racialized Social Democracy and the 'White' Problem in American Studies." *American Quarterly* 47 (3): 369–87.

Lott, Eric. 1993. *Love and Theft: Blackface Minstrelsy and the American Working Class.* New York: Oxford University Press.

Lucas, Samuel R. 1999. *Tracking Inequality: Stratification and Mobility in American High Schools.* New York: Teachers College Press.

MacLeod, Jay. 1987. *Ain't No Makin' It.* Boulder: Westview Press.

Mancini, Janet K. 1980. *Strategic Styles: Coping in the Inner City.* Hanover: University Press of New England.

Massey, Douglas S., and Nancy A. Denton. 1993. *American Apartheid: Segregation and the Making of the Underclass.* Cambridge: Harvard University Press.

McCarthy, Cameron. 1999. *Sound Identities: Popular Music and the Cultural Politics of Education.* New York: Peter Lang.

———. 1993. "After the Canon: Knowledge and Ideological Representation in the Multicultural Discourse on Curriculum Reform." In *Race, Identity, and Representation in Education,* edited by Cameron McCarthy and Warren Crichlow. New York: Routledge, 289–305.

McCarthy, Cameron, and Warren Crichlow, eds. 1993. *Race, Identity, and Representation in Education.* New York: Routledge.

McClary, Susan. 1994. "Same as It Ever Was: Youth Culture and Music." In *Microphone Fiends: Youth Music and Youth Culture,* edited by Andrew Ross and Tricia Rose. New York: Routledge, 29–40.

McCormack, Don, ed. 1999. *McCormack's Guides.* Martinez, Cal.: Donnan Publications.

McIntosh, Peggy. 1989. "White Privilege: Unpacking the Invisible Knapsack." *Peace and Freedom* July/August: 10–12.

McLaren, Peter. 1994. "White Terror and Oppositional Agency: Towards a Critical Multiculturalism." In *Multiculturalism: A Critical Reader*, edited by David Theo Goldberg. Cambridge: Blackwell, 45–74.

Mead, George Herbert. 1934. *Mind, Self, and Society*. Chicago: University of Chicago Press.

Miles, Robert. 1989. *Racism*. New York: Routledge.

Moraga, Cherríe, and Gloria Anzaldúa. 1981. *This Bridge Called My Back: Writings by Radical Women of Color*. Watertown, Mass.: Persephone Press.

Morrison, Toni. 1993. *Playing in the Dark: Whiteness in the Literary Imagination*. New York: Random House.

Myrdal, Gunnar. 1962. *An American Dilemma: The Negro Problem and Modern Democracy*. New York: Harper and Row.

Nagel, Joane. 1996. *American Indian Ethnic Renewal*. New York: Oxford University Press.

Oakes, Jeannie. 1994. "More Than a Misapplied Technology: A Normative and Political Response to Hallinan on Tracking." *Sociology of Education* 67 (2): 84–88.

———. 1985. *Keeping Track: How Schools Structure Inequality*. New Haven: Yale University Press.

Oakes, Jeannie, and Gretchen Guiton. 1995. "Matchmaking: The Dynamics of High School Tracking Decisions." *American Educational Research Journal* 32 (1): 3–33.

Ogbu, John. 1983. "Minority Status and Schooling in Plural Societies." *Comparative Educational Review* 17 (2): 168–90.

———. 1982. "Cultural Discontinuities in Schooling." *Anthropology and Education Quarterly* 13 (4): 290–307.

Olsen, Laurie. 1997. *Made in America: Immigrant Students in Our Public Schools*. New York: New Press.

Omi, Michael, and Howard Winant. 1986. *Racial Formation in the United States: From the 1960s to the 1980s*. New York: Routledge.

Orfield, Gary, Sara Schley, Diane Glass, and Sean Reardon. 1993. "The Growth of Segregation in American Schools: Changing Patterns of Separation and Poverty since 1968." Cambridge: Harvard Project on School Desegregation.

Ortner, Sherry B. 1998. "Identities: The Hidden Life of Class." *Journal of Anthropological Research* 54 (1): 1–17.

Paez, Dario, Cristina Martinez-Taboada, Juan Jose Arrospide, Patricia Insua, and Sabino Ayestaran. 1998. "Constructing Social Identity: The Role of Status, Collective Values, Collective Self-Esteem, Perception and Social Behavior." In *Social Identity: International Perspectives*, edited by Stephen

Worchel, J. Francisco Morales, Dario Paez, and Jean-Claude Deschamps. London: Sage, 211–29.

Palladino, Grace. 1996. *Teenagers: An American History*. New York: Basic Books.

Park, Robert Ezra. 1950. *Race and Culture*. New York: The Free Press.

Perry, Pamela. 2001. "White Means Never Having to Say You're Ethnic: White Youth and the Construction of 'Cultureless' Identities." *Journal of Contemporary Ethnography* 30 (1): 56–91.

———. 1991. "The Politics of Identity: Community and Ethnicity in a Pro-Sandinista Enclave on Nicaragua's Atlantic Coast." *Berkeley Journal of Sociology* 36: 115–36.

Pettigrew, Thomas F. 1989. "The Nature of Modern Racism in the United States." *Revue Internationale de Psychologie Sociale* 2: 291–303.

Pfeil, Fred. 1995. *White Guys: Studies in Postmodern Domination and Difference*. New York: Verso.

Phoenix, Ann. 1997. " 'I'm White! So What?' The Construction of Whiteness for Young Londoners." In *Off White: Readings on Race and Power in Society*, edited by Michelle Fine, Linda C. Powell, Lois Weis, and L. Mun Wong. New York: Routledge, 187–97.

Pinderhughes, Howard. 1997. *Race in the Hood: Conflict and Violence Among Urban Youth*. Minneapolis: University of Minnesota Press.

powell, john a. 1997. "Reflections on the Self: Exploring Between and Beyond Modernity and Postmodernity." *Minnesota Law Review* 81 (6): 1481–520.

Prager, Jeffrey. 1987. "American Political Culture and the Shifting Meaning of Race." *Ethnic and Racial Studies* 10 (1): 62–81.

Radway, Janice. 1991. "Interpretive Communities and Variable Literacies: The Functions of Romance Reading." In *Rethinking Popular Culture*, edited by Chandra Mujerki and Michael Schudson. Berkeley: University of California Press.

Rhomberg, Christopher. 1999. "Social Movements in a Fragmented Society: Ethnic, Class, and Racial Mobilization in [Clavey], Ca. 1920–1970." Ph.D. Dissertation, University of California.

Richards, Chris. 1999. "Live Through This: Music, Adolescence, and Autobiography." In *Sound Identities: Popular Music and the Cultural Politics of Education*, edited by Cameron McCarthy. New York: Peter Lang, 255–88.

Rist, Ray C. 1970. "Student Social Class and Teacher Expectations: The Self-Fulfilling Prophecy in Ghetto Education." *Harvard Educational Review* 40 (3): 411–51.

Rodrick, Stephen. 1995. "Hip-Hop Flop: The Failure of Liberal Rap." In *Rap* on Rap: Straight-up Talk on Hip-Hop Culture, edited by Adam Sexton. New York: Delta, 113–17.

Roediger, David. 1994. *Towards the Abolition of Whiteness*. New York: Verso.

——. 1991. *Wages of Whiteness: Race and the Making of the American Working Class*. New York: Verso.

Roman, Leslie G. 1993. "White Is a Color! White Defensiveness, Postmodernism, and Anti-Racist Pedagogy." In *Race, Identity, and Representation in Education*, edited by Cameron McCarthy and Warren Crichlow. New York: Routledge.

Rosaldo, Renato. 1989. *Culture and Truth: The Remaking of Social Analysis*. Boston: Beacon Press.

Rose, Tricia. 1994. *Black Noise: Rap Music and Black Culture in Contemporary America*. Hanover, N.H.: Wesleyan University Press.

Ross, Andrew. 1994. "Introduction." In *Microphone Fiends: Youth Music and Youth Culture*, edited by Andrew Ross and Tricia Rose. New York: Routledge, 1–13.

Ross, Andrew, and Tricia Rose. 1994. *Microphone Fiends: Youth Music and Youth Culture*. New York: Routledge.

Rundell, John, and Stephen Mennell, eds. 1998. *Classical Readings in Culture and Civilization*. London: Routledge.

Rutherford, Jonathan. 1990. *Identity: Community, Culture, Difference*. London: Lawrence and Wishart.

Samuels, David. 1995. "The Rap on Rap: The 'Black Music' That Isn't Either." In *Rap on Rap: Straight-up Talk on Hip-Hop Culture*, edited by Adam Sexton. New York: Delta, 241–53.

Saxton, Alexander. 1990. *The Rise and Fall of the White Republic*. New York: Verso.

Schuman, Howard, Charlotte Steeh, Lawrence Bobo, and Maria Krysan. 1997. *Racial Attitudes in America: Trends and Interpretations*. 2d ed. Cambridge: Harvard University Press.

Sears, David O. 1988. "Symbolic Racism." In *Eliminating Racism: Profiles in Controversy*, edited by Dalmas A. Taylor and Phyllis A. Katz. New York: Plenum Press, 53–84.

Segrest, Mab. 1994. *Memoirs of a Race Traitor*. Boston: South End Press.

Shrum, Wesley, Neil H. Cheek Jr., and Saundra MacD. Hunter. 1988. "Friendship in School: Gender and Racial Homophily." *Sociology of Education* 61 (4): 227–39.

Slavin, Robert. 1995. "Enhancing Intergroup Relations in Schools: Cooperative Learning and Other Strategies." In *Toward a Common Destiny: Improving*

Race and Ethnic Relations in America, edited by W. D. Hawley and A. W. Jackson. San Francisco: Jossey-Bass, 291–314.

Sniderman, Paul M., and Thomas Leonard Piazza. 1993. *The Scar of Race.* Cambridge: Belknap Press of Harvard University Press.

Steele, Claude M., and Joshua Aronson. 1998. "Stereotype Threat and the Test Performance of Academically Successful African Americans." In *The Black-White Test Score Gap*, edited by Christopher Jencks and Meredith Phillips. Washington, D.C.: Brookings Institution Press, 401–27.

Steinberg, Stephen. 1981. *The Ethnic Myth: Race, Ethnicity, and Class in America.* Boston: Beacon Press.

Tajfel, Henri. 1982. *Social Identity and Intergroup Relations.* Cambridge: Cambridge University Press.

———. 1969. "Cognitive Aspects of Prejudice." *Journal of Social Issues* 25 (4): 79–97.

Tajfel, Henri, and John C. Turner. 1986. *The Social Identity Theory of Intergroup Behavior.* Monterey: Brooks-Cole.

Tatum, Beverly Daniel. 1997. *"Why Are All the Black Kids Sitting Together in the Cafeteria?" and Other Conversations About Race.* New York: Basic Books.

Terkel, Studs. 1992. *Race: How Blacks and Whites Think and Feel About the American Obsession.* New York: New Press.

Thandeka. 1999. *Learning to Be White: Money, Race, and God in America.* New York: Continuum.

———. 1999. "The Cost of Whiteness." *Tikkun* 14 (3): 33–38.

Thompson, Becky, and Sangeeta Tyagi, eds. 1996. *Names We Call Home.* New York: Routledge.

Thorne, Barrie. 1993. *Gender Play: Girls and Boys in School.* New Brunswick: Rutgers University Press.

Tuch, Steven A., and Jack K. Martin, eds. 1997. *Racial Attitudes in the 1990s: Continuity and Change.* Westport: Praeger.

Turner, John C. 1996. "Henri Tajfel: An Introduction." In *Social Groups and Identities: Developing the Legacy of Henri Tajfel*, edited by W. Peter Robinson. Oxford: Butterworth-Heinemann, 1–24.

Twine, France Winddance. 1997. "Brown-Skinned White Girls: Class, Culture, and the Construction of White Identity in Suburban Communities." In *Displacing Whiteness: Essays in Social and Cultural Criticism*, edited by Ruth Frankenberg. Durham: Duke University Press, 214–43.

Valenzuela, Angela. 1999. *Subtractive Schooling: U.S.-Mexican Youth and the Politics of Caring.* Albany: SUNY Press.

Wallace, Michele, and Gina Dent, eds. 1992. *Black Popular Culture.* Seattle: Bay Press.

Ware, Vron. 1992. *Beyond the Pale: White Women, Racism, and History*. New York: Verso.

Waters, Mary C. 1990. *Ethnic Options: Choosing Identities in America*. Berkeley: University of California Press.

Wellman, David. 1977. *Portraits of White Racism*. Cambridge: Cambridge University Press.

Wells, Amy S., and Robert L. Crain. 1994. "Perpetuation Theory and the Long-Term Effects of School Desegregation." *Review of Educational Research* 96 (4): 691–706.

Wetherell, Margaret, and Jonathan Potter. 1992. *Mapping the Language of Racism: Discourse and the Legitimation of Exploitation*. New York: Harvester Wheatsheaf.

Williams, David R., James S. Jackson, Tony N. Brown, Myriam Torres, Tyrone A. Forman, and Kendrick Brown. 1999. "Traditional and Contemporary Prejudice and Urban Whites' Support for Affirmative Action and Government Help." *Social Problems* 46 (4): 548–71.

Williams, Raymond. 1977. *Marxism and Literature*. Oxford: Oxford University Press.

———. 1976. "Base and Superstructure in Marxist Cultural Theory." In *Schooling and Capitalism: A Sociological Reader*, edited by Roger Dale. London: Routledge and Kegan Paul, 202–10.

Willis, Paul. 1978. *Profane Culture*. London: Routledge.

———. 1977. *Learning to Labor: How Working Class Kids Get Working Class Jobs*. New York: Columbia University Press.

Wilson, William J. 1987. *The Truly Disadvantaged: The Inner City, the Underclass, and Public Policy*. Chicago: University of Chicago Press.

———. 1980. *The Declining Significance of Race: Blacks and Changing American Institutions*. Chicago: University of Chicago Press.

Winant, Howard. 1997. "Behind Blue Eyes: Whiteness and Contemporary U.S. Racial Politics." In *Off White: Readings on Race, Power, and Society*, edited by Michelle Fine, Lois Weis, Linda C. Powell, and L. Mun Wong. New York: Routledge, 40–53.

———. 1994. *Racial Conditions: Politics, Theory, Comparisons*. Minneapolis: University of Minnesota Press.

Wray, Matt, and Annalee Newitz, eds. 1997. *White Trash: Race and Class in America*. New York: Routledge.

Index

Academic achievement (racial differences in), 159–60, 171–72, 177, 186, 187, 196, 224 n.6

Affective resonance, 116, 117–18, 121–22, 176, 210

Affirmative action, 150; Clavey High School students on, 165, 167, 176, 178, 188; Valley Groves High School students on, 80, 82, 83, 101, 151, 154, 155–57, 175

African Americans. *See* Black(s)

Age (as factor in experience of racial-ethnic difference), 3, 35–36, 187, 206–9

Alternative rock music, 28, 29, 37, 48, 50, 68, 69, 113, 115, 116, 118, 119, 121, 129. *See also* Punk music

"Alternatives" (Clavey High School social group), 48–50, 157, 171

"American culture," 78, 79–80, 86–90, 95, 96–98, 178. *See also* Culture

Anger. *See* Violence

Anita (Clavey High School student), 76

Ann (Clavey High School student), 85–88, 91, 99, 131, 157, 173, 205

Anthony (Clavey High School student), 56, 57, 116, 171

Antiracism, 94, 179; possibilities for nurturing, 3, 5, 22, 190–98. *See also* Equal status projects

Anti-Semitism, 135, 141, 142–43, 145

Asian Americans: at Clavey High School, 14, 16, 17, 46, 48, 53–54, 60, 95, 101–2, 176; markers of, at Clavey High School, 50, 51; stereotypes of,

63, 64, 184, 225 n.12; at Valley Groves High School, 14, 28, 31, 35, 42; as white, 51, 89, 98. *See also* "Minorities"; Racial-ethnic difference

Attitudes (about race), 5, 8, 9. *See also* Racial identities; Racism; Stereotypes

Autobiography of Malcolm X, 138

Backpacking, 24

"Bad," 62

Baldwin, James, 21, 180, 185–86

Bands (school), 40, 42, 71–72

Barry (Clavey High School student), 51, 72, 84, 88–93, 95, 97–98, 165, 167, 173

Beastie Boys (musical group), 37

Bee Gees (musical group), 38

Beeman, William, 222 n.8

Berkeley High School (California), 226 n.21

Bettie, Julie, 203, 223 n.3

Billy (Valley Groves High School student), 25, 28, 30, 32, 77–78, 82, 90, 105, 106, 108, 109, 155

Black(s): at Clavey High School, 14–16, 46–47, 51, 53, 56–59, 125–27, 171; as dominant racial identity at Clavey High School, 1, 14, 18, 22, 44, 46, 60, 68–71, 125; influence of urban culture of, on whites, 67–72; and persistence of black-white paradigm in spite of multiculturalism, 59, 102–3, 226 n.18; social groups among, at Clavey High School, 48,

Black(s) (*cont.*)

60; stereotypes of, 109–10, 115, 172, 176, 184–85; at Valley Groves High School, 14, 28, 31, 35–36, 42, 123, 124. *See also* Affirmative action; Black identity; Blackness; "Minorities"; Racial-ethnic difference; Racial identities; Slavery

Black Caribs, 6

Black identity: Civil Rights movement's redefinition of, 7–8; markers of, at Clavey High School, 50, 51, 56–59, 67–73, 112, 130, 227 n.23; and power, 7–8, 102, 182–83 (*see also* Violence); as racial-ethnic identity, 211 n.2. *See also* Black(s); Blackness; "Minorities"

Black Muslims. *See* Nation of Islam

Blackness: performance of, 35, 63, 64, 110–11, 127, 131; toughness associated with, in white youth's eyes, 21, 51–52, 105, 107–9, 124, 128–29, 182–85. *See also* Black(s); Black identity; Racial-ethnic difference

Blame-shifting (as whites' response to accusations of white oppression), 166, 171–72, 176, 177

Blauner, Bob, 230 n.19

Blumer, Herbert, 133, 174–75, 182, 220 n.53, 237 n.7

Bobby (Clavey High School student), 65

Bobo, Lawrence, 148–49

Bonnett, Alastair, 239 n.23

Bourdieu, Pierre, 78, 231 nn.10, 11, 238 n.17

Boyz II Men (musical group), 68

Brian (Clavey High School student), 141, 142, 145, 148

"Butterfly" (dance), 70, 125

California anti-affirmative action bill (Proposition 209), 101, 175

Canaan, Joyce, 221 n.2

Carli (Valley Groves High School student), 31, 34–36, 78–80, 82, 83, 110, 111, 128–29, 153, 155

Carter, Prudence, 224 nn. 5, 6

Census Bureau, 7, 193

Cheerleaders, 39–41, 44, 62–63, 71

Chodorow, Nancy, 183

"Chola" clothing style, 59, 111

Cindi (Clavey High School student), 111–14, 117–19, 129, 149, 165–66, 170

Civil Rights movement, 7–8, 84, 136, 188, 189

Clarke, John, 223 n.2

Class: at Clavey High School, 15, 17, 18, 48–49, 170–71, 200–201, 242 n.1; as factor in experience of racial-ethnic difference, 3, 48–49, 51–52, 90–91, 117–18, 122, 147, 154–55, 158–62, 184, 201, 226 nn. 16, 18; middle, as author's research emphasis, 18–19, 200–203; performativity of, 48–49, 51–52, 203, 223 n.3; and power, 9, 154–55, 226 n.16; schools' role in construction and reproduction of, 10–11, 24, 33, 187; at Valley Groves High School, 12–13, 18, 200–201, 242 n.1. *See also* Working class

Classical music, 105, 113–15

Clavey High School: author's choice of, as research site, 18–19, 200–210; black as dominant racial identity at, 46–47, 51, 53, 56–59, 125–27, 171; cultural meaning of white identities at, 20–21, 24, 76–77, 84–96, 104–5, 111–23, 133, 150; curriculum at, 54–59, 98–100, 163–64, 167, 175, 187–89, 196–97; demographics and description of, 13–17, 45–46; interracial association as personal and up-close at, 2–3, 20, 47–72, 97–101, 105, 124–26, 129, 172–79, 181; race-neutral views at, 86, 173, 188; racial identity—not peer groups—as basis of social organization at, 44–72, 174, 188–89, 208; reactions at, to Million Man March, 21–22, 139–49; space in, divided by racial identity, 1, 60–

64, 111, 122, 195; white as minority
racial identity at, 1, 61–63, 67, 70–
72; whites' perception of variation
among minorities at, 96, 101, 123;
whites' self-perceptions at, 151, 157–
79, 191–92, 195. *See also* Multiculturalism; Schools

Clothing styles: at Clavey High School,
46–53, 68, 72, 149, 171; racial meanings embedded in, 21, 25, 48–53,
89–90, 112, 182, 186; at Valley
Groves High School, 27–31, 59, 111;
for youth, 10, 223 n.2

Colonialism, 42, 79, 80, 96, 97, 102

"Color blind" (race-neutral) views, 23,
189, 198, 220 n.50; at Clavey High
School, 86, 173, 188; at Valley Groves
High School, 31–33, 42–43, 72,
123–24, 127, 144, 146, 147, 153, 154,
157, 175. *See also* Race: as something
that matters; "Racelessness"

"Communities of Difference" (Fine,
Weis, and Powell), 197–98

Conchas, Gilberto Q., 225 n.15

Connerly, Ward, 175

Connolly, Medria, 131–32

Constitutive activities, 116, 120–22

"Cool," 61–63, 221 n.2

Country music, 24, 105–8, 113, 117

"Cowboys" (at Valley Groves High
School). *See* "Hicks"

Creoles, 6

Cross, William E., 215 n.13

Cultural assemblies (at Clavey High
School), 98–100, 125, 188

Culture: "American," as white, 78, 79–
80, 86–90, 95, 96–98, 178; definition
of, 190, 229 n.15; racial-ethnic minorities perceived by whites as having, 20, 82, 83, 86, 95, 96, 98–102; as
social process rather than static thing,
3; of whites as heterogeneous, 113–
19, 122; of whites as meaningless,
119–20, 122; whites' self-perception
as having no, 2, 6–7, 20, 24, 28–32,

75, 77–84, 87–90, 94, 96, 98, 105,
128–29, 150, 191

Curriculum: at Clavey High School,
54–59, 98–100, 163–64, 167, 175,
187–89, 196–97; at Valley Groves
High School, 13, 34–37, 187, 188,
196. *See also* Multiculturalism

Daniel (Clavey High School student),
94, 114, 118, 165

Dawana (Clavey High School student),
142, 145

Denial (as whites' response to accusations of white oppression), 166, 169–
71

Derek (Valley Groves High School student), 154

Disco music, 37

Dolby, Nadine, 224 n.7, 231 n.11, 232
n.23

Drama. *See* Performing Arts magnet
academy

Drinking, 25, 30, 221 n.2; and ethnicity, 92, 93

"Drip look," 46, 68, 149

"Druggies" (stoners), 29–31, 48, 60.
See also Hippies

Drugs, 29, 30, 221 n.2

Du Bois, W. E. B., 185

Duncan (Clavey High School student),
52, 53

Duster, Troy, 182, 232 n.15

Eagles (musical group), 105

Easy listening music, 113, 117

Ebonics. *See* English language: Black

Eckert, Penny, 24

Edwards, Mr. (Clavey High School
teacher), 56–57, 135, 139–40, 143–
45, 147, 148, 164

English language: Black, 17, 35, 51, 63,
68, 109–10, 112, 125; Standard, 17,
35, 50, 123; students with limited
competence in, 17, 55. *See also* Slang

Enlightenment, 23, 97, 185

Equal status projects, 64–67, 183, 197–98, 210. *See also* Integration

Eric (Clavey High School student), 84, 85, 91, 105, 163–64, 168, 170, 173

Ethnic identities: author's interest in, 6; at Clavey High School, 91–93, 97–100; symbolic, 83, 92, 94–97, 100, 228 n.4; at Valley Groves High School, 76, 88. *See also* "Minorities"; Racial-ethnic difference; Racial identities; *specific ethnic and racial identities*

"European American" clubs, 7, 54, 100, 197

European Americans. *See* White(s)

Exasperation (as whites' response to accusations of white oppression), 166, 167, 170, 176, 177

Experience (as shaping racialized musical tastes and leisure activities), 116–32

Fanon, Frantz, 185

Farrakhan, Louis, 135–42, 144, 145, 148, 149

Fear: whites', of groups of racial "others," 136, 141, 142, 147, 237 n.7; as whites' response to accusations of white oppression, 166, 168–69. *See also* Violence

"Feedback loops," 57, 176. *See also* Stereotypes

Filipinos: at Clavey High School, 16; at Valley Groves High School, 14, 28, 31, 42, 123, 124

Fine, Michelle, 197–98

Food: at Clavey High School, 47; preferred by American whites, 23, 76, 77, 84, 90, 92, 93; at Valley Groves High School, 26. *See also* Thinness

Football players, 39–41, 53, 64–65, 71, 93

Fordham, Signithia, 224 n.6

Forrest Gump (movie), 105, 137

Foucault, Michel, 6

"Fresh," 62, 109

Frith, Simon, 121–22

Fugees (musical group), 68

Fuhrman, Mark, 141, 143

Future Teachers magnet academy (at Clavey High School), 17, 55

"Gangster chicks," 111

Gangster rap, 114, 116

"Gangster wannabes," 48, 52, 53, 60, 108–9

Gans, Herbert, 228 n.4

Gap (clothing store), 27, 48–50, 60, 171, 221 n.1

Garifuna, 6

Gary (Clavey High School student), 65

Gender: effect of author's, on research, 208–9; as factor in experience of racial-ethnic difference, 3, 22, 51–52, 134, 148–49, 177, 178, 180, 184–85, 223 n.3; and performance of blackness, 111, 124; and power, 9, 148–49, 162, 165, 177, 178, 184–85; schools' role in construction and reproduction of, 10–11, 24, 187; of skaters, 29, 52

Germany, 92, 93, 95

"Ghetto people," 48

Giroux, Henry, 197

Gloria (Clavey High School student), 50–51

Goldman, Ron, 150

"Good," 62

Gramsci, Antonio, 78, 238 n.17

Grateful Dead (musical group), 30

Green Day (musical group), 50, 68

Grey, Mr. (Clavey High School student), 45–46

"Grunge" style, 46–49, 52, 171

Guilt (as whites' response to accusations of white oppression), 166, 168, 170, 176, 177

Guns & Roses (musical group), 114

Hairstyles, 27, 171

Hall, Stuart, 9, 73, 182, 197, 211 n.2, 227 n.23, 233 n.32, 241 n.45

Miskitus, 6

Mississippi Burning (movie), 146

Monique (Clavey High School student), 76

Mormon youth, 28–29, 80–81

Morrison, Toni, 231 n.5

"Muffies." *See* "Popular" crowd

Multiculturalism: at Clavey High School, 45–46, 69–70, 98, 163, 173, 187, 188–89; competencies in, 35, 51–52, 109–10, 128, 131–32, 185, 186; "conservative" vs. "left-liberal," 196–97; "critical," 197, 198, 241 n.45; lack of integration of, into curriculum, 98, 99–100, 188–89, 196–97; as maintaining white privilege, 229 n.14; vs. "melting pot," 8; persistence of black-white paradigm under, 59, 102–3, 226 n.18

"Multicultural week" (at Clavey High School), 68–69, 98, 99–100. *See also* Cultural assemblies

"Multiracial self," 21–22, 122, 128–32, 177, 180, 183–86

Murray (Clavey High School student), 64–66, 93–94, 164–65

Music: kind of, associated with blacks, 68–69, 112, 114–19, 121; kind of, associated with whites, 24, 37–38, 69, 105–18, 121; listened to by "popular" crowd, 28; as racialized, 182, 186; for youth, 10, 104–5, 205. See also *names of musical groups; specific kind of music*

Myrdal, Gunnar, 188

Nation of Islam (Black Muslims), 48, 135, 138–39, 142, 143. *See also* Farrakhan, Louis

Native Americans: at Clavey High School, 15, 16, 46; culture of, 84, 93, 101; treatment of, 79, 80, 93, 164

Nicaragua, 6

Nine Inch Nails (musical group), 115

"Normal." *See* "Racelessness"

"Norm-other" logic (in schools), 30–33, 47–53, 78–80, 106. *See also* "Us-them" relationships

Norms: minorities perceived as deviating from, 30–31, 98–100; "popular" crowd as conforming to middle-class adult, 28–31, 34, 36–37, 98, 106, 221 n.2; of white identity, 90, 91, 95, 96–103, 117, 176, 178, 181, 192, 196; whites as setting, 4, 6, 8, 10–11, 19–20, 23–24, 33, 36–43, 72, 96–100, 178, 187

Ogbu, John, 224 n.6

Oktoberfest (Valley Groves High School), 37

Oldies music, 113

Olsen, Laurie, 226 n.17, 227 n.25

Omi, Michael, 189

Orbison, Roy, 38

"Others": as depicted in media, 19, 21, 124, 128–29, 174–75, 181; as deviating from norm, 30–31, 98–100; identity as formed in contradistinction to that of, 2, 4, 9, 33, 84, 90, 92, 93, 95–98, 103, 123–27, 129, 174–80, 182–86, 197, 219 n.49, 229 n.14. *See also* Colonialism; Interracial association; "Minorities"; Multiculturalism; "Multiracial self"; "Norm-other" logic; Racial-ethnic difference

Pacific Islanders, 15, 16, 46, 60

Parades, 39–41, 71

Parents, 39, 41, 43, 58–59, 226 n.16

Parks, Rosa, 138

Past, 20, 80–83, 87–88, 91–97, 102–3, 197

Patti (Clavey High School student), 53, 56–57, 61, 62, 69, 114, 158, 164, 169

Pearl Jam (musical group), 105

Peer groups: at Clavey High School, 44, 48–49, 52, 53, 60; role of, in con-

ganization at Valley Groves High School, 31–33; as dominant mode of social organization at Clavey High School, 44–72, 174, 188–89, 208; performativity of, 10, 33, 35, 51–53, 61–63, 73–74, 131–32, 184 (*see also* Race: as arbitrary social construct); vs. "race," 3–4; vs. racial attitudes, 5, 8, 9; school space appropriated according to, 1, 26–28, 31, 34–36, 60–64, 111, 122, 195, 223 n.4, 227 n.21, 231 n.9; schools' role in forming, 10–11, 19–72, 187–89, 194–98; "social" vs. "cultural," 5, 73, 88; solidarities associated with common, 4, 5, 73, 152, 156–57, 162, 177–78, 195, 208, 231 n.9. *See also* Black identity; Ethnic identities; Interracial association; "Multiracial self"; Norms; "Others"; Racial ascription; Racial-ethnic difference; Stereotypes; White identity

"Racial Prejudice as a Sense of Group Position" (Blumer), 133, 220 n.53, 237 n.7

Racial profiling, 4

Racism: association of, with "hicks," 29, 33, 153, 154, 157; at Clavey High School, 159–62, 171–74, 176, 195; conditions which challenge, 64–67, 183, 197–98, 210; and group position, 133, 150–79, 220 n.53, 237 n.7; scholarship on "new" white, 3–5, 179; separatism seen as, 136, 139–41, 144, 145, 147, 163; tracking as, 20, 34–37, 54–59, 64, 98, 171, 176–77, 187, 194, 196; at Valley Groves High School, 36, 123, 151, 153–54; white pride seen as, 86–88, 100, 134, 166. *See also* Anti-Semitism

Rage Against the Machine (musical group), 39

Rallies, 38–39, 41, 62–63, 68, 69, 71, 114

Rancho Nuevo, 11–13, 78

Rap music: at Clavey High School, 68–69, 112–18, 121, 125, 129–30; commodification and diffusion of, 124, 129; gestures associated with performance of, 109–10; at Valley Groves High School, 21, 30, 37, 105–9. *See also* "White rappers"

"Ravers," 48, 52, 53, 112

Reggae music, 37, 69

Religious youth, 28–29, 48, 54, 80–81, 85

Renald (Clavey High School student), 62

Republicans. *See* Barry; Jonathon

Resonance, 116, 117–18, 121–22, 176, 210

"Reverse discrimination." *See* Affirmative action

Revolution or reform. *See* Social-political change

Rhythm and blues music, 68–69, 106, 113, 114

Richards, Chris, 231 n.11

Richards, Mr. (Clavey High School administrator), 45

Riley (student at Clavey High School), 114

Riley, Mr. (Valley Groves High School teacher), 77, 81, 82, 135, 137–39, 143, 146

River metaphor, 4–5, 180, 191

Rock and roll music, 24, 28, 29, 37–38, 41, 49, 50, 113, 114, 119

Roman, Leslie G., 214 n.9

Ron (Valley Groves High School student), 32, 124

Rosaldo, Renato, 229 n.14

Salt-N-Pepa (musical group), 68

Sanctions: for being a minority, 147–48; for exhibitions of white pride, 86–88, 134, 166; intra-racial, 148; for racial-ethnic boundary-crossing in schools, 21, 50–51, 186, 224 n.6

Sandinistas, 6

Sandra (Clavey High School student), 50

Teachers (school authorities), 187; at Clavey High School, 17, 45–46, 56–57, 201–2, 207; effect of stereotypes held by, on students, 10, 56–58, 225 nn. 14, 15; at Valley Groves High School, 14, 25–26, 34, 43, 77, 81, 82, 154, 201, 207. See also *names of specific teachers and administrators*

Teenagers. *See* Youth

Television. *See* Media

"Theme Day," 38, 69

Thinness (as component of white identity), 76, 84, 88

Thorne, Barrie, 211 n.3

Tina (Clavey High School student), 91, 170

Tootsie roll (dance), 125

Toughness. *See* Blackness

Tracking (educational), 20, 34–37, 54–59, 64, 98, 171, 176–77, 187, 194, 196

Trish (Clavey High School student), 51–52, 132

University of Texas (Austin), 6

Urban Outfitters (clothing store), 30

"Us-them" relationships, 20–22, 83, 86, 95, 100–101, 122–28, 180, 181; proximity of interracial association's impact on, 134–79, 182–84, 186, 230 n.18. *See also* "Norm-other" logic

Valentine's Day, 37

Valley Groves High School: author's choice of, as research site, 18–19, 200–210; curriculum at, 13, 34–37, 187, 188, 196; demographics and description of, 11–14, 25; interracial association as impersonal and distant at, 2, 20, 21, 33–43, 72, 101, 105, 123–24, 152, 162, 175, 181; location of, 7, 11; race-neutral views at, 31–33, 42–43, 72, 123–24, 127, 144, 146, 147, 153, 154, 157, 175; reactions at, to Million Man March, 21–22, 135–39, 143–49, 188; space in, dominated by

racial identity, 1, 26–28, 31, 34–36, 195; white as dominant racial identity at, 1, 13–14, 18, 20, 22, 24, 25–43, 67; white identity as cultureless at, 20, 24–43, 75–83, 97, 98–100, 105, 128–29, 133, 150, 191; white peer groups as dominating, 11–14, 26–43, 106, 208; whites' lack of differentiation among minorities at, 83, 101, 123; whites' self-perception at, 80, 82, 83, 101, 150–57, 165, 174–75, 188, 191–92, 195. *See also* Schools

Village People (musical group), 38

Violence: and black urban life, 109, 116, 158–59, 171; at Clavey High School, 94, 158–60, 168–69, 172–73, 177; metaphor of, at football rally, 39, 41; of racial ascription and racial "color-blindness," 220 n.50; at Valley Groves High School, 29; various kind of music as expressing, 118, 129–30, 186. *See also* Blackness; Sexual harrassment

Washington, Mrs. (Valley Groves High School teacher), 135, 136–37, 143, 147

Weis, Lois, 197–98

White(s): culture of, 23–24, 73–132; decline in majority status in U.S. by, 7, 193; as dominant racial identity at Valley Groves High School, 1, 13–14, 18, 20, 22, 24, 25–43, 67; as dominant racial identity in U.S. 23, 96, 150, 159–60, 187, 193, 220 n.53; as having no culture, 2, 6–7, 20, 24, 28–32, 75, 77, 78–84, 87, 88–90, 94, 96, 98, 105, 128–29, 133, 150, 191; as minority racial identity at Clavey High School, 1, 61–63, 67, 70–72; on the past, 20, 80–83, 87–88, 91–97, 102–3, 197; and persistence of black-white paradigm in spite of multiculturalism, 59, 102–3, 226 n.18; proposal of clubs for, 7, 54, 100, 197; relationship of, to other racial

Pamela Perry is Assistant Professor of Community Studies at the University of California, Santa Cruz.

Library of Congress Cataloging-in-Publication Data

Perry, Pamela.
Shades of white : white kids and racial identities in high school / Pamela Perry.
  p. cm.
Includes bibliographical references and index.
ISBN 0-8223-2877-1 (cloth : alk. paper) — ISBN 0-8223-2892-5 (pbk. : alk. paper)
  1. White children—California—San Francisco Bay Area—Social conditions—20th century. 2. Whites—Race identity—California—San Francisco Bay Area. 3. High school students—California—San Francisco Bay Area—Social conditions—20th century. 4. Race awareness in children—California—San Francisco Bay Area. 5. San Francisco Bay Area (Calif.)—Race relations. I. Title.
F868.S156 P47 2002
305.235'09794'6—dc21   2001051138